MONSOON VICTORY

By the same author:

THE CONSUL AT SUNSET
DRINKERS OF DARKNESS
GILLIGAN'S LAST ELEPHANT
THE JOURNEY HOMEWARD
SEE YOU IN YASUKUNI
WARRIORS AND STRANGERS
WITHOUT LOVE
THE YEAR OF THE LION

GERALD HANLEY

Monsoon Victory

WHITE LION PUBLISHERS
London, New York, Sydney and Toronto

First published in the United Kingdom by
Collins, 1946

White Lion edition, 1974

ISBN 0 85617 224 3

Printed in Great Britain by
Biddles Ltd., Guildford, Surrey,
for White Lion Publishers Ltd.,
138 Park Lane, London W1Y 3DD

To F.S.

FOREWORD

This is the story of the advance down the Khabaw Valley to the Chindwin. The advance began after the Japanese had been defeated on the borders of India in June, 1944. It was the first time we had advanced in the monsoon, and an East African Infantry Division was picked for the job.

Their job was hard, for the Khabaw was said to be a pestilential area, and the Khabaw Valley during the monsoon becomes a swamp. They pursued the Japanese and captured Kalewa, after five months of sustained effort, and inflicted the first big defeat the Japanese suffered in the war. This is the story of one Division of the Fourteenth Army, and of what it did in the first advance into Burma.

GERALD HANLEY

CHAPTER ONE

It was raining at Manipur. Sometimes the rain came in a sheet of water and the sky moved like a greyish smoke, swirling until it merged into the rain-blue hills.

It was the time of the monsoon.

In Assam and Burma when the monsoon comes, the land is deluged and the rain beats down for hour after hour like the grief of the dying season.

I arrived at Manipur in the dark and a few globes of yellow light were glistening on the spreading rain-pools. The station was swarming with troops and they had dumped their kit into mounds. The rain drummed on webbing and steel until it had sought out every crevice, and the troops sat as do all troops who have travelled far. They were hunched, and had ceased to avoid the piercing fingers of the rain. They let it pour on them, for they were now wet through, and it did not matter any more. Their only effort was the cupping of their hands to shield cigarettes from the running streams of water that flowed on their glistening fingers.

A thin steam rose from these hundreds of men. They had lost their identity in this world of monsoon night, and they waited for the calling of names and units. They had spent days in an Indian train and had chewed the cud of discomfort with the stoicism that seasoned soldiers possess. They had stared out of train windows for days at the beating rain which swirled in brown floods on to the paddy fields and jungle. They had coped during their journey with crooks, beggars, pimps and the various wallahs who sell tea, cakes and unleavened bread. They had slept on wooden boards covered with a black crust of soot, sticky with a sort of salty bitterness and surrounded by the bags, pouches and sacks that soon they would hang on to their bodies for the march.

Soldiers in Burma are like warrior-monks who must eke out their burning days on the bare necessities of life. The tremendous machine that feeds and supplies them will try to push in a pound of luxury, but usually a pound of ammunition, or bandages or Mepacrine must go instead.

These sodden soldiers sitting in the dark at Manipur had come from Britain, India and Africa to fight the Japanese. They smoked; and they thought in a hundred languages. Some had driven trucks in Bermondsey, herded goats on the plains of India and beaten drums after the reaping in Africa. All these men, white, brown, and black, had fought and endured in holes in the ground, had marched together and had spoken to each other in the bastard Lingua-Franca of soldiers from many countries.

It was the last day of July, 1944, and the green world that was disappearing under the racing water was the battleground of the Fourteenth Army. This army had fought the Japanese to a standstill during the battle that was joined for the possession of India. It was now driving the enemy like starving cattle back on to the borders of Burma and India. In a sodden morass of jungle and water, in rain that seldom stopped, the enemy was now staggering after leaving sixty thousand dead along the Burma front. Hurricanes of high explosives had destroyed the last fibre of that suicidal bravery and fanaticism peculiar to the Japanese Army. The rags of the enemy masses who had fought crazily for India were now drowning in a sea of rain and madness. Their death-wish was now satisfied, in a scene of degradation and chaos that has seldom been equalled. The smell of their dead filled the jungle. They died as animals die when the great sickness comes to the herds, hopelessly, reduced to a state where the very cells of their bodies had been destroyed by starvation, disease and dementia.

The troops on Manipur station were going in again. Some had fought in the Arakan country of the South and some had fought in the savage hell of Kohima. Soldiers have little to say. Their feelings are incoherent and are yet simple. When I looked at them I felt respect for them, for they had torn apart one of the most ferocious armies in the world.

The enemy had swarmed over the frontier of India frantic with victory. India would give them all the food and shelter they needed during the coming monsoon. They needed monsoon quarters in order to prepare for the final phase. The bloodiness of the fighting on that frontier, where men fought hand to hand in the jungle, blinded with sweat, will remain for ever in the memories of those who fought there and survived. The hills are steep and matted with jungle. The scenery is magnificent, and Japanese soldiers trapped in their foxholes wrote of its beauty in their grubby diaries. Some said it reminded them of the blue and gold hills of Hokkaido, while one saw a hill covered with cherry blossom where cherry blossom had never grown. Driven crazy, and outfought, starving and hopeless, the enemy soldiers stared out through the jungle at the hills of India. The thunderous fury of the artillery sought them out and the shells tore down their parapets, their camouflage and finally their morale. Overhead the sky was racing and fluxing, swelling into dark masses as the monsoon gathered itself for the months of rain. When the sky darkens at the time of the monsoon it is like the silent approach of a power that dwarfs humanity. The jungle that has sweated its green strength, and the earth that has cracked with thirst, can now drink until drowned under the force of water. This force lights a million candles in the earth which flower, riot and multiply until they die of their drunkenness. One glistening jungle plant will become a calendar of nature's life and death. The vastness of the jungle, lashed into a green brightness by the rain, gives off the scents of plants and flowers, and the bitter cloying smell of the teak hangs in the trees. In this place of swollen rivers and drowning jungle the soldiers of the Fourteenth Army closed in on the doomed troops of Japan.

The Japanese tore crazily at handfuls of boiled grass, at bitter roots and berries. Their hour had come when the rain burst on them and flooded their holes, bunkers and trenches. The smell of their dead was with them always and the hair of the living grew long and matted under the brown steel helmets. They watched the mountains of India disappear into veils of blue rain mist and their anguish knew no bounds, for some went mad where they crouched after the months of dynamic effort in a country which was stronger than man. When the British guns found an enemy bunker they turned on it and smashed it to pieces. The enemy could not believe that it was time to go; that they had failed in their greatest venture. They died with the grass in their mouths. Those who turned South knew that a hundred miles of drowning country lay between them and the Chindwin and the real anger of the rain had not yet shown itself.

'Go in now,' said General Slim, Commander of the Fourteenth Army, 'and destroy them.'

The eyes of the people had turned to the West. India was safe. The mass of metal that was to be thrown into Europe and the powerful armies that waited to attack, now drew the gaze of the world. In July the battle of Normandy was joined, and far to the East, in Assam, near Burma's frontier, a great British army went in pursuit of the Japanese in a scene of nightmare and death. This was the greatest defeat that the enemy had suffered in all Asia, and they were to die beside raging torrents, on hills that broke their dying bodies and in burning villages where they collected for their last moments.

As I waited at Manipur a soldier gave me a cigarette and talked about the fighting. He knew he had been in a great battle, but was not yet sure of the greatness of victory. He had seen villages blasted into ashes and littered with the calcined bones of the dead. For this heap of ashes men had fought like wild animals, driving each other in and out as the effort increased. The dead were littered in the jungle and the Japanese troops, driven by the weird power of their fanaticism, finally cracked under the courage and fighting power of the Fourteenth Army.

This soldier who talked to me in the raining night could not tell me of the heat, the exhaustion and the extra few minutes of effort that wins battles in Burma's jungles. He knew these things well, but could only hint at them, for they had become his daily life and were not surprising any more.

I was to find out all these things as he had done. I was to find also that the human body is the greatest machine in the world, for while rain and heat, insects and parasites work on it and worry it, the glow of the spirit in the envelope of tired muscles cannot be extinguished by metal, fire or the Yamato spirit of Japan.

The rain did not stop. At length a truck appeared, throwing up waves of spray. We piled into it and drove to the Transit camp, which lay in a sea of mud. With us were three British nurses, wet also, but cheerful. They wore khaki slacks and tunics; their raincoats had ceased to function and they shivered as did the men. These nurses who had served down in the Arakan had seen the skull behind the war. They had experienced all the hardships of Burma's jungle scene, and had tended the sick and wounded until their tired hands had worked without thought, automatically, yet still with tenderness. Now, in this atmosphere of wet misery, they wondered what the camp would be like. Would anyone be there to meet them. Would there be tea?

There must always be tea for the British when they are campaigning. It is made in drums, petrol tins and rusty kettles: it is hot and sweet and is as much a part of life as the snatched sleep and the staring-eyed night watch from the weapon-pit. Would there be tea to-night? This question was thrown about inside the bouncing truck like a ball, for we were thirsty, tired and chilled. At Manipur the country is high and the night is cold. One cup of tea with a cigarette would brush all this away and we could then open up our camp-kit and search for a dry blanket.

One of the nurses was tiny, with large eyes. She was feeling tired and ill. She hated riding in trucks, but had done so for the past two years: she could not get used to it and it was like sea-sickness to her. One of the other nurses held her hand and said we were nearly there.

We jumped out of the truck into inches of mud. Two Indian orderlies dragged the kit out and rolled it about in the mud for a while. No one protested: worse things had happened, and to explain to the two orderlies that we did not want them to roll our things in the mud would be too great an effort and they would not understand, for they were too sleepy. To explain things at this time of the night, in the rain, to two sleepy Indians would result in the exclamation of rage, the cracked note and the desperation that comes to those who cannot speak the local language. So they dragged the kit through the mud and we went in search of tea.

A British sergeant had prepared hot tea and sandwiches, and his thin, red face smiled as he led the nurses to the hut of bamboo poles and grass. These huts are called 'Bashas,' and great camps of 'Bashas' abound in Assam.

CHAPTER TWO

1

I was seeking the 11th East African Division which had just gone into action. They were somewhere south of Palel on the heels of Yamamoto's troops. This East African Division had trained for over a year in Ceylon, going through the hard routine of jungle training, which is about the toughest experience of all army life. Africans from Kenya, Tanganyika, Uganda, Nyasaland, Rhodesia. Zanzibar and the Belgian Congo, and even some leather long-service Somali N.C.O.s made up the Division. A great number of these men had seen service in Italian Somaliland, Abyssinia and Madagascar. They were now entering a war of a different type. A war in the jungle where a personal issue is very personal indeed and a soldier learns to rely on his own hands, eyes and feet. They had been told that the Japanese troops were fanatics and great fighters. They had seen posters depicting the height, weight, general build, colouring and peculiarities of the Japanese. They had seen pictures of the enemy's weapons and equipment and had learned of the tricks, traps and ruses employed by the small yellow soldiers in jungle warfare.

It is hard to describe the fighting qualities of soldiers like the Japanese, especially to Africans, and not make them appear as supermen. It is particularly hard when you wish your troops to be always on their guard against a ruthless enemy and yet avoid the impression that the Japanese never sleep, that they fight through the day and night.

Now, in early August, as the East Africans went into action, they were able to slay those enemy troops who turned to fight. The word 'slay' is particularly apt. When the Japanese soldiers showed fight they were slain; when they were found helpless they were taken prisoner, which is the most terrible thing (from the Japanese point of view) that can happen to them.

There is no such thing as a born jungle fighter, that is, as far as fighting with modern weapons is concerned. The jungle fighter has to be trained, and some people, when trained, are better than others because they may possess the characteristics that make good bushmen.

The East African has excellent eyesight, good ears and a feeling for the gifts of nature. He is adaptable and has an eye for camouflage. He will make you the finest bed in Burma with a few lengths of bamboo, and he can cut through iron-hard timber with his matchet as though it were cardboard. To see an *Askari* use a matchet or *Panga* (as it is called in Ki'Swahili) is to see an artist at work. The shoulder is not used: nor is there a straining or twisting of muscle: there is only the loose grip of the powerful fingers on the handle of the *panga,* and a rhythmic swing that is wonderful to watch. The steel bites through the timber easily, and only a few strokes are required. They can use their *pangs* for hours, seemingly without effort, but if a European attempts work with a *panga* his fingers are cramped and weakened after a few minutes.

This gift with the *panga* was to serve them well in their advance, for they were to chop their way through some of the thickest jungle in Asia, and then fight at the end of it.

The great mass of the East African askaris were completely unsophisticated men when they joined the army. They came in from their tribal territories, generally wearing only a long piece of cloth. They counted up to ten on their fingers and then started again. They thought that machinery was mystery, and they cut scars into their flesh when they were sick. These young men were the rawest army material in the world, and in peacetime it was considered that seven years was the time needed to produce a trained askari. The impact of civilisation on the African is considerable, and despite this they took to the army quickly, responding to the training with zeal.

They first fought against the Italians who had built up an army of great numbers, but little stamina, in the territories of Somalia, Abyssinia and Eritrea. The British forces swarmed over these territories in a matter of weeks and the East African troops caught the smell and feel of war for the first time.

Japan, when she became Britain's enemy, threatened to overwhelm even Ceylon, and at that time the first detachments of East African troops were sent to the island. As these troops trained in Ceylon more drafts arrived from East Africa, and the tempo of their lives quickened as they received new types of weapons, better transport and more intensive training.

As the 11th East African Division they were picked to enter the Burma theatre, and at Kakching, near Palel, the first East African patrols went out some time in July, 1944.

The pressure on the enemy was increased as the Division moved into the line, and in early August they were outside of Tamu, in company with a famous Indian Division who were then withdrawing for rest.

The rain increased in weight and the roads were running under inches of water. When the rain stopped for an hour the heat rose like fire and drew steam from the sodden clothes of the troops.

2

From the truck I was able to see Kohima, or what had been Kohima. It was now a mound of glistening black ashes surrounded by bright green vegetation. The killing and wounding that those ashes had seen before the final battle was not now evident. There was only the silent rain falling on the scene. Beside the road lay heaps of shell-cases and every few yards were graves of British and Indian troops.

To get to Palel I had to first pass through Imphal, which the Japanese had besieged hopelessly. I knew that the troops of the East African Division were now outside Tamu, which lies on the border of Burma and India and at the entrance of the ill-famed Khabaw Valley. The advance would go down the Khabaw Valley to Kalewa on the River Chindwin. This valley had the reputation of being one of the most pestilential areas in the whole world, and famed for the virulence of its malaria. In the monsoon it would be a sheet of water and its jungle was packed with close-growing bamboo which cut down visibility to a few yards.

For us it would be hard. For the wrecked enemy it would be

harder. They were lost and without hope and they would die in thousands.

I reached Palel at midday. It was still raining and the grass was flattened and muddy. A few tents were scattered under the side of the hill. This was part of the 11th Divisional headquarters. The officers, most of whom I had met in Ceylon, were having lunch from a small table made of bamboos. Their boots were covered with mud and the earth floor of the bamboo 'basha' Mess was rapidly becoming a red paste.

For the first time I ate Soya Link Sausage. This is a piece of chemical composition shaped like a sausage and possessing a taste so flat and boring that it is quite impossible to face it after three days' trial. Soya Link Sausage and Repatriation are the two subjects that troops in Burma will discuss any time and with considerable heat.

The Soya Link is packed inside a golden-coloured tin and is approximately five inches in length. When cooked it looks like a sausage, being brown and firm.

'Hello!' says the officer at breakfast. 'Sausage or Soya.' One prod with the fork into the chemical pasty mess and he knows that it is Soya. Therefore, it is uneatable, and is put aside.

The finest comment on Soya Link that I have heard was made to me by an American pilot who had food with us in a patch of jungle. We told him that Soya Link was an American invention, for he had refused to touch his portion. 'Sure,' he said. 'It's an American food but we don't eat it. It's for the British, who are doing us the favour of eating it.'

At Palel we borrowed a Jeep and drove on into the hills. Tamu lay on the other side of this hill range, and as we climbed through the mud the cold increased. Towards Burma the country stretched into blue ranges of high mountains with the jungle stretching like a carpet of black and green fleece. Great valleys fell away into blue and grey mist, and this mist seethed slowly, trapping the lights of the fleeting sun and casting them in long bars of lemon-coloured light across the jungle.

There was the smell of rotting flesh, rising and falling in waves. On our left was a line of trenches that the enemy had dug round a bunker position. The red earth had been opened by explosions and was now waterlogged. Somewhere in the holes were the Japanese dead, who had fought on as the rearguard. We had arrived at the war.

Farther on a few British Sappers were rooting about cautiously, probably looking for concealed wires, for in this war both sides plant a hundred kinds of death that may wait months before striking.

A Japanese tank lay half over the cliff and the precipice fell steeply for hundreds of feet into a valley of yellow bamboo.

A few miles farther on we spotted something leaning against a tree and holding a rifle. We became ferret-eyed and cautious. It was a dummy soldier, planted probably by the enemy. Somebody had tucked a tin of bully-beef and an empty cigarette packet into the dummy's breast pocket. The dummy was wearing Japanese trousers with the narrow ankles and a British green jungle coat. We could not see any wire leading from him to a hidden charge and were childishly disappointed. Dick Elley, the conducting officer, said consolingly: 'Well, never mind, they've probably removed it.'

There was a road leading away to the left and a notice which said:

'Danger. Mines!'

As we drew nearer to the front the litter of retreat grew more varied. We got out of the Jeep to see the first Japanese gun, which lay on the side of the road. It was a big gun with a long barrel and long trail and the wheels were steel-rimmed and obsolete. This was 150-millimetre gun, and had been abandoned together with two excellent heavy gun tractors, which the Sappers said they would have in working order quite soon. A clutter of heavy black shells lay near the gun, and as we passed on through the mud, chests of these shells lay burst open everywhere. Brown Japanese trucks had rolled down the cliff and lay twisted in the trees. It was evident that our troops had pounced on the Japs from here with great speed and were giving them no respite.

The East Africans were still moving into the line and their artillery had not yet arrived. The going was sticky and soon the roads became impossible to negotiate as the rain poured on day and night. When the sun made a brief appearance it burned as the sun always does after heavy rain, with a fierceness that dried the clothes in a few minutes.

A few miles from Tamu we began to see smashed gun positions, bunkers torn open like wooden boxes in the soil, legs sticking out of the earth and ammunition boxes carrying the white stencilled characters of the Japanese army. This was the first time I had seen their writing and it seemed strange that we should fight people who used this curious language.

Dead mules, swollen, with their shaggy coats darkened with

rains, hundreds of ruined mule-saddles and steel helmets covered with camouflage-sacking and string. Here the air stank of death, and gradually one realised that here was the war-zone where thousands of enemy troops were trapped, not only by the Fourteenth Army, but by nature, armed with primeval jungle and a sky that had not yet produced its real fury.

The smell of Tamu came to us as we drove down into the mouth of Khabaw Valley. It was a smell that was sweet and terrible. A smell that once experienced is never forgotten, and is only more sickening than the smell of dead animals because it is the smell of dead human beings who have lived and hoped. When human beings have died or been killed in hundreds the odour of their ruined bodies has a quality that is almost frightening. This may be because of the sanctity with which human beings have always thought of the dead. In war and catastrophe, when faced with this horror of fleshly disintegration all about him, man loses the somewhat hushed respect he has for the dead, and can live, work and fight in the atmosphere of decaying bodies with hardly a thought.

For Africans such scenes and atmosphere hold hardly any terror at all, nor are they disgusted. Perhaps it is because they are still primitive in many of their reactions and possibly because the dead are not their own. At Tamu, which held one of the most shocking collections of human misery, endurance and death, imaginable, the East African Askari went in to seek out those who still wished to fight and to kill them wherever they could be found.

3

Tamu stands at the point where the narrow roads lead off into the jungle for the Chindwin River. It had been a beautiful village, peaceful, with the scattered and crumbling pagodas that the Burmese build in thousands to ensure the peace of their lives after death. The Burmese lived there quitely until the Japanese swarmed out of the Far East and established an outpost of the Co-Prosperity Sphere.

Tamu, in early August, 1944, gave off a smell of dead that reached for miles around it. It had been bombed and set ablaze, then bombed again and again. The trees that still stood were gashed and ripped open by shards of steel. The road of liquid mud that ran through it had been torn open by bombs from the Hurricanes of the R.A.F. These great craters now filled with rain had sucked back the debris, the fragments of men and shattered trees, and through these craters the Jeeps felt their way while the occupants held their hands over their noses.

The big pagodas stood beside the road, their front walls torn away and piled up nearby where they had been lashed down by the blast of 250-pound bombs. The tall, fluted spire of the one pagoda hung by a shred of metal, and from inside the pagoda four great gold-painted Bhuddas stared out, placidly, yet with contempt, for their privacy had been destroyed. They stood on a high altar, massive, and like all statues of the Bhudda, powerful, stout, yet graceful. At their feet stood a row of snow-white Bhuddas, each about a foot high. The head of every smaller idol was gone, sliced off by the blast.

Over five hundred Japanese corpses were packed inside this small village of blackened sticks and rubble. The jungle had been torn down, ripped away, and blasted into splinters, exposing the frameworks of the enemy hospital buildings, barracks and offices. In the ruins of these buildings the enemy lay dead in rows, in heaps, in pieces. They choked the village. Many had killed themselves with grenades, and these lay like horrible broken dolls.

At the feet of the tall Bhuddas who gazed out on to the scene of lashing rain, craters and torn trees, lay Japanese troops who had crawled here to die at the feet of the idols. They were mixed up with the remains of boots, groundsheets, batches of field postcards in gay colours, hundreds of grenades and filthy bandages. They had dragged themselves in out of the rain and the explosions, worn down beyond all hope of recovery, insane, and finished as soldiers and men.

The dead lay in bullock carts, under houses, in trees, craters and trenches, half dressed, fully equipped and naked. Rifles, ammunition pouches, belts, thousands of rounds of ammunition and hundreds of grenades and mortar-shells lay everywhere. The bombers had torn this place to pieces, sprayed it with explosive cannon-shells and terrified the sick and dying who had collected here. Some were alive, demented by hunger and fever, who turned to fight like animals on the last tremor of the electric fanaticism that had brought them here. These were cut down by bullets. Some tottered about in circles, mumbling, out of their minds. They fell down and crawled about and were picked up by our troops. Batches of them were carried to the trucks as prisoners, and many of these died where they stood, with their minds unhinged by rain, cold, explosions and utter physical and mental exhaustion.

One, wounded in the arm and shoulder, was taken prisoner by a patrol of askaris. He was bent and in the last stage of starvation. The askaris helped him along when suddenly he stopped and pulled a grenade from under his wounded arm. To throw a Japanese hand-grenade it is necessary to pull a pin and then bang the grenade sharply before throwing. Generally the enemy bang them on their steel helmets. This one did not complete the action, for, as he fumbled with the grenade, he was bayoneted by the askaris.

When they had killed him they remembered the tales they had been told, the drills, the lessons and warnings. Here were the troops of Japan, beaten into a form of senility, their bodies and minds broken, yet they still wished to kill.

Tamu, pest and charnel-house, was evil and ghastly, and you drove through it swiftly, for the smell stayed on your clothes. The living Japanese were even more terrible to look upon than the dead, for they walked as mockeries of their prostrate comrades, like animated cadavers. Their feet, upon which they had marched, stumbled and tottered since June, without food and without hope, had been abused past all endurance. They were useless and could no longer support the owners, who, covered with sores and weak from a form of Beri-Beri, could not even lift their hands for food. There was a dreadful magnificence in this picture, for after marching from the Chindwin and fighting for months on the Indian frontier, they had been starved into weakness and had then fallen back still trying to fight. They had reduced themselves into horror for Japan, and yet must still die after all this effort which had taken them beyond sanity. They must still fight or kill themselves. They must not be taken alive by the enemy, for this was disgrace and shame. These subhumans who had lived through storms of explosives were now slain if they turned to fight, and generally only those who did not even remember their names in their madness were taken prisoner without a fight. They came out of holes, shouting in cracked voices, waving their hands, their hair thick and overgrown into the shape of enormous wigs. They wished to die. In their tortured and animal minds was the fear of shame and the memory of many warnings:

'If you are taken prisoner when unconscious, then stuff your tongue down your throat and choke yourself to death when you get your chance,' said an order of the Japanese Command.

'Kill me,' they cried. 'Kill me: kill me.'

The rain fell on them and they stumbled into craters filled with water, but they did not mind. They mewed like cats, wept, joined their hands together and muttered incoherently. Even now they were filled with menace, for despite their physical state the seed of whatever it is that drives them still remained. When I saw them my first impression was that such obedience and endurance deserved a better end than the bursting grenade pressed against the chest. For an Emperor or an Army to expect this of its soldiers after being reduced to the state of wild beasts seemed too much. But they like it, and those who cannot bring themselves to do it (and there are many of them) become sick with remorse after capture, and yearn for the death they cannot give themselves. In Burma it is a good thing when they kill themselves, and those who cannot do so are taken prisoner and treated humanely according to the rules of war.

At Tamu I realised for the first time with complete conviction that the Japanese as they now behave and feel are a menace to the whole of humanity. It is improper to see fulfilment in a self-inflicted death and is unholy to welcome it as glory to the dead, the living and the unborn of the family. It is not right that human beings should willingly, like dumb animals, suffer a thousand indignities of the flesh and spirit and then commit suicide, either by grenade or by charging in ecstasy on to the machine-guns of the enemy.

The Japanese are not supermen, but they possess a contempt for death which is so great that it is stupid and pathetic. It is also degraded, and though it has an air of sombre greatness at times it is sad and evil. Such people should have tails or horns and should not stand upright. They should live in herds and endure nature as do the beasts of the field, for normal men with their love of life cannot live in the same world with a people who go to death as do elephants when their time has come to die.

I repeat that one sees pathos in the sight of small yellow human beings who have done all and more than was expected of them, yet wish to die for their failure. You wonder what can be done with them. Soldiers know the answer, especially those who have fought against them. Even the most primitive African has feeling for life and shuns death. For the Japanese soldier death is a leap into the shrine of Yasukuni, and is like a drugging perfume, even when it comes with tearing steel.

The askaris stared wide-eyed at the pictures from nightmare which they saw at Tamu in the pouring rain. They sniffed the smell of the corpses, and when they found enemy troops who opened fire they rushed in to kill them. They had come a long way from their villages in East Africa and had arrived in this curious hell of water and corruption, impenetrable jungle and violent death.

They were able to fling themselves on to an enemy who had been built into a legend, and destroy them. They felt the power of their weapons, and though they knew that these living wrecks were not the same men physically as had marched from the Chindwin to India, they never forgot that one day they would meet fresh, well-fed troops who would try their fighting qualities in jungle warfare.

CHAPTER THREE

1

Some have earlobes that hang for two or three inches like great pendulous circles, and upon these they used to hang rings of copper and brass. The practice of piercing the earlobes and stretching them is now dying out, and there is even a certain shyness in those who possess these signs of their tribal life. The askaris wish to be like Europeans, though there are many who never change and remain as unsophisticated as in the days when they lived with their tribes.

Many have chains of scars cut into their faces; in lines running down the cheeks, in circles radiating from the eyes and in curving rows upon their chests. This practice, too, is dying and there are many, who, having learned the ways of the white man, now wish their faces were clear and unscarred.

There are eaters of maize and banana and drinkers of cattle-blood. Some spent their lives with cattle, wandering over lonely plains where the yellow thorn trees cast a sparse shade and the hills roll jaggedly away up the rift valley. There are others who scratched the red earth around their huts and planted maize, living the quiet life that passes like a dream in Africa.

Experts with bees, and some who have hunted for meat in the rocks and bush. Some from tribes who have been powerful in the days when the spear ruled Africa, and others whose tribes have the new power of the white man's ways with cattle and crops and medicine.

These East Africans come from a land where the rain—and lack of it—has ordered life, caused catastrophe and the migrations of people, and has meant the beginning and the end of life. They do not come from a country of jungle, nor are they accustomed to great heat. They are not born jungle fighters, though many of the tribes are of ancient fighting races. Even those who had lost the feel of the bush and sky had never quite lost the memory of it in their bones.

They are not big and powerfully built, but are well knit and strong, with the greatest part of their strength in their cheerfulness and good humour. They are not fast thinkers, but sure and steady when they understand the way. They are not jet black, but run from very dark brown to a light coffee-colour. Some, from the races of the North, have hawk faces, and others have the heavy short jaw and thick lips from Central Africa. Those with the hawk faces are generally learners; sharp-eyed, alert and highly strung, as compared with the plodding and sometimes puzzled men who come from a different race.

The unspoiled East African has a dignity that can surmount many of the trials of life. He has also a sense of humour and can mimic many types.

As a soldier, when well-trained and disciplined, he has proved himself to be first class. By nature the East African is lazy, though as the tempo of his gradually changing life increases so also does his sense of responsibility. To produce soldiers from the mass of men who joined the army in the first two years of the war was a task that required patience and understanding of a high order. The African tends to be capricious and unbalanced when the guiding hand is missing. He will spend all his hard-earned money on a red silk umbrella or a brightly painted box, neither of which he can make use of. He is easily tempted by rogues, and is quickly impressed.

When they came from their tribes to the recruiting posts they were the rawest material in the world.

They jumped out of moving trucks, not realising that they would strike the ground and hurt themselves. Many had never known violent movement or speed. Others, when they were sick, wished to be burned with hot irons, for sickness was a demon stranger who must be sent away. The facts that are known to the white man were quite outside the lives of the average recruit. Such things as clocks, pills, telephones, engines, bullets, antiseptics, dynamite and electricity, pressure-gauges for tyres, compasses, dial-sights, maps, keys, boots, cigarettes, mosquito-nets and prophylactics were to enter their lives as strange and new things, and they were to learn how to control them and to direct death, save live, and destroy achievement, ugliness and beauty. The war, which had started somewhere in the homes of the white men, had absorbed all his muscle, this striving for knowledge and this ignorance which in most cases was abysmal.

They were able to reach out and accept almost all that the white man offered, for they were not tied by ancient taboo, not crushed by cruel gods, or separated by religious or racial hatred. Pork, beef and tobacco: they could accept all without shame or fear, and because of this they were fortunate in many ways and unfortunate in others. Without the restraint of taboo and ancient fear, and unhampered by any religious book of rules, many accepted all, including the evil, and were destroyed as Africans.

Many white men preached goodness and a great number lived badly, and from all this the African drew experience, and when the army life entered into his consciousness and absorbed him he grew both as a man and a personality.

The British officers and non-commissioned officers who trained this army of East Africans spent long hours in the sun with them, made hundreds of thousands of inspections, paraded them for the taking of quinine pills, made them bathe regularly and keep their hair short. They told them a thousand times 'Do this. Do that,' and taught them how to wear uniform and keep it clean. Then they trained them to kill efficiently, which is the first duty of soldiers in war, and how to save their friends when wounded. Drivers, painters, carpenters, cooks, signallers, artillerymen, infantrymen, medical-dressers, muleteers and military policemen were trained through thousands of hours of patience and understanding.

The mass of infantry learned how to use the rifle, grenade, bayonet, mortar, Bren-gun and shovel. They learned to take cover, to rush swiftly and with economy of movement, to creep, to leap and to do what they were told. They were taught how to march and how to rest, how to cook for themselves and how to protect themselves from disease.

From the brightest and most reliable of the troops who were beginning to assume the air of soldiers were picked the African non-commissioned officers. Under the guidance of tough old regular N.C.O.s these young ones learned to watch, to ignore, to chide and to demand obedience.

From a vast milling and confusion came lines of fit, well-fed troops, who kept their eyes front and did not fidget.

The final test is battle.

2

In Ceylon they trained and worked as they had never done before. The hot jungles were very different from the hills and plains of Africa, and in this trying climate they learned what real exhaustion was, and when their bodies and minds became used to the dark green light of the jungle they found that they could use nature and its trees and colours for warfare against an enemy who had shaken the world.

In Africa they had worn khaki, with long shorts that reached below the knees and long puttees. When they were ready after the last Divisional training effort in Ceylon they were issued with the green jungle battledress of thin, tough cotton, and they knew then that they would soon leave for Burma.

The passion for writing and reading had gripped them and every man had learned even a few words. In their spare moments they sat down with stubs of pencil, pushed out their tongues, and with much labour wrote a letter to Africa. The troops from Nyasaland and Uganda showed more skill and were familiar with the printed word. The others worked patiently. Soon the output of letters to Africa increased, became vast.

The East African Division was given its own vernacular paper in Ceylon, which was called 'Heshima.'

This paper is printed in Ki'Swahili, the Lingua Franca of East Africa, and Chinyanja, the language of Nyasaland and Northern Rhodesia. It gave them news of the war and of home. In the front of the paper a character called 'Bwana Kiko' (Kiko means pipe) wrote on a variety of subjects, and more often than not issued words of warning about the dangers of this and that and instructed them upon such subjects as saving money, venereal disease, alcoholic excess and goodwill.

Most of the officers of the Division came from the army in Britain, as do nearly all the British N.C.O.s. From Rhodesia, Nyasaland, Tanganyika, Uganda and Kenya came officers who had known the African for years, but the great majority of them were from Britain, and have gained all their knowledge of the African while commanding them in the army.

This Division, made up of most of the tribes of East Africa, was picked as the spearhead of the advance down the Khabaw Valley to Kalewa on the Chindwin River. As a spearhead they would fight in the monsoon and would liberate territory that the Japanese had held for over two years. As things stood in August, their greatest enemy would be the monsoon, for the Japanese could offer only token resistance, but the kind of resistance that doubles the labour and ordeal of the rain and the jungle.

In Burma the Division was issued with the new monsoon-cape, which was of stiff and heavy waterproof material, and equipped with a hood. Later this was withdrawn and gas-capes were issued, for they were lighter in weight, easy to roll up and carry, and were green or coloured with camouflage paint.

Steel helmets were abandoned; the branches made a clinking

sound against them and they were heavy. Also the enemy did not have a great deal of artillery left. So the Division went into action wearing khaki slouch hats.

All khaki webbing, sheets, vests, towels, mosquito-nets and any other light coloured material, was dyed dark green before the troops entered the battle zone.

A green and black army passed through the mud, and with the evil-smelling ruins of Tamu as the axis of their operations they went in pursuit of the enemy.

Divisional headquarters was at Moreh, where the hills sloped down to Tamu. On the glistening red hillside, half hidden in rain mist, a litter of tents grew into a headquarters, and as the monsoon grew in strength this headquarters settled itself in for the first phase of the campaign, which was the capture of Sittaung on the Chindwin, far up North of Kalewa.

The Chindwin runs from North to South and was swollen into a fast torrent. The Japanese troops were desperate to reach both Sittaung and Kalewa and escape from the fury of artillery, planes and rain. One force of survivors from the Imphal debacle took the road to Sittaung, while the other headed south to Kalewa.

The task of destroying these troops was formidable, for both weather and disease might hamper movement and mobility. It rained with a shattering intensity. The askaris, lovers and dreamers of rain, were unable to believe that this happened every year and went on from April to October.

In August an Askari asked me when the rain would end, and when I told him October he could hardly believe me. 'But, Effendi, it has been raining for months now. How can there be enough rain to last until October? Why is there so much? How can people live here?'

3

I stood at the side of a river. It swirled and foamed, fed by black clouds that were gathering over the jungle. Three dead Japanese lay on their faces and the water washed over their heads. They had come here for their last drink. They wore black rubber jungle boots, muddy puttees and khaki breeches and tunics. They had been dead for days. They also wore respirators slung over their shoulders, and though they had thrown away all their other equipment they had kept these respirators. Nearly every corpse I had seen lay with respirator slung, for as we were to find out later, they had been told that the British would use poison gas to keep them out of India.

Across the river were several big bamboo huts packed with corpses. The sick had collected near the river and the stragglers from many battalions had stayed here when they fell down into the mud and their friends stumbled on.

This gloom was intensified by the rain and the looming jungle. The mud which sucked at the feet and slowed up trucks added to it. It was like being cut off in some far, unknown land, of eternal water and vegetation. You were conscious of people dying horribly down the road and knew that you would come upon them as they lay in all the attitudes of final moments.

There was a feeling of satisfaction in this, for one never forgot that these Japanese troops, had they been fit and well, would have been fighting and on the offensive. It was satisfying to know that they were experiencing, even if in a far more terrible manner, what they had inflicted on the peoples of the East during the past seven years.

This had never happened to them before. Their machine had never failed them, nor had they been deserted and cast aside to the whims and angers of nature, and enemy fire.

The Burmese, gentle, two-faced and uncertain, turned on them, and would give them no food and no hiding places. The Japanese were cast off and left to wander and die. They cursed the Burmese, and especially the puppet of Rangoon, Dr. Ba Maw. Against this individual, Japanese officers made threats, telling the Burmese what they would do to him if ever they reached Rangoon.

'Ba Maw told us that the Burmese would help us in our conquest of India, but when misfortune came to us the Burmese turned on us and were traitors,' shouted a Japanese lieutenant to the villagers and headmen south of Tamu. 'We will make him pay. We will castrate him,' screamed the lieutenant. He then asked for flour and was refused. He found some and asked villagers to grind it for his men. They refused, and the officer, together with his dying men, set to grinding the flour in the middle of the village, while the Burmese looked on with sneers.

The Burmese were proud of having done this, and probably had been as proud before under other circumstances. Life is today and to-morrow, and money. It is never yesterday.

Because of the rain the artillery of the 11th East African Division was having difficulty in getting through. Up to now, no real resistance had been met and the African troops had been in the fighting for over a fortnight. They learned war quickly, under hard and ideal conditions. They began to sleep in the rain, march and fight in it, and began to think of it as something permanent. They began to look like first-line troops, for dirty, tired soldiers wearing equipment and with rifles slung look men indeed.

CHAPTER FOUR

On August 13th I watched the first interrogation of prisoners. A wire cage had been hastily put up beside the road at Moreh, not far from Divisional Headquarters. Inside this cage several wrecked human beings lay on their faces and moaned. The doctor had seen them, and these were passed as men who would recover after a little food. Even so, they were terrible to look upon, being emaciated and unable to think. They could walk after a fashion but were still in the grip of the nightmare of the last five weeks. They were in rags and two had their feet bandaged. They had come straight from the forward area and would now be interrogated before being passed on to the Corps headquarters.

Opened tins of bully-beef and packets of biscuits lay beside them. Only one was eating: he was doing this with a wolfish intensity and was tearing swiftly at the lumps of bully-beef, stuffing them into his mouth and looking round wildly and with a certain fear. He was breaking the code because he was human and starving. He was alive in this valley of dead men who had endured until the end for the Emperor and the Army, and he was eating. Actually he looked close to hysteria, for several times he stopped and opened wide his eyes, his mouth trembled. He stared at something I could not see. He continued to eat with sharp and desperate movements. Perhaps he thought that the British were going to kill him, and there was probably solace in this thought, for he could enjoy this meal to the full and then die.

The others did not move; they lay still on their faces, thinking or raving quietly. They were all small men with powerful hands and their hair was matted and had grown into thick, black shocks of coarse fibre. Only two wore boots. The others were barefooted and these they had wrapped in filthy rags. Over their heads was stretched a tarpaulin and the rain ran from it in streams and poured through their shelter. They did not attempt to divert it by scratching a channel with a twig. They let it run under their bodies. What was rain now, or pain, or death. They were prisoners and were finished with Japan and their families.

Twenty or thirty Africans stood around the cage, fascinated. They stared and said nothing. They had not been to the front yet and these were the first Japanese troops they had seen. They did not speak but leaned on the wire and drank in every aspect of these captured men.

The Japanese did not look at them. When I walked up with Major Harston, the Senior Supply Officer of the Division, one dragged himself on to his haunches, pressed his hands together and bowed.

So it was true, they really did this. The Africans were fascinated and looked at us with a sort of pride, then grinned. It was evident that they felt a sympathetic contempt for these puny, broken prisoners.

What scenes of battle and desolation these prisoners had seen one could only imagine. They belonged to Yamamato Force which had been cracked open and then thrown back. Holes in the ground filled with water, and artillery that registered on them when the planes were not diving down to release bombs and flails of cannon shells. Grass eaten from the mess-tin and officers who were unbalanced by defeat and failure. Then the long, unreal journey through the mud and jungle to the collapsing-place where they had crashed on their faces, right out of this world.

The first prisoner to be interrogated was a young man with large, long, black eyes, and an expression of hopelessness and defeat. He wore a thin vest of bloodied cotton and a pair of khaki breeches which, though they normally laced up at the ankle, were now open so that the strings trailed in the mud. He was helped along by two askaris who gripped his arms. He was dragged, for his feet made only the movements of walking. They were bare, torn and caked with blood and dirt, looking as though they would never be able to carry their owner again. He made gasping cries and turned his head right and left. The high pile of hair that stood out in spikes from his head made him appear even younger than he was and, if possible, more pathetic. He was terrified of the Africans and had obviously never seen such men before. The Africans were powerful Ja'luo tribesmen from the shores of Lake Victoria-Nyanza, and they dwarfed this sick man, who had probably terrified many people in his time. They tried to hurry him and he cried in Japanese:

'Kakki! Kakki!' which is the Japanese word for Beri-Beri.

The Africans laughed and stole looks at him until they reached the lean-to office of the Interrogating Officer, who was a British lieutenant, with the bored air that Interrogating Officers usually affect during interrogations.

The prisoner stopped in front of the large wooden box that served as a desk and swayed about until he fell down. He was helped up again by the Africans, and he then pressed his hands together and bowed with great dignity to the Lieutenant.

He sat down on a four-gallon petrol tin when told to do so by the Lieutenant and bent his head as though in prayer. I did not realise at the time that he was tottering on the edge of hysteria, but the Lieutenant seemed to know all the signs. ('He is going to break down shortly and cry,' he said to me; 'they nearly all do. It's damn strange.')

He gave the Japanese a cigarette, and just then a large mess-tin of tea was brought in with some tin cups. When the prisoner was given a cup of tea his mouth twisted again and one side of his face began to twitch.

'Don't look at him for a moment,' said the Lieutenant, and then engaged me in trivial conversation until the wretched prisoner had recovered himself.

He asked a few questions and the prisoner replied at once, but stopped to drink greedily from the tin cup. The tea brought a speck of light into his eyes and he gasped as though about to collapse again.

They talked for a few minutes in the guttural Japanese tongue, and then suddenly the prisoner gripped his head in his hands and began to weep brokenly, drawing in long, sobbing breaths and in such a manner that his whole body shook violently. He sobbed on and on, while the Lieutenant watched him with a gleam of sympathy, yet covertly, for with the Japanese one can never be sure what is about to happen.

The Lieutenant did not say 'I told you so,' it was too pathetic for such comment, for here was a man who had broken down in front of other men and there was no secret and no reserve left, and there was embarrassment among the Africans.

'He is crying because he has remembered how he was deserted by his officers,' said the Lieutenant. 'He said he marched until he could march no longer, and after falling down several times he found he could no longer get up and he called out to his officer. The officer simply told one of the men to throw him a hand-grenade, and this was done, but he was afraid to kill himself when the others had gone.'

This man, who had gone through sufferings that few men have experienced, was now hysterical because he had not killed himself. How were we to defeat these people, not in Burma, but in the whole of the East? when they regarded death as the answer to both victory and failure. Death was something casual that you produced for yourself out of a steel globe of high explosive and with little sorrow. I cannot quite put into words what this meant to us. I can only say that it meant destroying a whole people if they were all to act in this manner. How can people make fine machinery and deal with the problems of physical life in a manner that shows brilliance and yet behave as though the world and all its works matter not at all. This power, or this whim of sub-humanity, is the most perplexing thing of all about the Japanese.

This youth, who sat with his head in his hands, as though all the trouble in the world was his, was twenty-eight years old. He was good-looking, even in his present state. He had worked for five years at the Nakajima airplane factory in Japan, and had been a riveter. When he described the work he had done there the interrogating officer had not understood the expression he had used, and forgetting all his tears and his anguish the prisoner stood up to demonstrate. He did it with smiles; holding an imaginary riveting machine and driving in invisible rivets with a perfect imitation of the accompanying noises.

The Japanese are like that. They shift from one extreme to the other, even in their diaries. Some of the saddest human conclusions on the war are to be found in the diaries of the Japanese troops, and yet they fight as fanatics, apparently without thought of home or family. They have a mentality for which we have no measuring-board. They do not remind you of any other people. They are a people apart. You realise this when you find a packet of charms from a Japanese temple in the same bag with a perfectly made toothbrush sealed up in a cellophane bag. Both are made in Japan.

Outside in the cage the other prisoners were still lying in a semi-coma, moaning softly. A British N.C.O. with a Tommy-gun slung over his right shoulder nudged one of them and said: 'Here, you little bastard, drink this.' He held out a cup of tea to the prisoner, who clasped his hands and tried to bow. He had to be helped. Soon they were all given tea and bully-beef with biscuits. They drank avidly, making long, loud sounds of pleasure. They picked weakly at the bully-beef until the tea gave them strength, when they ate it with relish.

It was hard to believe that these were the people who had ravaged China and who had torn apart the life of a great country. How could they know that their planes had attacked Pearl Harbor when their diplomats had been engaged in negotiations? It was quite obvious that they did not care.

These little men could know nothing of politics and of the shifting scene of intrigue. How could they imagine that their flesh and muscle was merely part of a vast reaping machine that tore rubber, rice and sugar from the territories they had lately captured. They would die anywhere, anytime, anyhow, for the Emperor.

Looking into this cage one realised the terror and horror of the Japanese war machine which drove on like an engine of steel and flesh, uncaring. When they were told to die they died, until they made the air where they had breathed horrible with the scent of their sacrifice. If you looked at this cage in the rain merely as a collection of barbed wires holding several emaciated men, there was nothing more than pathos in the scene. But when you remembered the mass frenzies on the streets of China and killing at Hong Kong, when crazy with victory, they ran riot, the cage took on a new significance. The wire imprisoned a few of the most dangerous men in the world. Because they believed in their horror and in their politeness: because they believed in Japan with everything that made up their bodies and souls, and because they lay in dirt, uncaring and spent, they proved all this. People say that the Japanese are only part of a machine, like cogs: but the cogs do their work without complaint.

The Japanese soldiers care as little for the lives of their enemies as they do for their own. How can you expect mercy from a people who spend their lives as water. Their Yamato cult, their surprises and their training drove us out of the East, but could not finally conquer. The spirit of humanity is still triumphant and will always win.

In a captured order of the day, written by General Sakurai Tokutaro, Commander of the Japanese 51st Division Infantry Group in Burma, was written:

> 'If your hands are broken, fight with your feet. If your hands and feet are broken, fight with your teeth. If there is no breath left in your body, fight with your ghost.'

This is no cheap phrase flung from a balcony hung with eagles of ice-cream: this is an order that will be obeyed and is given for that purpose, and not for printing in newspapers for a worried public. It is well to repeat that the Japanese are not supermen, but they are the most formidable fighters of the Axis when measured in terms of savagery and sacrifice. Where the

Commander can stand on a hill and watch a heavy twenty minutes' bombardment on a German position and say with fair certainty, 'Well, those Jerries have had it: mop them up,' he cannot say the same for the Japanese. Even after the bombardment the infantry must dig them out, kill them and burn them, if the Japanese have not done it themselves. They have produced a new horror in the war by the quality of their mass dying. British, Australian and American soldiers have killed them like rats, in holes, trenches, bunkers and forts, with a hundred kind of weapons. They have been sealed up by bulldozers under tons of earth, blasted out with phosphorous and then calcined with flame-throwers. And more are sent up to die in waves. The infamy of this murderous casting away of thousands of deluded human beings cannot yet be truly appreciated. It appears as if the Japanese like to die in this manner.

Looking into the cage, one reflected on this. The threat of death meant nothing.

August 15th was a very full day. I had heard the Japanese speaking their language and had seen how they reacted to capture. The most interesting note in all the day's happenings was to find that the enemy could weep, not only in battle hysteria, but with the bitterness of men who feel they have been deserted.

At this stage I had no real conception of the greatness of the victory won by the Fourteenth Army on the borders of India. One slouched along in a corner of Burma's immense jungle, and could not see the full picture of the enemy's retreat. I did not know then how the Fourteenth Army's fighting spirit had split open and utterly wrecked a powerful army that had marched from the Chindwin to India. But gradually, as we passed south, and I began to understand what the Fourteenth Army stood for and what it had done in South-East Asia, I was able to see that this offensive that we had started would go a long way indeed into Burma.

In the tent on the side of the hill at Moreh, small rivulets swelled into pools and ran over boots, into haversacks, and then flowed under the bed. The rain drummed on the golden canvas overhead, raced off and came in to join the growing pools. I scratched new channels into the mud with twigs and tried to coax the water away into another direction. After half an hour I gave up: one grew resigned. Rain dripped through on to the blankets, formed pools, spread and then soaked everything within reach. This was going to continue for a couple of months. We sat in the mouth of the tent and looked out at the silver sheets beating on the jungle. Below us, columns of askaris slopped along, hunched up under their capes, their rifles slung, muzzles down. From the boots up to the waist they were bright red with mud, their battledress turned black with the rain. They marched, each deep in his own thoughts, heading for the Sittaung track. Artillery bumped and swayed beside them, throwing up sheets of dark-red water. Twenty-five-pounders on thick rubber wheels, manned by askaris who were about to open fire on the Japanese for the first time.

In Divisional Headquarters the atmosphere was one of great busyness. The really hard part of this campaign was going to fall on the Supply and Transport who would need to supply rations, petrol and ammunition, no matter what kind of weather prevailed, or what terrain faced them. Without supplies, the division could not move.

Planes came over and made the first air-drop of supplies to us on a strip of road near Moreh. They came in low and fast, showering the supplies on to the dropping zone. A bag of maize struck an askari and killed him on the spot. Supplies with great speed and weight, undamaged by the force with which they hit the ground.

The Supply and Transport of the Division had had no experience before with supply by air, but quickly grasped the technique. Officers of the Service Corps developed a trained eye for a likely dropping zone, and in a short time the air-supply machine worked smoothly, in all weathers.

The askaris working on the supply drops became expert at judging speeds and dropping places, and there were few accidents. Generally, every man left the vicinity and lay low until the planes had unloaded their cargoes.

This Division was now becoming well knit as a fighting machine. The reasons for the repetition so many times during training of certain points became apparent to all, especially to the private soldier. In action, the memory seizes on the automatic action performed a thousand times for the instructors, and gives it a meaning which the granite or grass of the training station could never give it. Flying bullets shout in a louder voice than the sergeants, and the rush bored at a dummy position becomes something different in battle; something filled with menace that must be swiftly performed.

Discipline is the first and most urgent requirement of troops in battle. Discipline is a patch in the brain that has been put there by the army, and which controls the nerves and muscles and will to fight and endure under orders. This discipline is something quite apart from all other human reactions and when deeply rooted in good soldiers, will carry them through any hell devised by the enemy. Not the discipline of thin-faced fanatics who are lost without their leaders, but something else, where officers and men are in bondage to each other and will perform their duties until completed.

Discipline means that excited soldiers will not open fire without orders and thus expose their position. The soldier who opens fire on his own may commit all his comrades to wounds and death. Disciplined soldiers lie still, even though roused to the high nervous pitch of battle excitement and will wait for orders. In the jungle such discipline is all-important, for the hidden eye is peering and the ear feels the atmosphere like a moving antennae. A crackle or a shout may bring down the chattering fire of a machine-gun.

The askaris began to lift branches aside with the delicate touch of the artist and to steal the quick, sweeping look at what was revealed. The Japanese, highly praised by us as jungle fighters, make noises like bunches of monkeys. This is a curious thing because they have always been described as the finest jungle fighters in the world, but many legends died in 1944, and they were killed by the troops of the Fourteenth Army.

Where were the small calibre, fast-firing rifles described in our press in 1942 as being part of the Japanese armoury. It was said that armed with these small calibre weapons the enemy troops could carry hundreds of rounds of the small calibre ammunition in their pockets and operate for miles on a handful of rice.

True, the Japanese rifles are of small calibre, being ·256, but they weigh over nine pounds and are longer and heavier than ours. The ammunition is not small, and is, in fact, about the same size as that used by the Italians, and has no special quality, but is, in fact, poorer and less powerful than ours. The rifle is cumbersome, and though serviceable, is not as good as that used by the Allied armies.

'The enemy can live on a handful of rice and can travel for miles and miles.' This is another handover from 1942. True, the Japanese are frugal and physically are very tough indeed, and can march great distances; but the story of the handful of rice is not quite what it appears to be. Man cannot live by rice alone, even the Asiatics. Most Japanese soldiers serving outside of Japan suffer from Beri-Beri, and this is a disease that can destroy the fastest moving army. It helped to break them outside of Imphal, and has ravaged them everywhere they have fought in South-East Asia and the Pacific war zones.

It is laid down by their Command that the Japanese troops shall receive the equivalent of three thousand calories a day, which is about the same number supplied in the British Army. The enemy needs the same bodily sustenance as do other troops, and without it they sicken and die. Our system of a balanced vitamin-ration in tablet form is far superior to that of the Japanese Army which supplies its troops with yeast tablets. Yeast is good, but deteriorates and has not stopped the Beri-Beri and other results of ration deficiencies which have softened the bones of many enemy soldiers.

The Japanese supply system is a sketchy affair and has generally been based on victory. When victory has not been awarded them the enemy have starved to death. When they left the Chindwin, to attack India they carried fourteen days' rations. India would give them the rest. India gave them nothing, save hot steel and misery, and the weak supply machines, that endeavoured to feed them in their plight, was destroyed by Allied bombers. Grass cannot offer three thousand calories per day, and so the mighty and almost miraculously frugal soldiers of Japan lay down and died together with their legend.

'Fight with your ghost.' It is difficult to do so, even for the Japanese. The ghosts whom we were pursuing in August, 1944, were unable to walk properly and their feet and teeth were useless also. The splendid machine of the human body, though lit with the strange spirit that had conquered the East, could fight no longer, not even with its ghost.

The Africans fell on them with bayonets and matchets, and pressed down through the mud to Sittaung.

CHAPTER FIVE

Two of the greatest inventions of the war are the bulldozer and the Jeep. The former is huge: a monster of powered steel, which when in action resembles some berserk shining bull with lowered head. Without bulldozers the Fourteenth Army could never have pressed on with their heavy equipment as fast as they did. Trucks bogged down in mud above the wheels have been dragged, pushed and worried out by bulldozers of every type. Some trucks laden with a great weight of steel bridging material sank helplessly in the red mud, and all ranks peeled off their jackets and laboured until they were ready to drop. Behind, the bogged truck lines of Jeeps and trucks came to a standstill and the expert Tommies, never losing a moment, brewed fast mess-tins of tea as they waited.

The bulldozer clattered along, and in a few minutes the truck was pulled out on to the side of the road. With a rush, all the traffic surged, splashed and rolled forward. Jeeps carrying the painted insignia of the 33rd Indian Corps, the red shield of the Fourteenth Army, one or two with the phoenix of the South-East Asia Command, and most wearing the black rhinoceros head on the white circle of the 11th East African Division, flitted in and out among the bigger trucks. If you were bogged down, you stayed there until the flood of traffic had gone and then you sent for a bulldozer. The bulldozer cruised up and down the roads, looking for those in distress, helping where they could, but in August it was not possible to work on any concerted plan until the advance had got some way forward.

The bulldozer may find a part of the road that is rutted and has become a trap for all traffic. The Indian driver backs his monster for some distance, with the big blade lifted and looking rather like a polished stanchion attached to the front of the tractors. When the bulldozer is ready to charge this steel pusher is lowered and the blade sinks into the soil while all the power of the engine exerts itself. Tons of earth and mud, tree stumps, Japanese skulls, are pushed aside leaving a hard, flat surface. The machines we saw in August were the small fast types, rather like whippet tanks. Later in the campaign we were to see what a team of big bulldozers could do with one of the most heartbreaking roads in the world.

The Jeep is like a good pony: like a person with a good, strong heart and like everything that will not admit defeat but tries again. Jeeps have done the most amazing things: have crawled almost sideways up muddy slopes while the driver, heart in mouth, leans forward after the manner of a horseman urging on his mount and clasps the steering wheel with anxious hands. Jeeps have gone through rivers when the exhaust blast under the water makes a sound like a high powered motor-boat engine. Crawling across acres of mud and across felled and broken trees, they have taken ammunition and food where no other form of transport could go.

The affection felt for the Jeep is something that is usually reserved for a domestic animal. Drivers have gone through ordeals of travel in their Jeeps, and patted the steel of the Jeep's bonnet in their admiration. Plastered with mud, filthy and faithful, these machines have never failed in their task. It is doubtful whether any other steel contraption has compelled such affection on the Fourteenth Army's battlefields, which extend for thousands of square miles of dense jungle and mountain.

After we had burned Tamu's hundreds of corpses, the engineers started on their task of keeping the road to Sittaung open. 'Road' is a word that lost its meaning during the monsoon but will do to describe the tortuous ribbon of red mud that led to the first objective on the Chindwin. To get on to the main track to Sittaung after Tamu, it was necessary to cross three torrents of water. All bridges had been destroyed by the enemy or washed away. The first of these rivers was negotiated by the slow and boring method of fixing a collapsible assault boat to a cable and pulling it across. The troops and supplies went across in batches and the infantry sat down in the shade of the side of the road and waited their turn.

It was interesting to watch the East African troops as they gradually turned into the patient, trained soldiers of the great Fourteenth Army. Marching in mud that sucked at the boots and gaiters, with a sodden steaming pack and a rifle that must be always clean and ready, is a test of fitness and training. The sweat-salt runs into the eyes in streams and tastes sharply on the lips, and the engine of nerves, cells and muscle burns a fuel that is costly and precious. The uniforms of marching troops in Burma sometimes show streaks of glittering whiteness. These are the body salts that have been cast out and dried, and must be replaced quickly.

Salt tablets are an issue to the men and these are taken with plenty of water. Without replacement of lost salts and fluid comes heat exhaustion accompanied by high temperature and, quite often, death. The exhaustion that comes to marching infantry who have floundered through mud and rain, in one moment soaking the clothes and equipment through and through, in the next, burns with a sharp, eye-searing heat, is something that the troops do not talk much about. They lie down in their rest periods, quietly, appreciating, as few people have done, the peace and boon of relaxation. They must get up again and go on and as they march they tighten this strap, loosen that belt, shift that weight just a little and stare with a dulled fascination at the glistening neck of the man in front. And always these men know that the end of their march will probably not be as the ends of other marches during the days of training. There will be no flopping down with a cigarette while the cooks brew tea. Here, in Burma, there will be digging and probably fighting. To go into action after a long march through tropical heat imposes an excessive demand on the human body, but it has been done again and again for over two years in Burma. From the Arakan, to the Khabaw, to Mogaung and onward, men have done it, pressing on the tired body, never falling out, never giving in.

Few soldiers write in their letters home of the sick, reeling sensation that accompanies the march in the heat of midday. In the mouth of the Khabaw Valley, the askaris learned all these new notes in the scale of jungle warfare and they pulled their battledress jackets down until they hung only by the belts, and marched stripped to the waist. Their black skins which were designed to absorb the sun, flashed as the long back-muscles clenched and unclenched. Their slouch hats drooped, and the sharpnesses and softnesses of cheek bones and noses were lost in glare and sweat-polish that wiped out line and shape.

To the tune of the song that they had sung about Mussolini in Italian Africa, they now sang of Tojo. They were not sure who Tojo was, for their grasp of the global war was still in process of growing, but they knew he was one of the demons of Japan.

They called the enemy 'Jampans,' which is the nearest they can approach to the pronunciation of the word 'Japanese.'

It was strange to stand by the side of the road and watch them go by. Three, four and five years before, they had never handled anything more lethal than a spear and they had never heard of Burma or Japan. Now they were pouring through the mouth of this pestilential valley in pursuit of Yamamoto's troops. They were trained and hard. They were able to bear the burden of Burma's capricious days and carry heavy mortars on their shoulders, ammunition and rations. They were committed to fight in one of the toughest theatres of the war, and had already smelled endless corruption, they had seen what privations the jungle and the rain could inflict on man.

The stranger who looked at these askaris would see them as black men from an indeterminate part of Africa. Many people confuse East and West Africa, and some think that Nigeria is near Kenya. In any case, they are regarded by the stranger as black men from Africa who still may be secretly cannibal. The askari with a Bren gun, and wearing jungle battledress, hides much turbulent history under the uniform, but the life he lived before he went to the army was of a hundred different natures. The askaris of the East African Division are drawn from the country between Nyasaland far south, to the barren deserts of

Kenya's northern frontier, and even from the banks of the Nile.

Heads of every shape known in East Africa can be seen among them. Faces that are thin and sensitive and others that are chunky and poorly formed are to be found in the ranks. Some are tribesmen whose lives were filled with ritual and rooted in animism, while others come from tribes who have never developed their lives much further than the height of the maize they grew.

The rhythms and songs that in the north are accompanied by the clapping of hands, for the nomads seldom carry drums, and the more sultry drum music of the country farther south are mingled here under green uniforms.

There was even a grey-haired Zulu who worked in the stables of Johannesburg. How did he join the East African Division? He moved and wandered as have the tribes of East Africa for centuries, moved by impulse or contact with other men.

Some are swift of thought and are passionate, and others are slow with the steadiness of those who have lived in security. The army machine has placed a strain upon them that has forced the slow flow of their characters into new channels. They have acquired new appetites, and have come to understand that the pills, mosquito-nets and prophylatics have a real purpose which they fulfil admirably. With all this has come the ache of separation from home, the eating of strange food and the suffering of new pains. Also, there is the separation from the family group and the barren life of celibacy.

The fast, electric, and petroleum fed tempo of their lives in war has no relation whatsoever to the slow, drifting sunlight of their peace-time lives. The war has uprooted them and pushed them into situations to which they cannot swiftly accustom themselves, and despite this they have done well as soldiers, equipped with the best arms and equipment that the army can give them, and a good-nature that is their own.

The fighter-bombers that screamed overhead in threes, flashing past like slivers of light; the bulldozers that mashed trees and soil into a heap and then flung them aside, and all the new engines of battle like heavy tanks, big guns and flame-throwers, thrilled them and made them feel that this was the big war they had really come to at last.

An air-strike by fighter-bombers when seen for the first time is an experience that for excitement can hardly be surpassed. The planes come in low and fast, loosing their two bombs on to the bunkers where they explode in a shattering burst of flame and debris. Others bore in, peeling off until they have the sights on to the target, when they open fire with cannons. The cannon shells burst in strings of white-hot flashes up and down and across the target.

The area is one of flame and concussion, and the jungle is seized as if by giant hands, ripped out of the ground and flung to the four winds.

For the askaris their first air-strikes were experiences that lifted them to the highest pitch of excitement. This was a side of the war that they had only heard about, when dozens of fast planes came in and flung high explosives with great accuracy and fury on to the Japanese positions.

As the troops slumped down towards Sittaung, the administrative machine of the Division was taking a grip on the country, and dumps, field maintenance centres, field hospitals, gun-parks, repair shops and bakeries were springing up in the jungle, beside swollen rivers and under the shelter of cliffs. The stream of fighting troops gradually swelled and by the time the forward elements had pushed their way through the scattered and stinking corpses that were everywhere on the Sittaung track, the enemy had established positions with fresh troops and was trying to fight a rearguard action.

Bundles of Japanese currency, smelling of the dead they had been taken from, were brought into the Intelligence Officer's truck which was fitted up as an office. This dreadfully scented currency, which filled the truck with its odour, came from Sumatra, and had been taken from the body of a well-equipped, and what the police might call well-nourished, enemy corpse. If the enemy were pushing in troops from Sumatra, it might mean that a new regiment or even a new division was moving up against us. The Intelligence staff pored over maps and known enemy dispositions, sifting all information after the manner of the Intelligence, but could not at this stage say what was in the offing.

At a place called Jambo Hill the forward troops of the brigade, moving on Sittaung, came on to stiff opposition and preparations for battle were made.

The artillery was slowly coaxed forward, after crossing the rivers and pushing through the mud that was deepening under the feet of the marching troops and the wheels of the few vehicles that could make their way forward.

The enemy position called 'Jambo Hill' was probably given that name to commemorate the first pitched battle of the Division's campaign. 'Jambo,' a Ki'Swahili word, is a form of greeting, and is used throughout East Africa by those who speak

Ki'Swahili. Jambo Hill was considered to be held by about thirty men with rifles and light automatics. It covered the bend in the road and was placed well back in the jungle, yet with an excellent field of fire. As a road block it was well chosen, for the approach to it was through very thick jungle. It was decided to bring down artillery fire on to it and then clear it with infantry.

From the river below Tamu the Hygiene Squads were working on their gruesome task. They had established a routine for dealing with the enemy dead. One Japanese steel helmet filled with flame-thrower mixture was poured over the corpse and a short trail of the mixture led away from it. A match was applied and a blast of hissing flame enveloped the dead. The grenades that the Japs always carry blew up in the terrific heat, and the squads passed on to the new task.

One of the Hygiene officers, a short, ginger-haired and eternally cheery Scotsman, kicked open the door of a 'Basha' which was some distance from the road. Five Japanese moved inside, but he was faster and ripped off a long burst of Tommy-gun fire into them, killing the lot. In a few moments they were ablaze and the Scotsman was furious because a brand-new enemy map-case had received part of his burst and was ruined.

The atmosphere had ceased to be unreal and it was surprising to walk a few yards and not find corpses. How many thousand had died in the jungle will probably never be known. Some came out on to the line of communication weeks after we had been there and they were killed as soon as they appeared. Many skulked in the jungle, living on anything they could find, until eventually they walked into one of the East African patrols and were killed or captured.

The picture of what had happened to the enemy troops who had entered India was now becoming clear to us and we could see with what desperation they were trying to escape. They continued to die ahead of us and we came on them everywhere. Some had been injecting themselves with camphor in an effort to keep on their feet. Near three newly dead soldiers lay tubes that had contained liquid camphor. One haversack held about thirty full tubes. I saw those who had swayed on the edges of the cliff along which the road ran and had then crashed headlong to death below. They were eating the bitter ashes of a defeat they had never known before and they could not stem the rush of the askaris towards the Chindwin.

The retreating enemy who passed beyond Jambo Hill now hoped to escape under the protection of those who were holding the position but the attack went in with all speed to destroy this obstacle.

A battalion composed of Nandi and Wakamba tribesmen of Kenya was picked to go in and take the position. This was the youngest battalion in the Division and many of the old sweats from the other East African territories were surprised when they heard that 'the young soldiers' were given the first attack of the campaign.

The 'young soldiers' sharpened their heavy *pangas* to a razor keenness, and waited for orders. They wanted to go in and kill the 'Jampans' with these murderous blades. The heat of the jungle was not diminished by the rain, and below the waiting askaris who lay hidden in the jungle, the twisting sea of mud that was the road had become silent and glistened redly in the sun, that was sinking beyond the trees. To-morrow morning, when the white mist curled at the boles of the teak trees and there was the chill of the early morning, these askaris would go in to their first attack on a prepared enemy position. Seven or eight thousand yards behind them as the shell flies, over the jungle, hills and ridges, the artillery was preparing for the morning.

The fixing of times for death and forms of devastation, the working out of strings of pencilled figures that would bring terror to men in the morning, is a curious thing and is done like a drill. The red and blue pencil-marks on the map and the swift calculations with the protractor while you watch, can never even convey what the bursting shell will do in the morning. The science of bringing death into focus while you drink tea from a mess-tin has an anonymity all its own, and every man engaged in it is working with the assurance of a Pontius Pilate. When somebody tries to kill you from a distance, you cannot believe that it is meant for you. It is surely for somebody else, and there must be some mistake. This is quite wrong, for when gunners and bomb-aimers throw their loads of steel, they have worked meticulously to kill you, and you are merely a cipher, like X or Y, and your fear of death does not affect the world.

When the sun went down beyond the jungle, men and weapons were ready to fight a small battle, but one that was historic for the Division, and would be the culmination of long training and many lectures, drills, exhaustions and boredoms.

CHAPTER SIX

1

The artillery officer shouted loudly and deliberately, taking his time over orders to the African gunners who were stripped to the waist. Their bodies glistened like black silk. The British N.C.O.s watched them with satisfaction for the battery was about to fire for the first time against the enemy.

Standing with me, about ten yards behind the guns, was a deeply sunburned British sergeant. He leaned on a spade and said: 'You're standing on a grave I've just fixed up for some of the little yellow men.' He grinned. Like everyone else in the valley, he was becoming callous. He added: 'We couldn't have them lying around like that. Near the Mess too!'

There was a flash of orange flame from one of the guns and a flat, sharp detonation. Then another farther down the line and another. The piercingly loud voice of the officer leaning over his map cut in again, detailing ranges to the guns. There could be no mistaking his orders. They came like the peals of a new bell and the men on the guns responded quickly and surely.

Somebody brought tea. While we sipped the hot, brown stuff from the mess-tins the sergeant patted the soil and twigs of the grave with his spade. 'We should knock a few more off this morning,' he said with a false gravity. 'It's terrible, isn't it?' He shook his head sadly. 'Nice little chaps, too. Do anything for you.'

Then the whole battery fired together and we heard the sucking noise of the shells passing through the air.

Comments were coming through from the forward observation officer of the battery, who was now lying two hundred yards from the Jap positions. The battery was firing smoke shells for registration and eight thousand yards away the F.O.O. was forced to whisper his instructions, so close was he to the Japs.

Another few shells were fired and the officer at the map passed the word round that the F.O.O. had now crawled to within forty yards of the enemy. When the F.O.O. was satisfied with the range, the guns would open up with fifty rounds 'Gunfire,' and every gun would fire as fast as possible, prior to the infantry assault.

Two men worked on the punctured tyre of our Jeep. We would have to travel fast and along hilly roads to reach the battle area. When the Jeep was ready, we set off through the jungle.

Where the road was steep we came on to heaps of dead enemy troops. Few wore boots and all had carried a mess-tin in their hands. From somewhere they had obtained rotten rice and this was still in the mess-tins. They had been unable to eat it. Many we took prisoner were 'dehydrated,' as the troops called it, for the cells of their bodies had been destroyed by privation and they could not absorb water or food, which passed straight through them. Nearly all of these cases died.

The groups of dead we now passed had collapsed on the hills. Their long rifles lay near them, rusted and useless. Several lay on their sides with their hands arranged under their heads as if in sleep. We passed trucks riddled by fragments of bullets and on the front of each truck was the big, white, steel star of the Japanese Army. From these brown-painted trucks hung dead men and some lay across the steering wheels, and many lay where they had crawled into the shade. There was no sadness in any of this. It was quite correct and proper that these barbaric soldiers should have suffered and in some way atoned for the feverish murder and pain they had dealt out for years in the East. This was the kind of beating that they would understand, for they had now seen war as they had never known it before. It was a pity that so many should be misled and cast to death in this manner, like useless horses in the knacker's yard, but sentiment and certain sanctities were murdered under Japanese bayonets at Hong Kong and other points East. In the craze of killing, burning and destroying, they had never visualised this day when death, which they value highly, turned them into a herd of wandering dwarfs and then slew them unhurriedly.

The radio voice of Japan, which had cracked excitedly during descriptions of the chaos and terror caused by the soldiers of the Emperor, had promised India to Greater East Asia. This voice had gloated with pride in the stupid suicidal deaths of Japanese troops.

In the Khabaw was a horror that the Japanese radio announcer could not imagine. A madman, with hair standing like a bush from the shrunken head, in rags and unable to talk, does not look like a hero, or a warrior of Yamato. He looks like a swindled human being who has been turned into a trained animal, and when they died in heaps, the pity of it all is purely abstract, for these, who can cry over the beauty of a bird's wing, are murderous beings.

2

We crawled up over the gluey mud and still the dead were with us. The enemy were still falling out of the marching columns, and their Command could not save them.

Shells began passing over us in twos and threes. The artillery had started to concentrate. We reached a bend in the road where there were many troops and a headquarters, high up on the wooded slope, was full of movement. The last flight of shells passed over as we entered the camouflaged headquarters.

A little way beyond and looking out over the rolling carpet of jungle was General Fowkes, Commander of the 11th East African Division, wearing a slouch hat and holding a map in his right hand. He showed us the enemy position on his map. Below us, some hundreds of yards away, plumes of smoke were rising out of the dense mass of teak and bamboo, and then a Verey light burst like a red flower and showered sparks as it sizzled down again. It was seven minutes past twelve as the red success signal burned out. The General smiled. Everybody smiled.

From this point on the road was impassable, and troops were laying down thick bamboos across the deep mud.

With the General we started off through the jungle, walking alongside the yellow telephone cable which led to the forward companies of infantry. Askaris stood to attention and smiled back when the General congratulated them. In Ki' Swahili they said it was a big day. They were excited and happy, and they passed us with rifles at the short trail and with fixed bayonets. The going was hard, up steep hills that took the breath away, and the jungle had collected the heat and held it. The atmosphere was that of a hothouse.

The narrow track suddenly widened into a large clearing littered with wounded. They lay still and without uttering a sound. Askaris who are hurt seldom complain unless they are frightened. They have a great faith in the European doctors, and are not afraid. The Bwana M'Ganga (doctor) will arrange everything, and they lie still until he arrives.

At this spot I saw the most considerate and gentle men I have yet met. They were Indian stretcher-bearers who were operating with the forward troops. They said nothing, but squatted with grave faces and calm eyes, while they fanned the flies away from the wounded askaris. They never made a fast movement, nor did they turn sharply when addressed. They acted as if they had cared for wounded man all their lives and they produced an atmosphere of peace and confidence. Two Indians were removing the jackets of those askaris not already attended to.

In the middle of all these dozen or so wounded askaris lay one of their officers. He was very young and the black face-paint which the officers apply when they lead Africans into battle had been half-wiped off. From the dirty, strained face, his two blue eyes stared with a hard brilliance now accentuated by the painted face. He was naked and the dressers had attended to his wounded leg.

General Fowkes went over to the young officer and said: 'Well done. Well done. Is it hurting you, son?' The officer smiled and nodded. 'I know what it's like,' said the General, 'I had four myself last time.'

He then spoke to the askaris and knelt down to ask how they felt. They said they felt well and the General said he was proud of them, and of what they had done that day. They were glad of this and smiled faintly.

The Indians fanned them with long, slow strokes and stared up with their flat, black eyes, seeing everything and yet not losing sight of their patient's needs. We walked back on to the narrow track that led to the captured position. Four Indians carrying a body on a stretcher approached us, and perhaps because they conveyed it by their aspect, we knew the British officer on the stretcher was dead. A big shell dressing was bandaged against his white skin and he appeared as though resting after a long march. He had been very popular with his askaris and already they missed him and said so.

The climb up to the Japanese weapon-pits was steep. We looked down from the positions in which they had fought and for the first time I realised what it means to rise out of cover with your rifle and bayonet and attack through thick jungle. You cannot see the enemy machine-gunner, but you know he can see you, and he is waiting until you present the target he wants. Then the lash of metal comes sweeping your way and the hidden eyes follow your every movement.

In the captured weapon-pits the Nandi and Wakamba askaris had installed themselves and had set up Bren guns pointing towards the line of enemy retreat. The number two's on the guns squatted beside stacks of loaded Bren magazines. Already they looked seasoned and tough. They said they wanted to go on and kill the 'Jampans.' They grinned, and their teeth flashed like snow against the sweaty black faces. I asked them if they were tired, and one said:

'No, effendi. We are not tired. We are Wakamba.'

Two of them drew their sharp *pangas* and swung the heavy

blades softly. These two had used their *pangas* already and I saw the result of their work. A well-built Japanese lay on his back with his shoulders pointing downhill. One blow had severed the neck right through and the black eyes were placid and large. This one had hidden himself and then tried to escape, but the two Wakamba had dropped their rifles and as swiftly as they had fallen on an antelope in their time, they killed him with *pangas*. The sun flashed on the mustard-coloured skin of the Jap's chest and the two askaris who had killed him looked on without excitement. One of them plaited bamboo leaves into his hat as camouflage.

There was something sure and steady about these 'young soldiers,' and it was plain to see that they wished to go on and fight again. One of them said a curious thing, yet something which would not surprise those who know East African natives well.

'Why do our officers rush in front with us and get killed?' said this young Wakamba. 'Our major is dead. He trained us for over a year, and we knew him and he knew us. Now he is gone. Why don't the officers show us the enemy positions and we will attack them, and we will still have our officers when the fight is over.'

An askari lay sprawled on his face, dead. His hair was cropped two inches above his ears in the regulation fashion, and for some reason this seemed strange and sad. It had probably been cut the day before.

Another sat with his back against a tree, a field-dressing clamped against his chest wound. Suddenly he leaned forward and groaned and a thick spray of blood shot out of his back. He was not afraid. Two medical orderlies came and swiftly and gently they carried him away.

Down below us in the jungle somebody fired a long burst of machine-gun fire, and it swept and rolled among the trees. Everybody flattened out in the weapon-pits and watched their front. Another burst, this time shorter and with more urgency in its note. There were thirteen dead Japanese below the position killed in the attack by the artillery, and those Japs who had survived were now being hunted down by the askaris. The bend in the road, once dominated by this captured position, was now useable and four Jeeps had appeared loaded with rations. When the firing broke out the Jeeps stopped, the askaris jumped out and with their rifles and bayonets at the on-guard position, they fanned out into the jungle ahead of their vehicles.

This was something they had done a hundred times in training, and I watched them perform the action swiftly and with their eyes front. They did not seem to realise that this was the war, for there was no urgency in their attitude but rather was there careful litheness.

They knelt down and waited, ready to open fire under the corporal's orders. Their Jeeps were still ticking over and the much-needed load of rations glittered in the sun. Canned beef; soya link sausage; peas; flour; fruit and rice. Not far from where I squatted, a dead Jap knelt with his head on his knees half-supported by a tree. This was a few yards from the position in which the Japs had spent days. They had not attempted to burn or bury this dead man who had obviously died within the last couple of days. Once the enemy had fought with fury in order to retrieve their dead. Now they were sick of dead men and did nothing about their removal. Also, as often happened these days when the British artillery and the Allied planes gave the enemy no rest, the shell-fire and bombing forced the Japs to stay in their holes and any man that died or was wounded outside was left there. The enemy was forced to answer Nature's calls wherever and whenever he could, and this was nearly always a worrying business for them.

Allied planes were now beginning to drop delayed-action bombs in the vicinity of the Jap bunkers and trenches, and these went on exploding at various intervals and throughout the night, so that it was not safe for a man to rise and walk about.

The filling of water-bottles and the bringing up of rations became a problem of the first order for the enemy. These seemingly small matters wear down the nerves and cause men to do stupid things. To all this the ceaseless rain and the baling out of flooded positions and bad rations, when they were obtainable, added their weight of annoyance.

Somebody made a signal and the troops rushed back to their Jeeps. One sat in the back of each Jeep with a Sten gun cocked and ready. Then the small convoy started to bump and grind its way forward round the bend that was no longer covered by enemy gun-muzzles. Jambo Hill was ours and already the signallers were winding out their new lengths of cable. Two askaris from Tanganyika trotted along at the side of the road where the mud was firm, and from the iron drum that they held between them, the red cable snaked out and fell into the grass. They trotted past me, both singing a tribal song that ran up and down on five notes.

The memory of the Japanese cut down by the *pangas* stayed with me all morning. The savagery of his death seemed to bring a new aspect of killing into the war, because Africans when they kill do so with ferocity and thoroughness.

In ten years one might see the two askaris who did this first hand-to-hand killing, sitting under a thorn tree listening to a flute. They would probably be wearing blankets, or skins, while they watched the humped cattle with idle eyes. It would be strange then to look at them and say: 'These two slew a Japanese soldier in Burma with their knives.'

When we got back to the headquarters of the brigade we found the American Field Service ambulances waiting to move out with the wounded. The Americans who drove these ambulances were fine types of men, to whom no terrain was too difficult, nor any assignment too hard. They were a friendly crowd and had been drawn from all the corners of the United States. Many were rejects on medical grounds from the American Army, and could have been sitting in easy jobs back in their home towns, but as one of them said to me:

'This job gives you the feeling that you are doing something for the war. I sat on my fanny for six months in the States and one day I up and went. Everybody can drive a truck these days. The American Field Service was formed in the last war when few people could drive automobiles. Now, you might say, we are superfluous, and I guess we are, but—he grinned—I guess we can still make trucks do a few things that some other Joes can't. It's a nice idea, anyway.'

They wore British jungle battledress, with a red strip on the right shoulder carrying the words 'American Field Service.' They had beer when no one else had it. Good American beer in small bottles, quite unlike the vile stuff produced in India for the British troops. They did not hoard this beer. One American gave me a lift in the Jeep ambulance which was carrying two wounded askaris. He passed me a bottle of beer as casually as offering a cigarette. He had not much of it, either. But the generosity of Americans is something quite out of the ordinary and they are so natural and easy to approach that many of us suffer embarrassment. But this form of embarrassment is purely a luxury which the American has come to recognise with a sense of fun.

The American ambulance drivers did more good for the name of America than they will ever realise. Nearly everybody who came into contact with them liked them at once. They knew their job and they knew how to live. One, who always went far afield, and liked to go in with the troops to see 'the fun,' used to drive them straight out of the battle area and knew their names as well. This man was a tall and very fine looking youngster with black hair. He liked soldiering and was never happier than when searching for minefields and booby-traps. He is now missing and I am told that he was last seen heading off into the jungle with an East African patrol on the kind of show he liked best.

Another A.F.S. driver I met wore the Africa Star with the clasp of the Eighth Army. He was proud of the silver eight, and said: 'Sure, I got two other rows of medals, but I don't wear 'em. This is plenty.' And he tapped the Africa Star. He meant the silver eight, of course, which is coveted by a host of British officers and men.

Gradually the Americans learned Ki'Swahili and the askaris took pleasure in teaching the 'Amerikani' a few words. 'Okay?' the American driver would say as he guided the Jeep over the bumpy road. The wounded askaris would turn their heads to him and grin. 'Okay, effendi,' they answered.

CHAPTER SEVEN

On August 20th the troops who took Jambo Hill were edging up to a position slightly off the Sittaung track, called Pyinbon Sakan. In peace time there had been a rest-house at Pyinbon Sakan, perched on the hill and overlooking the road. It was now showing the effects of blast. The enemy had dug themselves into the place and it seemed that they intended to stay.

Twelve Hurricanes passed overhead and attacked Pyinbon Sakan with twenty-four 250-pounders. They then bored in and sprayed the hill with cannon shells.

It was considered that the Japanese had a company on Pyinbon Sakan, and the hammering from the air continued.

We had not seen one enemy plane up to this time, and enemy air attacks were considered unlikely occurrences owing to the destruction of most of the Japanese air force during their assault on India.

With the five Japanese divisions annihilated by the Fourteenth Army went most of the enemy air force. In August we had complete air superiority and the Dakota aircraft that dropped supplies to us did so without any fighter escort.

It was March, 1944, when the Japs set off on their advance into India. One hundred thousand troops were employed in the great effort to crush the Fourteenth Army and seize India. After crossing the Chindwin they had to scale the great barrier of mountain and jungle which lay as though guarding the Indian frontier. Their air force covered them and made attacks ahead of the advancing troops, but were countered by the Third Tactical Air Force which started to attack all along the Chindwin where the enemy had his bases.

This major operation was an all-out effort and though the enemy did break on to Indian soil and raise his flag there, it may be said that he came to choose his cemeteries.

General Metaguchi said to his troops:

'This operation will engage the attention of the whole world and is eagerly awaited by a hundred million of our countrymen. Its success will have a profound effect on the course of the war, and may even lead to its conclusion. We must therefore expend every ounce of energy and talent to achieve our purpose.'

The Japanese radio announced the destruction of the British troops who had tried unsuccessfully to stem this tide of one hundred thousand fanatics. Well trained, and merciless, the enemy troops marched with very light kit and they were fast. In their advance they were mauled badly by our retreating columns which were falling back on to the Imphal plain. They could not have realised that they were entering an area of battle where they were to be massacred.

For a fortnight the British and Indian troops fought to defend Kohima which the Japs wanted as a bridgehead into India. The slaughter went on in a hell of artillery and mortar fire, but the enemy had come up against something steely and resisting. They attacked like maniacs and were cut down and mangled in the death that they had been trained to seek. Kohima was relieved, but the Japs came again under a screen of artillery and mortar fire in a last all-out effort. This also failed.

The savage fighting that raged for Imphal and Kohima cost the Japanese thousands of their crack troops, and on June 22nd, at Milestone 109 on the Kohima–Imphal road, two corps of the Fourteenth Army linked up and then drove to Ukhrul where the Japanese were killed until their taste for death was glutted. Ukhrul will live in Japanese military history as the cemetery of a vast host of their dead and as a lesson in warfare.

Without food, without medicine and without air support, the enemy fell back towards the Chindwin, down the Palel–Tamu road, and the Tiddim road, and the pursuit began.

On August 25th Pyinbon Sakan, near Sittaung, was gradually turning into a torn heap of red soil and only a few patches of vegetation remained. The R.A.F. kept up the bombing attacks until this tiny hill lost its original shape and the enemy pulled out in the night.

For the first time the East Africans came under shell-fire when the enemy opened up with seventy-five millimetre guns beyond Pyinbon Sakan. Gradually the Japanese resistance stiffened and the dying Japs either died or were rescued as they neared the Chindwin.

We had been told that the Khabaw Valley was one of the most malarious areas in the world. It looked beautiful with its blue mountains and darker jungle, while the stretches of paddy field glittered in a green light so bright as to be almost sickly. This valley did not look malicious. But on August 25th, thirty-two men of an engineer unit went down together with malaria. This made everybody take their mepacrine with a solemn regularity and the Khabaw, after showing its teeth, went on looking beautiful, even when half-hidden in rain.

Every askari and every officer and N.C.O. took one tablet of the yellow mepacrine nightly. This drug acts as a suppressant to malaria and though the face goes yellow after the first few tablets, this wears off and no other effects are felt. It is possible that mepacrine kept the advance going down the Khabaw Valley and as we passed through its entrance we noticed that the large voracious mosquitoes started to search for blood at five o'clock in the evening when it was still quite light. They were so hungry they could not wait for night as mosquitoes usually do, but came humming about with a persistence that was quite surprising.

The first cases of a disease called scrub-typhus appeared and the anti-typhus squads went out into the jungle to search for infected areas. Where the tiny scrub-typhus mite was found, a notice was placed which stated, 'No camping,' and the areas were put out of bounds. Scrub-typhus is a killer, but many recover and it will not be long before medicine has found the answer to this pest.

After we had been a few weeks in the jungle, people began to sicken. Some developed sores, or went down with stomach trouble.

There were those who thrived on the atmosphere of the jungle, but this did not make them fall in love with the almost animal life of the jungle troops. Some were affected by the dark-green gloom which filled the arches of the teak trees, and there was certainly a baleful atmosphere when it rained that made you feel cut off and away from all the world. The rain became phenomenal for those of us who had never dreamed of such down-pouring sheets which fell for hour after hour. We were able to realise after a few weeks of this life how hard life had been for the troops who had fought in Burma since early 1942, hardly remembered by any save their own relatives.

The Burma front was a long way off and people watched Europe. Across the world to Burma was a great distance and the troops said that the Fourteenth Army was the forgotten army. In this judgment they were right, and not until it was feared that the Japs would take India did the world turn its eyes to Burma and wonder what kind of men made up the Fourteenth Army. It is not possible to put down on paper what they went through and how they went on living their almost troglodytic lives for months at a time when they baled the rain out of their living holes and stared out across the mountains at the Japanese positions. The hills of the Arakhan have probably seen more stoicism than any other terrain in the world. Across razor-backed hills that rolled on and on like the waves of the sea, British, Indian, African and Japanese troops sought each other out in bloody hand-to-hand fights, sprayed each other with bullets as ambushes leapt to life on jungle trails and squatted for hours, watching, until the eyes ached.

The heart-breaking road into the Arakan was made again and again and the rain crumbled it. Bridges were washed away and troops were cut off.

Now, as the enemy fell back on to the Chindwin River, there were signs that all this deadlock would dissolve into movement as the offensive into Japanese-held Burma swelled in power.

When the one hundred thousand troops of Japan's Burma Expeditionary Force were broken and turned into a rabble it gave us the opportunity for a great advance, and we all knew that as we floundered along in the mud and rain, it was probably the last fight the Japanese would ever make this side of the Chindwin. Behind us, gigantic preparations were going on after the tiring struggle against the Japanese offensive. When the roads dried, we knew that a river of men and material would pour down and across the Chindwin. The task of the East Africans was to clear the Chindwin of all Japanese and hold it for the attack into Central Burma.

The monsoon was worse than we expected, and as traffic ceased to function the infantry battalions took off their jackets and started to lay thousands of logs across the mud in an endeavour to make the road even 'Jeepable.' Because of the jungle the sun could not reach the black mud of the road. Sometimes it stayed out for a couple of hours and burned fiercely. The jungle was cut away from each side of the road, a back-breaking task.

While the troops closing on Sittaung were outside of that place, the other forces of East Africans were forcing their way down the Kalewa road, and had reached Witok. The rivers were racing and carried logs and masses of bamboos with them and the remains of bridges that had been torn from their foundations. Physical effort on the part of Europeans and Africans reached a peak, where men worked in a daze no longer conscious of their tired muscles and straining chests.

The Europeans worked stripped to the waist beside the Africans, until their white skins turned a dark, nut-brown and the sharp smell of African bodies mingled with the bitter, dead scent of the dying teak. Labour that turns the muscles into a set of cords and blinds the eyes with a film of salty sweat can never do more than tire, even in Burma. Because if the logs that are hewn fit side by side on the muddy road and the guns that are pushed go forward, then there is a satisfaction that is understood well by soldiers under orders.

The companionship of the army in the field is something that is understood only by those who have experienced it. It entails that men shall do the hardest things together and even derive a pleasure from it; a pleasure that has to do with the certainty that no matter what happens you will be together, and it will be easy that way. This companionship of men is far deeper than anything known. Men who have served together have experienced things that may be described by them in an expression that no one else would understand, and when they meet years later in a fair city the memory of the times of hardship they spent together are brought alive again. The war—any war—creates a set of comradeships that survive the pleasant anodyne of family life, which of all life's pleasures is the most disarming. So that when men who have known the fears and burdens of Burma's day meet again in some far place, they will have a contact that is outside everything else that surrounds their daily lives.

This will also be so for African soldiers, who, though they are less likely to meet the men of other tribes again after the war, will remember forms of companionship that will not come their way again.

This is the quality that makes war bearable for men. War is easier for men than for women even though they face war that is not anonymous as that of the bombers over a dark city. They face war where the human eye measures you for the kill at a few hundred yards. They are more fortunate than the women who wait, if only because of the comradeship which they enjoy in the midst of carnage.

For askaris, the barrier of tribes had to be overcome. Even now you will find that those askaris who speak Chinyanja as a language do not like to speak Ki' Swahili, for, as they say themselves, they are not of the race that speaks Ki'Swahili. In Kenya a tribe like the Nandi regard the Wakikuyu, who live near them, as quite another people with hardly anything in common with the Nandi. And they are quite correct in this attitude. East Africa has absorbed peoples of many races and cultures and though the twain meet in uniform and in a common Lingua Franca, there has never been the suggestion that the Nandi is the same as the Wakikuyu, or the Wanyamwezi the same as the M'nyao.

Those who really know and understand the East African, know that the phrase East African does not describe or lump together all these nomadic, pastoral and agricultural peoples, and also those who sort letters in cities, and those who deliver vegetables to white women, and all those others who live on the edge of the white man's world. The British people know little about the black and brown peoples who live in the Empire, mainly because they still believe in a world of Bosambo and bead necklaces, which are still considered as explanatory of Africa. This Africa still survives, but the future that Africa is forming is a matter of indifference to British people.

A soldier dead in the jungle may have white, brown or black skin, but death has abused his body in the same way and with the same steel. There is a difference only in the spheres of eating, thinking and living, but not in dying. The African soldier will understand this if he has not already understood it and it will give him a sense of security and a wish to live fully and without darkness. The kindness and friendship of British European soldiers towards Africans is something that draws the best from Africans, for the soldier has little colour-bar, and few scruples about sharing the same mess-tin of tea.

The African has a future that will give him happiness and he is fighting for it now, even though he does not know it. There are people who will see that he is given the gifts of the life he has fought to defend, but few Africans are aware of it.

When you see an African soldier lying wounded or dead in Burma, you are conscious of history, and you realise that though this African received his wound or death blow in a great struggle, there will be few Africans who will demand payment for it. They will be claimed again by the life they left, but which we are slowly destroying. The machine has come to them and one day they will live in it, but they should be prepared for that day.

The peoples of Africa need education and help. They have not agitated for it. They have been magnificently calm. The white men are eating their old system of life away with petrol, rubber, medicine and enlightenment. Having fought to preserve that gift of enlightenment, let us see that they receive all of its goodness.

There are people who have lived years in Africa who say, 'The old wog. The good old wog. He'll go back again to the old life after a few months of agitation. As soon as he gets that skin or blanket on again, he'll forget the novelties the army gave him. What do they want money for. They don't need it. They can live on a handful of flour.'

Well, there they were, stripped to the waist, wound with straps holding packs and haversacks. Two grenades stuck in their belts by the hooked springs that secured the strikers. Tatooed, scarred, burned by curing irons of their tribes, credulous still, despite the years of life in the army. They believed in their white Bwanas who led them and who would die with them in battle. Though the white Bwanas had a better idea of what this war was for than had the askaris, the latter brooded not at all on this. It was the war.

When one askari was asked by a visiting officer what he was fighting for, he said: 'To get more land for Kingi Georgi.' He believed it. In Africa, men had always fought for land and cattle, and women. They did not fight to make Africa safe for anything. They fought for something you could hold in your hand and see with your eyes.

When they struck Japanese and saw them die, they felt that this was why they had come to Burma. They did not know that there was also a spiritual reason, and several other reasons that nobody couldn't quite describe. When they passed Pyinbon Sakan, they wore their kit with an air of experience. They had stopped loading themselves with souvenirs. They were too heavy and awkward to carry. One day they would throw them away. They knew how to rest without removing their kit and had learned how to use the jungle, more luscious and riotous than anything they had ever seen.

Many white people in Africa ask: 'What are they going to be like when they come back? Difficult?' Not necessarily. If people are given a fair reward and a share in the dignities and works of life, they are never difficult. If it is recognised that Africans have soldiered like other peoples of the United Nations and are helped to live the kind of life they want, they will not be difficult. If a man comes to join the army wearing a blanket, smeared with red ochre paint, it does not follow that he must return to that life if he wishes to live another life wearing trousers and no red ochre.

All this has very little to do with the advance on Sittaung, save for the fact that I thought about it all when I saw them forming up to advance, grinning and cheerful, and with a belief in the white men who led them.

The African soldiers are the responsibility of the British people, but very few of the British people or the Africans realise it. If the people of Britain could have seen them laden with kit, sodden and singing the songs of their villages as they advanced on Sittaung, they would have been proud of them.

CHAPTER EIGHT

1

The road down into Sittaung was so bad that the Jeep bounced about until the driver's hands were stiff and tired from the constant struggle. Enemy dead lay all the way down the sides of the road. Even when you are used to them, the Japanese dead look weird and like small men from some other planet. The dead Asiatic face under the round steel helmet, with the smooth lemon coloured skin, and the thick, soft mouth, cannot give any inkling of their strange spirit as soldiers. Their eyes are long and narrow and as though cut and shaped by a sharp blade, so well defined are the lids against the soft, unlined skin. The black eyes are like obsidian, even in death. Sometimes I looked at them and wondered how much they had seen in their years of soldiering, China, Manchuria, Singapore, Burma and perhaps without ever having received leave to Japan.

The Japanese are called up at twenty, and graded into several medical categories as in other armies. Grade A1, is called *Ko,* and demands that a recruit be not less than five feet tall and in good physical condition. Grade B is called *Otsu,* and C, B and D follow with lessening standards of health and height. Category D, for example, means that a man is less than four feet nine inches in height, and for the sake of harmless fun it might be worth while mentioning here that the Japanese Army rifle is very long, so that the sight of category D on parade is probably an interesting spectacle. As in the British Army, recruits in poor condition are given a course of diet and treatment and are then examined again.

All A1 and B category men are fit for active service anywhere. Life in the Imperial Japanese Army is hard and the training rigorous. The life led by the ordinary Japanese peasant fits him well for the life in the army, for hardship is no novelty to him. The army life is probably better than anything he has experienced before, for he is certain of his food and shelter during his service.

The standard of cleanliness is quite high, though the personal urge of the Japanese soldier as regards cleanliness is not pronounced, and smells, filth and squalor move him not at all. As soldier material he is first class, and as a fighter is unquestionably brave and obedient. His stupidity is great, and as a tool of the Imperial will he is hard cast, but perhaps too highly tempered and he shatters instead of bending when the strain is too great.

Compared to the Japanese troops with their long, hybrid and borrowed culture and their unusual outlook, the Africans are fine human beings who share the same love of peace and family as the men of other races. The Japanese love their families too, and will certainly come to love peace one day if the beating they receive is heavy enough, but before all this they must serve the Imperial will.

There are people who hold the opinion that the Emperor wishes secretly for peace. The Emperor wrote a poem about a year after Pearl Harbor in which he hinted at the joys of peace. It was assumed from this, by some, that the Emperor wanted peace and loathed war. With Malaya, the Philippines, Burma and all the other conquered places in the hands of the Japanese Army, it was the right time to write such a poem, for peace is indeed a beautiful thing, especially when you have got what you want.

The slaves who die for him every day in swathes, and who rush to new forms of death in coconut groves and jungles, may not see any special significance in the poem, if they have read it. It is unlikely that Japan will join the United Nations as 'Free Japan,' even if the Emperor wanted it, and the Japanese soldiers may cry, leap from cliffs or do the grenade trick, if told to lay down their arms.

Only experts can say if the Japanese Army has such a thing as a morale that will snap completely, and the sadness of the experts fills the world. I have not heard any experienced soldier who has fought the Japanese for a long time say with certainty what he thinks the Japanese will do. Some say they will commit mass hara-kiri, and others think that Japan will collapse into chaos. We have no measuring board for the Japanese outlook. They are like no other people, and the pathos of their situation is peculiarly their own. They are stronger than their machines, and this is the trouble. They have not enough faith in the machine, and have not learned to be lazy. 'Spiritual Strength' is one of their axioms of life.

When his service starts as a recruit he is called a *Genekihei,* which means 'new soldier.' Once he was sent to China for his training and in that country he could become used to the brutishness and terror of the Imperial war. In China he learned to perform part of the act in deliberate ravishment so that he appeared to the world as a monstrous dwarf in the midst of a great people. In the country from which Japan had borrowed so much, he was able to commit enormities until he appeared to the Chinese as a pathetic human beast in search of a fitting death.

When he was trained, and became a superior private, he was called *Jotohei,* and wore three white stars on each red collar-patch. He could march great distances wearing a heavy set of equipment and had learned never to complain. He was fit to die anywhere under any conditions, for the Emperor and the army, and ever so often, small white caskets went back to Japan containing the ashes of those who had found the great reward. The spirit that drove two sub-lieutenants to compete with each other in China for the greatest number of victims for their Samurai swords, was to branch out into new pastures where the dreamy life of millions of brown people was to suffer a cataclysm.

As hundreds of thousands of *Jotohei* have now died, there must be a great rejoicing at Yasukuni shrine where the ashes of the dead are brought. The death of soldiers is regarded as a sacred and splendid thing, and is a cause for rejoicing among the living. At what point do the living weep from bitterness and loss, and what number of dead will cause them to ask for peace? Only the experts can say.

What is the mysterious thing that drives the Japanese troops to their mad deaths? What is it that prompts them to kill themselves? When they stand up in their muddy holes, with their hair matted and lousy, their minds cracked at last under the hail of crushing fire and steel, to stare out for the last time at the earth before death, what do they see? Do they see the gun flashes multiplying like bands of white and red light on the hillsides and see the earth erupt before them into smoke and flame and whizzing metal? Before the last screaming bayonet charge when they fall as grass under the blade, what do they think of? Allied soldiers have killed them until they are sick with the slaughter and the enemy dead lay packed in gaps among rocks and trees.

These little men write in their diaries of home and family with a yearning that is familiar to all soldiers. What is the thing that cancels out the wish to live and return to that home and family? And what is it that makes them obey orders that no sensible man on earth could think of obeying? They will sit in burning dugouts if told to do so.

One Japanese private was found sitting in a shell hole with three dead comrades beside him. They had been dead for days and the stench caused the two British officers who discovered him to vomit. The Jap private was sitting with a pair of bamboo chopsticks, picking grains of rice out of his pocket and eating them. He was surprised to see the two officers and he tried to fight. They took him prisoner. He had sat with those stinking and crawling dead for days. He had been told to stay there by his officer.

'Sub-human,' said the senior officer of the two. 'Sub-human.' No other explanation fits. How can they stand bombardments that drive them crazy and then still fight, when other more intelligent men would pack up? They are animal-minded men, for only animals could stand the degradation and rottenness of their lives.

The Emperor, whom the Japanese call *Tenno Heika,* has been shown a devotion by his fighting forces reserved hitherto in this world for the propitiation of Gods. The Japanese soldier feels that if Japan fails in the war, it will be the fault of the soldiers and not of the Emperor, for he can do no wrong. He can be failed by his subjects who, when they are seized by the peculiar half-mystical, half-animal ecstasy that comes to them in battle, will die blindly for him in the swamps and jungles of South-East Asia and the Pacific islands. There is never a uselessness in dying as far as the Japanese soldier is concerned. Death is the last great gesture in the soldier's life, and it is this thought that may have sustained so many of them through storms of shellfire in order to inflict casualties on our troops up to the last moment. It cannot be considered that the Japanese position is captured until every Jap in it is dead or unconscious.

Their army discipline is based on the personal pride of the soldier, and is rooted in Emperor-worship and 'face.' It is said that it is punishment enough for the soldier's name to be read out on parade together with the charge against him. They also have 'disciplinary units' to which it is disgraceful to be sent, for the only true honour is to be with a fighting unit.

To become an N.C.O. a soldier does a six-months' course of training, and usually he went to Japan for this. Under present conditions it may be difficult for them to go to Japan and they have probably established big training bases in the captured territories of Asia. At the end of the N.C.O.'s course there is an examination and those who come out first can be drawn upon for officer material. Men who come second can receive rank up to sergeant and those who come third are returned to the ranks.

The pay of the Japanese Army is very small and may best be described as pocket money. Leave, privileges of all kinds and mail are not given the important place they have in other armies. Equipment, food and the daily life are simple things, and the main effort is to fight.

If a Japanese soldier is taken prisoner by the enemy he is counted among the dead and his family is informed of his death in action. The prisoner can never return again to Japan. The Japanese troops who were captured by the Russians on the Manchurian frontier in 1939, are said to have been settled in Manchuria after exchanges had been made.

If men are expected to die in battle, even by suicide, rather than be captured, then it is not possible to give them the normal training in what to say when captured. This must be a great problem to the Japanese Command, for while the massacre goes on, those who are taken prisoner by us look upon themselves as disgraced and finished men. It is likely that a time will come when the Japanese must accept the fact that prisoners are bound to be taken in a successful Allied attack and they will probably teach their troops what to say when captured. This will mean a denial of the former principle that all should die rather than be captured. To undo all this mystic and uncivilised myth of suicide will be a difficult and risky undertaking.

'Do your best to avoid capture,' said the order of a Japanese commander; 'No matter how extreme and difficult the situation which must be faced. Kill yourself if necessary and uphold not only your own honour, but that of the *butal* (unit) and the Imperial army. If you are taken prisoner while unconscious, upon regaining consciousness do the following:

1. Make your escape and return to your unit as soon as possible.

2. Kill yourself unhesitatingly if there is no hope of escape.

For the honour of the Imperial army, hundreds of thousands have been flung again and again on to barbed wire, steel and concrete until wiped out. They have formed up in milling herds for the last charge, weeping and howling, and then have raced into the scythe-like fire of Allied machine-gunners, uselessly, and without any other intention than to die when all is lost.

When the East African askaris saw their first enemy suicides they clicked their tongues, but it did not worry them greatly. It was a good thing if men wished to kill themselves instead of causing trouble.

One came out of a hole in the ground holding his throat and screaming. He wanted to die, but even though this wish of his was not understood by the askaris, he died. They killed him with *pangas,* for he looked dangerous.

2

To become an officer, a man does twelve months' training. A probationary officer is called *Minarai Shikan,* and the commissioned officers are given ranks which correspond, in implication, with the units they command, viz:

Rank.		*Command.*	
2nd Lieutenant	*Shoi* (little)	Platoon	*Shotai*
Lieutenant	*Chui* (middling)	Company	*Chutai*
Captain	*Tai* (big)	Battalion	*Daitai*
Major	*Shosa*	Regiment	*Rentai*
Lieutenant Colonel	*Rentai*		
Colonel	*Taisa*		

The Japanese regiment is equivalent to a British brigade and consists of three battalions. The word *Butai* is used in the same sense as the British army word 'unit.' A Japanese soldier may say he belongs to *Yamada Butai,* which means the unit commanded by the officer Yamada.

The enemy are devotees of the sword, bayonet and flag. Believe it or not, the Japanese light machine-gun, which approximates in design, weight and length to our Bren machine-gun, is fitted with a bayonet standard and boss, and will take the Japanese regulation bayonet so that the machine-gunner can fight hand to hand.

The officer's sword (*Katana*) is a beautifully made and balanced weapon, with a curved, thick blade, and can cut like a razor. The officers can fight with them and they are dangerous weapons, but have failed miserably when confronted with automatic fire.

The flag runs in various types, the richest the one embroidered with chrysanthemums. The one commonly found by our troops is a square of white silk or cloth carrying the red sun, and surrounded by a collection of Japanese characters, many of which are words such as 'Loyalty' and 'Honour.'

Flags and swords are eagerly sought by the Allied troops and in such places as Calcutta there are people who will pay high prices for these souvenirs. Nowadays there are Indian blacksmiths who make Japanese swords out of old car springs, and thus the honest fighting man returned from the front with a sword to sell may not receive the price he expected. Mother India has an answer to most money-making efforts on the part of private persons, and if the Indian tradesman sees a market, he cannot resist it. India is a wonderful country, and there are people there who could outwit any ambitious Satan.

Many enemy troops wear a cloth belt round their waists which is supposed to bring them luck and protect them from harm. Although this belt does not seem to possess the gifts attributed to it, there is no doubt that it has beauty. It goes by the name of *Sennin Bari,* and is a belt of a thousand stitches. One I saw was embroidered with a splendid tiger crouched to spring and was about twelve inches wide in the middle and tapered to each end. The thousand stitches were done in red silk, and ran in neat rows round the belt. An officer (and there are people who will do this kind of thing) counted the stitches again and again and found only nine hundred and ninety-nine. Nobody would argue with him, for this would entail counting on the part of the doubters. The patient officer who could only find nine hundred and ninety-nine stitches after many attempts, held the opinion that the thousandth stitch had been purposely omitted by the woman who made the belt for the owner, possibly because he was unfaithful. The owner actually met a very expert machine-gunner, which can be described as bad luck, though the Japanese may not think so.

The enemy troops also wear a leather bag round their necks, and in this they keep a small bone seal bearing the ideograph of their names. With the seal is enclosed a small tin of red paste which is used as ink. With these seals the enemy soldiers sign their names on pay-books and other documents. Many of the seals are carved from ivory and are often exquisitely made. Charms of red rice paper wrapped round tiny swords are also carried. These come from the temples of Japan and are meant to bring luck.

The askaris collected these things and stared at them for a long time, not being able to grasp why men should carry such stuff. They showed an interest in the enemy soldiers' religious outlook, but grasped as little as the average European. The enemy soldier's religion is as weird as his military outlook, and people vary in their opinions concerning the average Jap's philosophy and ideals. One wonders if even the Jap knows what they are. There is a great lack of information, generally, only people who have lived in Japan can speak with certainty of the Japanese religious point of view.

Askaris hoping for loot were disappointed. The enemy did not carry much in the way of luxury. Everything he had was for fighting and for food and sustenance.

The story that the enemy fight with small bags of rice round their necks, and can do so for days, was not borne out on the Khabaw front. Some wore the little bags of rice, but it had gone rotten, for the owners could no longer eat it, so far gone were they in physical privation.

Their clothing is not particularly remarkable, and is in fact far inferior to ours. They still use the old-fashioned tunic with the collar that buttons up tightly round the neck. The trousers are of the breeches type with lace-up ankles. Puttees are wound in a very haphazard fashion and there is no apparent rule for wearing them, as we found the enemy wearing them in a dozen different ways. Their boots are of two types. They use the ordinary army ammunition boot of tough, brown leather, studded and steel-tipped, and there is another type known as *Tabi*. Tabi are made of thick, black rubber, with tough uppers of black cloth. There is a separate compartment for the big toe, which gives them a very strange appearance. They are excellent for wear in the jungle and are very strongly made. Probably they were originally made for patrols, but we often found the enemy wearing them and they seem to have been highly favoured for long marches.

The forage cap is ill-fitting and has a short peak. On the front of the cap is sewn a small yellow cloth star. There are strings at the back of the cap for increasing or decreasing the size according to the size of the owner's head. This cap can be worn under the steel helmet.

The steel helmet is of thin steel and is shaped like a deep bowl. There are three pads inside it and inside these the owners often carry papers and photographs. On the front of the helmet is a small, steel star and the whole helmet is painted a dark brown. Camouflage sacking wound with string is almost always worn over it when troops are in action. As a method of stopping fragments, the helmet is poor. I have seen helmets that have been shattered into pieces, unlike the British helmet which can be dented, torn open, but never breaks in pieces.

Their weapons, though of far poorer type than those used in the Allied armies, are serviceable and well made. The light machine-gun, which greatly resembles the British Bren, is a good weapon, and the arrangements for sighting and alteration of the gas-port are both ingenious and useful. But what they gain on these adjustments they lose on such things as the awkward bipod and the changing of the barrel, which is difficult and takes considerable time.

The safety catch of their rifle is most unusual, but resembles that used on the Italian rifle Modello 91. There are several types of Japanese grenade. All are inferior to the Allied types, and where possible the Japanese will use our grenades against us. One curious thing about the enemy hand grenade is that when the pin is pulled it is not necessary to throw the grenade at once. Before it is thrown it is necessary to bang it sharply against a hard object, which releases a creep spring and starts the action. Therefore the enemy can pull the pins from a dozen grenades and keep them beside him during an attack on his position. All he need do is pick up each grenade, bang it and throw. Many times we found stacks of grenades with the pins removed beside captured foxholes.

Their water-bottle is about the smallest used by any army and though this may be a sign of toughness, or lack of metal, the climate of Burma is tougher, and men need bigger water-bottles than those used by the Japanese.

The infantry pack is smaller than the British type, but many strings and loops are attached to it, so that masses of equipment may be tied on to it. Their gas respirator is inferior, but quite well made, and in some respects resembles ours. It has spare eyepieces. The accessories for dealing with mustard gas burns are highly detailed, and such things as anti-dim for use on goggles and anti-freeze mixture sprays are kept in the respirator haversack.

The askaris tore the rubber wallets out of these haversacks and used them to keep tobacco and papers in, for they are completely waterproof.

The Japanese Army, though poorly equipped by our standards, is well found for battle, though as the avalanche of metal and equipment that we are using against them grows in power, it will avail them little.

In the ranks of the enemy are some who doubt. Few can say what they feel until they are given the opportunity to desert and only a few have done so. One was a lieutenant of considerable culture and education, who found himself in the hell of the Imphal fighting just after the monsoon had begun. The situation for the besieging Japanese had become desperate and when this lieutenant saw his opportunity he came over into the British lines. He was ragged and starving, but he had not lost hope in the world he had believed in. He had been a student of economics, and when his turn had come to go into the army, he had gone without a word. It is not possible to do otherwise in Japan when the time comes to go out and fight with the Imperial army.

This intelligent man, wearing the two stars of a lieutenant, had always doubted, but could say nothing. For him the world had been bigger than that surrounded by the waters that lapped the shores of Japan. The world was a place for men to live in and discover things. When he found himself with a platoon of half-mad troops, who wept aloud when they saw the only Japanese aircraft that had escaped the Allied fighters overhead, the seed of doubt grow stronger. He was expected to lead these tricked fanatics on to the British machine-guns with a cry of *Banzai,* and to watch them crumble before him. Then, if he survived the machine-gun, he was to do it again, and again and again, until the starving troops were wiped out.

One day, when the rain poured on them, he left and before he reached the British lines he threw away his sword. It was a couple of hundred years old and had belonged to his family. It was the curious evil link with the world he wished to desert.

When this man had left Siam with his troops for the Burma front, they had a feeling that an offensive was starting. Siam had been splendid and life there had been as pleasant as a man and a student could wish. Clean clothes and fresh, untainted air.

When they left the Chindwin with the expeditionary troops for the attack on India, they had carried fourteen days' rations. They were told to find the rest in India. They were told also that the Indian troops fighting alongside the British were finished and were waiting to revolt and kill their British officers. Fantastic though it may appear, they were also informed that the Germans had landed in England and that only India remained as a rampart of the British in the East. Because the

British were almost defeated and could not fight on, they were going to use poison gas against the troops of the Imperial Japanese Army. Therefore every man would carry a respirator. It is not known whether for propaganda reasons, or because he believed it, a certain senior Japanese commander shaved off a beard he had had for years. This commander was known to the troops of the Japanese expeditionary force in Burma as 'The Saint.' He would stop on the roads and sit down to talk to the soldiers, and his face was well known with its silky beard.

When he shaved it off he explained that he had done so in order that he could fix his respirator swiftly when the British used poison gas, as they were certain to do in order to defend India.

When I was told this story by an officer who was concerned in the case of the Japanese lieutenant, I remembered that every corpse we had seen from Moreh to the outskirts of Sittaung had carried a respirator, at a time when they could hardly support the weight of their shirts.

From the Chindwin through the mountains to the borders of India is a long and terrible march on fourteen days' rations, but the Japs marched swiftly, and their advance was indeed swift, until they came up against the defences and the smashing power of the artillery that waited for them. They were far from home, in a world of rolling mists and rain, and in jungle that frightened them.

The lieutenant deserted and came into the British lines. He told stories of the mass starvation and of men weeping like children in their foxholes, cut off, lost and doomed. There may be many like him in the enemy ranks, but they can say nothing, not even a word, until they desert.

For them the Emperor is not God, nor did he come from Jimmu, who arrived out of the side of Amaterasu, the sun-goddess. He is a man who lives an unknown life in the palace, and who must read daily of the screaming khaki lines of his troops being mangled and blown off the earth, for an idea, for something, for whatever it is that drives them.

What can be done when the war is over for this race of slaves who live in a land of fairy legend, surrounded by the harnessed power of machinery and invention, who drive heavy tanks, fire machine-guns, use flame-throwers and who believe that the Emperor is descended from a sun-goddess?

What can be done for prisoners whom we have seen lie on stretchers, weeping, as though suffering from some melancholiac sickness, because they have lost honour, have disgraced their families and have lost Japan?

The bombardment is not too terrible for them, because children who burn themselves with the forbidden matches will never do so again.

The Japanese have many great qualities which have been twisted into the last channel of all, for a few.

Outside of Sittaung and near Bhamo, and as far south as Buthidaung, this did not concern the Fourteenth Army at all. They had a more terrible job to do than that of the neat phrase to explain mystery. They were killing Japanese every day and they slept in water in order to be ready to do it again in the morning.

On September 4th the askaris entered Sittaung, tired, soaked with sweat and under a burning sun. With faint steam rising from the wet earth, they stared at the Chindwin River, oblivious even to the same scent of dead as had been their companion since the end of July.

CHAPTER NINE

As soon as we stopped our Jeep, it became black from end to end with flies. I had never seen flies in such numbers before, and I had been in fly-infested areas. The bonnet, the wheels, and then the whole vehicle was covered with one crawling mass of flies. They settled on the hands and face with a sickening casualness.

We rushed away from the Jeep, waving our arms, and the flies followed us. The enemy dead lay in all their usual attitudes, and here they appeared more pathetic by reason of the fact that they had reached the Chindwin River after surviving the march from India. They had died, forsaken.

This was Sittaung on the Chindwin; smashed to pieces, and turned into a sort of fantastic ploughed field in which patches of jungle still survived, and from which protruded strips of twisted metal and human remains. The craters overlapped each other until they reached the river. They were filled with green water, and in one of them, a Japanese from whom the trousers had been blown, crouched like an enormous frog, floating as though suspended in a chemical solution.

The war seldom looks just as Hollywood films it. The sense of magnificence is lacking. The troops with the four-day growth of beard never look as handsome and as devil-may-care as the film director would have it. And there is lacking the artistry achieved in the wreckage, and the sombre sense of history as portrayed by the experts. There are no pretty women concerned with the laying on of hands, nor is there the powerful and inspiring music slightly off-scene as the guns open fire. Instead, there is something tawdry, and something that repels. Only the spirit of the men who fight in it is great, and they are not conscious of their romantic aspect. A heavy pack and a filthy uniform do not allow the soldier to stand aside and watch himself. The three dimensional view of the war and the soldier can only be enjoyed at the cinema. In the scene of ugliness and destruction the soldier is truly great by virtue of what he stands and achieves and it has been the misfortune of the soldier's children that they must experience this fact for themselves, rather than understand it from the story of what Daddy did in the war, or wars. The troops of the Fourteenth Army will live in history, not only because they faced the most stubborn and fanatical of enemies, but because the will that took them to victory was composed of so many races and so many varied tongues and religions.

Sittaung, lying ruined and torn up in the bright, hot sun, had seen the British and the Japanese come and go. The Burmese had fled long ago.

Houses had been sucked off the ground by bomb-blast and dashed down again into bundles of planks and corrugated iron. Over this place the R.A.F. had wheeled and dived for days, crushing everything that might harbour the enemy, and spraying with fire anything that moved. The Japanese had fled in haste, and their half-buried dead stuck out of the ground beside those who had been killed in their tracks.

In this devastated place one Japanese soldier had been found alive. He could not understand what was said to him in his own language. He shook his head and grinned idiotically. His ears were filled with maggots and he was about to die. In this stinking place he had been left by his friends. He was no use to anyone any more. He was used up.

Beside the river lay bags of rotten rice stacked one on top of the other. Rations for many men, now useless. Life-jackets were scattered everywhere, and khaki cloth containers of the curious enemy magnetic mines. Wallets, ammunition pouches and haversacks. There was even a fan of stiff, brightly coloured paper, and hundreds of gas-masks were piled under the trees. The Chindwin threw off an oily light, and slivers of bamboo floated down on the silky surface. On the other side patrols of askaris were moving after the enemy. The blue mountains in the distance seemed to swim away in the heat-haze of the afternoon, and there was silence on the river, not even a bird note disturbing the stillness.

In the jungle that stretched from the river to the distant mountains, several thousand Japanese troops must have been moving. Information as to their desperate situation must have been scanty, for many units were lost, others destroyed, and the general dislocation of their battle system did not allow of anything other than flight. One of their main escape routes had now been closed with the capture of Sittaung. Parties of survivors were hiding near villages in the jungle, and many of them still hoped to escape. Many others died near the road within sight of the Chindwin. With the enemy, it was every man for himself, and the Africans took the hindmost when they showed themselves.

All the way from Imphal the leaflets of the Psychological Warfare unit had told the enemy the truth. These leaflets had been showered on them from planes, and they told the enemy troops that there was no hope for them. In their starving state, as they ate their grass and roots, they were able to read *menus* dropped from British planes. These *menus* carried a list of the food they would receive as prisoners, food dear to the Japanese heart, in contrast to the muck they were eating in their frightful monsoon retreat. Other leaflets were dropped over central Burma and were addressed to the troops who would soon be meeting their ragged and ruined comrades who managed to escape across the Chindwin. These leaflets said that when they met the survivors of the great Indian border debacle, they would hear and see for themselves that what British leaflets had told them for months was true. The Japanese propaganda which spoke of German-occupied England, and a weak British Army on the Indian border, would be proved lies by the fleeing and starving enemy troops who might cross the Chindwin. Many of the enemy carried these leaflets in their pockets, and were found dead with them. They were not asked to surrender; the leaflets spoke of an 'honourable arrangement.'

This assault on the minds of completely deluded human beings was carried on incessantly. The truth, plus the shattering effect of their defeat, had its effect. They must have begun to think for the first time on the importance of being alive. This truth would have its effect first on the individuals who thought beyond the foresights of their rifles, and who would feel resentment for the lies they had been told. It would probably take longer to affect the others who made up the masses of the enemy army. When a complete platoon or company surrendered, it would be possible to say that the morale of the Japanese Army was cracking. Even when one or two fit and well-fed individuals surrendered voluntarily, it would mean something, even though they were one or two out of a vast army. It would mean that they had begun to think freely, to compare, and to doubt.

The leaflets conveyed bare truth. When they were told that new weapons would be used against them, they saw and felt the effects of the new weapons, both on the ground and in the air. The truth hurt in many ways, in many places.

On the outskirts of Sittaung the sappers were clearing a minefield. It had been hastily laid. Haste and anxiety were evident in everything the enemy did. Even their suicides were hasty.

The badly laid mines were symptomatic, not only of anxious haste, but of the inability of the enemy to make full use of the powerful weapons he had borrowed from the West. These Western weapons were controlled by Eastern minds, which, though they had shown a certain ingenuity in the cyclone of their 1942 campaign, had not yet learned to exploit fully the powers and potentialities of their war machines. When they retreated out of India, they came along roads over which tall cliffs towered. They were desperate, but they did not think of blasting the cliffs down on to the road. They kept blowing up small bridges, and the British sappers laughed. The enemy artillery never made full use of its opportunities, and counter-battery work by enemy gunners was rudimentary rather than the expert work of trained men.

In 1944 the Japanese were learning what the proper application of high explosives could mean, retreating under a rain of it from guns and bombers. They also learned that a properly planned line of communication is vital when fighting a highly trained and well-armed enemy which had denied them the monsoon bases of Kohima and Imphal. The hysteria of the attack and the fervid certainty of victory ignored this problem, and the collapse of their communications under the monsoon and the bombers of the Allied air forces had left their army to starve and die. They had learned their first great lesson in warfare. They did not lack fighting spirit or courage. They lacked a certain coolness, and the knowledge that even a divine mission of the Sons of Heaven must eat, especially at the ends of long and arduous lines of communication through monsoon jungles. They had also been unable to believe that Japanese troops could be beaten and hammered into utter defeat.

If they are allowed military colleges in the new world, Imphal will be on the main sand-table of the lecture hall. The importance of supply and transport, and a proper appreciation of the enemy's fighting spirit, will be stressed in lectures to military students. The facts of a mismanaged war which caused the massacres of Japanese troops in South-East Asia and the Pacific may have proved to the enemy that the flexibility and planning of free men is more powerful than the electric hysteria of the enslaved.

On the west side of the Chindwin from March to August, 1944, close on eighty thousand of their troops had perished, and many thousands had sickened of malaria and Beri-Beri because the climate had not noticed that they were supermen. The only reward of the dead was the knowledge that they would live in the shrine of Yasukini for ever, and of the living that they were failures as men and soldiers of the Emperor. It was ironic that semi-savage troops from Africa could show more humanity and feeling than could the semi-cultured barbarians of Nippon.

On the thirty miles of track leading to Sittaung the Hygiene Squads had burned over eight hundred enemy dead. Those who had died rolled in their blankets, in the jungle, were left. The stragglers who were afraid to surrender died like pathetic animals. It is to be wondered if all this will affect the poetry of the Emperor. It could be made magnificent, even epic, but only when viewed from afar, and through Yamato-coloured glasses.

While the East Africans entered Sittaung, the Fifth Indian Division, one of the most famous in the Fourteenth Army, had reached milestone 100 on the Tiddim road. They too, were pursuing the enemy towards Kalemyo via Fort White, while the Eleventh East African Division was pushing towards Kalewa. Separating the two divisions was a sea of jungle, but they would join together near Kalemyo where the two roads came close together.

On September 6th East African patrols struck out north and south from Sittaung, but though they found no enemy in the area they came upon two hundred Burmese villagers, who, like all people caught up in wars, were sheltering until peace came. They reported that Japanese stragglers had been killing themselves in considerable numbers. It was the same old story. The enemy were still living on leaves and grass, and the sick were left to die. These villagers wished for peace and they asked if air raids and fighting would continue. Their lives had been uprooted in such a way that only a few cattle and a little rice remained to them. Down the Khabaw Valley this shortage of rice had been felt by most Burmese. The Japanese had forced all able-bodied people into working as coolies on the lines of communication, and the result had been the stoppage of nearly all rice cultivation.

While they carried rice to the forward Japanese troops, the Burmese had slit open the sacks, flung rations over the cliffs, and returned for more. They had not said much, but had done what they could to hinder the Japs, not so much out of patriotism as out of unwillingness to co-operate with the Japs. They had watched the Japs come stumbling back in retreat, begging for food. The Burmese became more bland than ever, and said that they had none, and the Japanese officers had cursed them with tears in their eyes. With a certain amount of quiet pleasure the Burmese described all this, and their pleasure was heightened by the knowledge that with the arrival of the British air raids would cease. They had become as civilised as the peoples of Europe in their knowledge of air raid precautions, and having experienced the twentieth century they could now sink back into the pleasant life of the Burmese peasant. Their villages had been destroyed by bombs and shells, and they had seen their pagodas used as strong points by the Japanese. Their problem was now food and clothing, and the Civil Affairs Branch which was to follow the British troops into Burma was already dealing with this matter.

While patrols searched the country on both banks of the Chindwin near Sittaung, the East African force which had started down the road to Kalewa had reached beyond a place called Htinzin. Here the mud and rain became worse. It was so bad that infantry battalions took off their kits and became roadmakers. They piled logs on to the mud in an effort to make a corduroy road, and pegged down thousands of bamboos. The trucks mashed them down into the mud, and again the Africans brought logs and trees until these too, disappeared into the black and evil-smelling mud. Stretches of logs ran for hundreds of yards and over these the vehicles crept slowly, sometimes slipping into the mud where they generally stayed. As the trucks moved over the logs, their wheels cast the timber right and left until the timbered road was ruined. A jumble of logs and mud was all that remained after several vehicles had passed, and the wet, tired troops started again on their job. On all this the rain hissed hour after hour until the askaris who stared at the black sky could hardly believe that it rained like this for months every year. They came from a country where rain was precious and uncertain, and this squandering of water by the sky was something that they wrote home about, often at great length.

A driver might stick in the mud twenty times in an hour. He would sit down beside the bogged wheels until the mud reached to his chest, and by feeling at their base with his hands, manage to pack sticks and branches under them. With a loud sucking noise he would then stand up from the mud. One more try, with a revving and roaring of the engine, and the vehicle came out, hovering on the edges of the trenches dug by its wheels, until the sweating driver leaned forward like a horseman, and perhaps she would fall back into the trenches spraying the air with mud from her turning wheels. Clenching his white teeth, the African driver would have another try. While he worked, the rain poured down, filling every rut and hole.

Through this watery muck the infantry marched, often up to their knees. They marched stripped to the waist, and the rain cooled them, making their black and brown skins appear as though lit with a silvery light. To march thus, in a sort of daze, while carrying heavy weapons and equipment, becomes an automatic movement, and a slopping up and down movement of boots and sodden trousered legs.

The patrols fought sharp and vicious engagements in front of the marching columns. Sometimes these fights were scattered over large areas, and attacks on enemy positions were made without artillery support, for the guns were still miles back, ploughing their way through deepening mud, which stopped all traffic save Jeeps, and these had a hard fight of it and were often defeated.

Those who have been stuck in deep mud with a heavy vehicle, and have dragged themselves from wheel to wheel in order to pack sticks under the tyres for the next effort, know the fury that comes of desperation. They know also the dulled acceptance that replaces fury, and which allows the body to work in a sort of coma. In September beyond Htinzin there was much anxiety mingled with fury, for the trucks contained the essentials of life for the troops, and death for the enemy. The drivers worked until they were dropping with sleep, pressing on and on through the miles of water-logged mud to the forward troops. When the traffic stopped, the stuff was man-handled.

Dakota planes, despite black and dangerous skies, flew low over the jungle dropping supplies of all types. The pilots could see the troops below them stuck between rivers that raced and milled, and bogged trucks scattered down the road through the jungle. The infantry who received the supplies watched the planes come in over the trees glistening with rain. They could see the tiny figure standing in the plane's doorway, kicking out the bundles which burst into white flower of parachutes. Parachute loads that stuck high in the trees were retrieved by felling the trees. It was not always possible to climb after them because of enemy snipers.

Often the enemy lurked along the edge of the dropping zone hoping to steal food or grenades. In their starving state, as they lay in their foxholes, their thoughts must have been bitter as they watched fifteen or twenty heavy planes dropping food and supplies to the African troops opposite them.

Since entering the Khabaw Valley, not one enemy plane had attacked the East Africans, nor even flown over them. The sky over Burma was dominated by the Allied air forces, and over the Khabaw R.A.F. fighters and fighter-bombers went as they wished. The supply planes flew without escort, and the Japanese troops could see for themselves that their own air force had been destroyed.

The 11th Division had now been over a month in the line, and though hampered by the rain and mud, the machine was beginning to move as all the units came through the mouth of the valley and increased the pressure. The jungle can swallow a division of troops, and thousands of men and machines can disappear like many ants into a hill. To control a division in the jungle, feed it, and at the same time pursue a cunning enemy over almost impossible terrain is a task that requires work through the day and night, and allows for little rest.

At Divisional Headquarters there was a continual buzzing of field telephones, and the staff officers kept in touch with fighting units despite broken cables and growing difficulties as the monsoon increased its downpour. Reports coming in through the day and night told of four Japs killed here, five there. Reports telling of bridges washed away or blown up by the enemy, and of patrols who were cut off between rivers. One told of an officer whose mind had become unhinged and who had developed a phobia about water. For him the world had become one mass of flowing water, and he could not be evacuated owing to the swollen rivers. He felt that the waters had trapped him. Reports said that the medical officer with him had managed to fetch him for a certain distance down the road, and after a battle with the mud they had reached a river but could not cross. There were wounded and sick askaris whose number grew daily, and they could not be evacuated, for traffic could not move.

The rain did not stop; it increased in volume until the mud itself disappeared under the water. People stopped trying to keep dry. It was no use trying any more. The horrors of Burma have been overdone many times, and there has been a tendency to picture the place as one impenetrable jungle crawling with snakes and leeches. Very little of it is like that, but it would be difficult to over-colour the discomforts of the muck and rain of the Khabaw Valley in the monsoon. The monsoon campaign in the Khabaw was more one of physical endurance than one of continual battle against the Japanese. It was worse for the Japs. There was comfort in this for the African troops.

CHAPTER TEN

1

I made an attempt to reach Witok down the Kalewa road together with Clive Harston, the senior supply officer of the division. We took American K. rations with us, and filled water-bottles. With the American K rations, hot water is not needed to make the soup, coffee, or the lemon beverage they contain, and water, cold, from the water-bottle is used.

We drove through Tamu in a Jeep, and even now, after the burning it is still horrible, for the Hygiene Squads, overworked in these days, had missed many of the dead. Tamu was deserted, and the big bomb craters were still filled with brown water. The golden Bhuddas stared out as they had stared upon the enemy dead, as impassive as ever. While we were there the Burmese who were moving some of the statues had made friends with the askaris of a supply unit, who were helping them to move the idols. When the askaris saw the Burmese carrying the statues with an air of great reverence, they stopped their trucks and offered to help. The way in which they did this with signs was quite touching. One African joined his hands together as though in prayer and raised his eyebrows. The Burmese stared at him and then nodded, with smiles.

'Is it part of the God worship?' said the Africans, with their signs, and the Burmese said that it was.

The askaris then helped to load the idols into the trucks and the dozen or so villagers climbed in after them, when the whole party drove a few hundred yards to the new site.

This spontaneous act on the part of the askaris did more good than it is possible to describe, for I later talked with a Burmese officer of the Civil Affairs, who told me that the story had come back to him through the Burmese, and they were very impressed with the good nature of 'the black men.'

The Burmese had no idea as to where the black men came from, but they liked their good nature, and told the Civil Affairs officers so. The drivers who helped carry the statues were rewarded by a big meal of curry and rice, which the askaris love dearly. Food to the African is always the best answer.

We entered the jungle just as the rain began. Already we had come across bogged trucks, and soon we started to find the first trucks of a valuable bridging train, sinking, one could describe it, by the stern. Laden with steel bridging and pontoons, they weighed tons. The mud enfolded them and sucked them down. The rain became heavier, and drivers who could do no more sat glumly on the side of their trucks and the wheels of each vehicle were invisible, so deeply were they bogged.

We edged our way through, feeling the logs underneath the mud rolling and slipping. On this kind of road, where the 'road' of logs was hidden under the mud, you never knew the moment it would end, and your Jeep would simply fall off the logs where they ended, into many feet of mud and water. This happened to us. Up till then, wrapped in gas capes, we had remained dry, but as the Jeep sank down well above the axles, we knew that we had 'had it.' We each waited for the other to get out, and then got out together, stepping into feet of muddy water. Now it did not matter if one became plastered in mud from head to foot.

While one revved the engine in low gear, the other pushed until hidden in a spray of mud and slush which clung to the uniform and became thicker as the struggle continued. The face, arms and indeed the whole body became encased in a cloak of mud, and the Jeep did not move. We went on with this effort for over half an hour and then another Jeep appeared, bouncing and crawling along through the lake of mud and felled trees. Against the jungle the blades of rain flashed in millions of silvery lights, and these trucks which had given up the struggle yesterday glistened in the downfall.

When one Jeep pushes another out of the mud by creeping up behind it and then applying all the pressure that the gears can summon, it is called 'a kick up the backside,' though the troops in Burma word it somewhat differently even if the meaning is the same.

We were given a kick up the backside by the obliging officer in the Jeep, and then we bounced once again on to the treacherous surface of the logs under the mud. After an exhausting half-hour, during which we clung to every means of support offered in the body of a Jeep, we stopped to have lunch.

2

The American K ration is done up in a small neat box of rectangular shape which fits easily into the haversack or the thigh pocket of the battledress. The box is of cardboard and is painted with a thick yellow wax, and this protects it against all the ravages of the tropics, and of the monsoon in particular. Printed on the side is a list of contents, and with instruction as to preparation. The cardboard container is so strongly made that it must be ripped open with a knife. Inside were cellophane wrappings containing two packets of 'energy biscuits,' three lumps of sugar, one packet of coffee (soluble in cold water), one bar of fruit compress, one stick of chewing gum, a packet of four 'Camel' cigarettes and one tin of pork and beef compress. This makes a satisfying meal, but if eaten continually becomes boring and depressing, particularly to British soldiers who are used to bulk in the form of stews, soups and hashes. But for a patrol operating for long distances in trackless jungle, the K ration is the answer, though there are now various types of British jungle ration which are even better than the American K ration. Though not as compact, they are more satisfying and possess greater variety. Rations in battle play a great part in the maintenance of morale, and troops will shout with excitement to see tins of steak and kidney pudding come up with the bulk ration issues, after weeks of the soya link.

It can be said here that the Fourteenth Army has had to deal with the soya link sausage often when they thought they could face it no more. The brass-coloured tin that stands on the corner of the mess table, or in the corner of the foxhole, gradually assumes an air of evil triumph. Though with all their hearts they hated soya link sausage, the troops saw it come up again and again, by plane, Jeep and mule. Beyond patience many flung it to the ground and would not or could not eat it.

Seac, the newspaper for the troops in South-East Asia Command, ran a column of letters, and the highest proportion of them from the officers and men of the Fourteenth Army dealt with repatriation, soya link sausage and medals. Sometimes the subject of soya link held the area for weeks at a time, and then fell before the gloomy spectre of repatriation, but again the soya link would nuzzle into the columns and soldiers wrote of it with bitterness and even fury.

One soldier wanted to send a soya link sausage to Sir James Grigg for Christmas, but was probably dissuaded from doing so by his officers. Whenever Sir James Grigg made a new pronouncement on repatriation for troops in Burma, it was termed 'Another piece of Griggery-pokery' by the aforementioned troops.

'First it was ships,' said the troops. 'We had no ships. Now it is because we have no troops to spare from Europe, and before that it was because we didn't know what the invasion of Europe was going to mean.'

They talked Soya Link and repatriation until they were sick of the subject.

Then they talked about medals.

And when the troops in Burma talk about medals, the air seems to crackle.

The soya links continued to come up with the rations, and the African askaris ate them with zest, until one day they also stared with a glassy eye at the freshly opened can with its sour, chemical smell.

Askaris like bulk, even more than British troops. In Africa they ate *posho,* which is maize flour cooked into a porridge and with this they took meat.

The field service scale for the East African askaris is composed of the following items. Maize-meal, or rice, or atta, fresh meat, ghee, vegetables, potatoes, ground nuts, sugar, salt, tea, tinned milk, fruit and a weekly issue of cigarettes, tobacco, or the snuff beloved of the East African tribesmen and which is sent to Burma from East Africa. This snuff is very powerful, being made of crushed native tobacco and with a sprinkling of soda or pepper. In East Africa the tribesmen carry it in little buck-horns and offer it to each other when they meet. It is tapped from the buck-horn on to the back of the hand and then sniffed up. When white men take this snuff for the first time there is great amusement among the Africans as the white man groans, wheezes, closes his eyes and gasps for breath, and then finally is convulsed in a series of powerful sneezes.

The field service scale ration is issued under conditions of static or semi-static warfare, but the aim of the supply officers is to issue this ration when and wherever they can.

For jungle patrols, however, the ration is of a different order, and is known as the light-scale ration. This is done up in a cardboard packet, and consists of biscuits, chocolate, tinned meat, tinned cheese, milk powder, sugar, tea, salt, cigarettes, matches and one compound vitamin tablet—the vitamin C which wards off scurvy, and vitamin B which counters beri-beri. One is issued to each man on patrol, and both British and African troops use them.

There is another form of ration known as the composite-pack which is sealed up in a four-gallon petrol tin, and contains rations for eight men. While the light-scale is an individual ration and is cooked in the individual's mess-tin, the composite-pack is a communal ration and is shared among eight men, and can be cooked in the petrol-tin container. All troops in the forward areas of the Khabaw Valley carried a two-day reserve ration to be used only in an emergency.

The monsoon created such emergencies when front-line troops were forced to nibble into their precious reserves, but the Supply Corps saw to it that these occasions were rare.

There is yet another quite different type of ration called the jungle ration, which is done up in a sealed tin about the size of a service mess-tin. This is opened like a sardine tin, with a key, and the tin itself is used as a mess-tin for cooking the ration. The jungle ration is highly concentrated, and is a mixture of all forms of energy food. It contains lots of sweet stuff. Chocolate, sweets, sugar, biscuits, lemonade powder, compressed tea tablets and two cubes of porridge compress. There is also a tin of salt tablets, and a packet of matches, pressed meat and a tin of twenty good British cigarettes.

Another ration that appeared spasmodically during the Khabaw campaign, was the twenty-four hour ration pack as issued to the troops who invaded Europe in June, 1944.

All these various rations have been tried out on the Burma front, and are the result of long planning by experts. The soya link will be defeated soon, as South-East Asia receives the best that can be supplied to it, when conditions in Europe permit.

The greatest problem in Burma is that of supply, and if a Supply Corps cannot operate, an army will crumble. Mountains, swollen rivers, blocked and destroyed roads and jungle that must be hacked away, are only a few of the difficulties in the way of the Supply Corps. Often the line of communications runs for over a hundred miles through the jungle and mountains, and over this arduous country went Jeeps, mules, oxen, elephants, and when none of these could get through, the carrying was done by men. As the air power of the South-East Asia Command increased so also did the carrying capacity of the supply planes which gradually struck farther afield as the Fourteenth Army moved deeper into Japanese-occupied Burma. In mid-September, 1944, the Dakota supply planes came through thick cloud and rain to drop rations and ammunition, and there was not a man on the ground who did not admire their courage and determination.

The dropping of supplies from the air has become a scientific process. In Burma it means everything. Gradually the Air Force proved that almost anything could be dropped by air, providing there was a parachute strong enough to hold it in its descent.

It meant that warfare had changed, and that great bodies of men could strike into the jungle, carrying only their fighting equipment and they did not need to worry about lines of communication, dumps and bases for supplies. When they needed supplies, they called for them by radio, and the planes flew in and showered down all the necessities. Having replenished their pouches and haversacks, the men could move on, unworried about their rear. If the enemy got behind them, the force could move elsewhere, and when the planes came again, they were ready to move on, armed and rationed.

The askaris soon learned to distinguish those planes that were piloted by experts and those which were flown by learners. The experts swept in quickly, without much preliminary inspection, and dropped their loads smack into the centre of the dropping zone. The askaris soon learned the numbers of these planes and knew that there would not be a long search through the jungle for the supplies as with the less experienced who dropped their cargoes.

The inexpert at supply dropping sometimes began their unloading while over the centre of the zone, so that the long 'stick' of parachute loads continued to fall far into the jungle, while only one or two of the loads touched home. Arguments as to whether bad dropping was the fault of the pilot or of the man in the plane doorway who kicked out the loads, went on all over the field.

Working with each brigade was a composite platoon of the East Africa Army Service Corps. When a brigade was 'on air supply,' the composite platoon looked after all air drops, gathered all supplies from the dropping zone and established them in dumps. From here they split them up and sent them out to the brigade units.

An air-dropping zone that has been in operation for a few days looks like a laundryman's nightmare. Hundreds of snow-white parachutes festoon the trees, and litter the ground. The white canvas containers for the supplies lie everywhere, and as fast as the composite platoon troops gather the rations, ammunition, the general supplies, another small body of troops gather parachutes and containers and stack them in heaps for return to the rear air-strips.

When fifteen or twenty Dakota planes fly in line over the zone, they unload supplies at a terrific speed, so that the whole area is covered with stores of all kinds. It became a wilderness of fallen trees and muddied parachutes. Petrol, Jeep engines, hand-grenades, Penicillin, Mepacrine, blankets, rum rations and twenty-five-pounder shells came down with loaves of bread, marrows and onions. The collected mass of stores is an amazing sight, for on a big dropping zone when many planes have unloaded, there is a mountain of sacks, cases and parcels of all types.

On one occasion a note was found inside a case of rations, which said: 'Stop eating so fast, you bastards, we can't pack the stuff quick enough.' This had been written by a desperate packer far back on an airstrip in Assam, for as the troops who had taken Sittaung filtered down the Kalewa road, the whole division went on to air supply, and the consuming power of a division is tremendous when viewed from the packer's end.

There was argument, especially among supply officers, as to the relative value of road transport and air transport. In September, 1944, the air supply was keeping the advance moving into Burma, but the supply officers considered that it was a much more costly method of supply than road transport, though they knew it was the only means available in the monsoon.

First the packing of all these various types of supply takes hundreds of man-hours where the ordinary road transport does not. In packing air cargoes a packer can never be anything but careful, and cannot load his supplies into the plane as easily as he can into a truck. The packing of parachutes, the consumption of petrol on the flight and the hours of flying by the pilot, all tend to make air supply more expensive in every way than road transport.

It is true that whenever possible the supplies to the front were sent in by road, but during the monsoon, the air-supply planes were in the air in all weathers, and when their story is written it will be seen how much is owed to the Allied air forces for the advance into central Burma. Flying over jungle and mountains, often in blinding rain, they dropped supplies to the Fourteenth Army along the Burma front from Myitkyina to the Arakan, and then repeated the operation ad lib.

3

After finishing the K ration, we started up the Jeep and crept forward again on to the mud and logs, heading for Sunle, where the forward troops had been the day before. The road became worse, and we came on Jeeps that had been grinding away for hours, while officers, N.C.O.s and askaris, all stripped to the waist and glistening with rain, pushed and pulled at the sunken vehicles. Trucks laden with bridging material had been given up as hopeless cases, and their drivers sat hunched up in the cabins, sucking at damp cigarettes. If ever there was a wilderness of mud and water and defeated machinery, it was the Kalewa road in September. The order had just come through that all traffic was to cease, and ours was one of the last Jeeps that still moved on the road.

A long column of infantry marched through the mud. They were askaris from Uganda, just moving into the line, and even to see them soaked with rain and carrying heavy packs, made the onlooker feel something of their physical effort. They were singing a song of their country in Lugunda, their own language, and I remember one officer with an enormous moustache tramping along in front, who was singing it too. The officers and British N.C.O.s carried rifles and bayonets like the men, for when they went into action, the askaris were led by them, all badges of rank having been removed. We crawled along between the marching lines of troops who grinned and waited to see us stick.

In a couple of weeks I was to grin like that, as I marched past stranded trucks, for in the monsoon the feet of men won the day. No mud defeated these thousands of feet, nor did the thickest jungle stop them.

Enemy trucks were parked all along the track, nearly always with the driver dead at the wheel or near the vehicle, and some of them had committed hara-kiri with grenades, or as this custom was called by a few in the division, 'hoity-toity,' or 'willy-nilly.'

The jungle near the Sunle Chaung was mostly teak, and these tremendous trees shut out the sunlight, and the roads could not be bared to the sun without a great deal of labour involved in cutting down the trees. As it had to be done, gangs of infantry worked with the sappers, and they were soon able to let in a little sunlight which shot down in golden beams through the damp gloom, like the light into an ancient cathedral.

The work of the sappers during the monsoon went on without a stop. They pulled boats across rivers and sent them back again, hour after hour, as battalions waited to cross. Each boat carried only a few men, and they carried on in this manner while pontoon rafts were assembled so that vehicles could cross. In the burning sun they worked until they were ready to drop, and the skins of the Europeans turned the dark colour of chocolate. They ate their rations straight from the opened tin, and washed it down with mess-tins of tea, and then went straight back to the ferry. Other gangs of sappers cut culverts to drain away the water from the roads, and as fast as they worked, the rain kept up with them. They slept beside their jobs, under a sheet of canvas, and surrounded by rations, spades, weapons and flowing mud. Each man in the division, when it was time to sleep, made himself a small private world in which he dumped his kit and waited for sleep or an enemy patrol.

The river at Sunle was wide, deep and furiously fast. Hundreds of troops squatted in the shade of the jungle, waiting to cross, and those Jeeps that had made the trip were being carried across the river one by one on the back of an old truck which could just make the crossing.

A few yards on the left of us, and on the bank of the river itself, a divisional truck lay shattered. It had run on to a landmine yesterday, and three askaris were killed instantly. A British sergeant was blown over the bonnet of the truck but was unharmed. The mine was one of our own that had been planted with many a hundred others during our retreat before the Japanese offensive. The maps which contained the information as to the positions of these minefields were still on the way to the division, and were anxiously awaited.

It was not safe to go far into the jungle without taking the greatest care, for the hidden wire or peg might cause an explosion that would kill or maim many men. This jungle had been sown with various booby-traps and mines, by both Japanese and British, and men as well as mules were often killed during a careless stroll.

We waited at Sunle River for a couple of hours, but the mass of traffic that waited would take priority over us, so we turned back and began churning our way through the mud again.

The trip back to Divisional Headquarters was easier, the mind and body had become acclimatised to the rain, mud, felled trees and torrents.

CHAPTER ELEVEN

In a special order of the day addressed to the 11th East African Division, issued on August 31st, General Slim, Commander of the Fourteenth Army, said:

'In my last order of the day I told you you had defeated the Jap armies opposing you and that it remained to destroy them. The extent to which you have done that is shown by the fifty thousand Japanese left dead on the soil of India and Northern Burma, the great quantities of guns and equipment you have captured, the prisoners you have taken, the advances you have made and the flight of the remnants you are still pursuing.

'To the Fifteenth Corps in the Arakan fell the unique honour of being the first British-Indian formation to hold, break and decisively hurl back a major Japanese offensive. Theirs was an example of tenacity and courage which inspired the whole army. The 4th Corps met the main weight of the Japanese Assam offensive, and, in one of the hardest fought and longest battles of the war, shattered it. 33rd Corps in their brilliant offensive from the north not only drove a large Japanese force from what should have been an impregnable position, but destroyed it. Together the 4th and 33rd Corps have swept the enemy out of India.

'The troops of the L. of C. areas, not only by their gallantry and steadfastness in action, but by their tireless devotion behind the immediate front made a contribution essential to victory.

'What you owe to our comrades in the Allied air forces I need not remind you. Our whole plan of battle was based on their support. There would have been no success had they failed us. Their share in our combined victory was magnificent, and historic.

'There is not a division or brigade in the Fourteenth Army which has not proved its superiority over the enemy and knows it.

'The 11th East African Division, a late-comer in the field, has lost no time in making its mark and showing itself to be of the highest fighting quality. Great things are expected of you, and the Fourteenth Army is proud to have you among them.

'To the officers and men of the 11th East African Division I send my congratulations. The Fourteenth Army has inflicted on the Japanese the greatest defeat his army has as yet suffered. He is busily trying to build up again and reinforce his broken divisions. He will fight again, and viciously, but we have paid him something of what we owe. There still remains the interest. He will get it.'

These were the words of one of Britain's great generals, who had caused an army to do magnificent things against a hitherto unbeaten enemy, in a zone of operations that was almost forgotten by the Allied peoples. The 'Forgotten Army' would be remembered by the Japanese.

The bayonets of this jungle army were pointing at Mandalay, and now that Myitkyina in North Burma had fallen, the way would open swiftly, especially after the monsoon. It was not known at this time just where and when the enemy would stand and fight, but there was little doubt in September that he was bled dry, and would need time to push new troops from Southern Burma up to the front. The policy of pursuit and ruthless destruction of the enemy was being followed all along the Burma front, and despite the bad weather the Allied air forces flew out to strafe and bomb any enemy target that presented itself.

The enemy was getting the interest. In small patrol clashes with askaris from every territory of East Africa, he was getting it. Three and five killed, and seven wounded. Every day it went on; and on the Tiddim road, British and Indian troops were doing it too; and below Myitkyina it was happening, and near Maungdaw in the Arakan. The mass killing of the battles of Imphal, Kohima and Ukruhl had stopped, but dying from hunger and sickness, and from the bullets of fast patrols, went on.

Though the askaris had not developed the same point of view concerning the Japanese as had the Europeans, they were daily becoming conscious of the importance of their fight into Burma. Physically, to begin with, they felt far superior to the Japanese, but they never underrated them as fighters. Having met a defeated enemy, after two years of propaganda which informed them of the Japanese will to fight and conquer, they felt on top of the world. They had used their bayonets and *pangas* on the enemy, and even if the pursuit was an ordeal of the first magnitude they slopped on through the warm mud.

The kind of warfare that prevailed in early September is described in the following official divisional report:

'A patrol went into Yedok on September 7th. As they entered the village they heard a vehicle start up. They went towards the noise and saw one Jap disappear into the bush leaving mess-tins full of rice and a diary behind. The patrol smashed the vehicle, and left a grenade as a booby-trap. When they left they heard the grenade explode. They also heard light machine-gun fire from the direction of Yedok, presumably firing at nothing. In the village, tracks of approximately ten men were seen on a track running west from the village.'

The advance down the road at this stage of the monsoon was made possible by the still figure staring with unwinking eyes, and the fast movements of patrols who engulfed enemy patrols and shot them up with rifles and sub-machine guns. The patrols operated ahead of the main body and carried the war to the enemy.

Reports said that the enemy were digging positions some considerable distance beyond Yedok at a place called Yazagyo, and when the Japanese dig positions, they dig them well and cunningly. R.A.F. recce planes swept over the enemy territory and pin-pointed targets, and also sent back word of enemy field-works and dispositions. The enemy was still trying to screen the retreat of the broken troops from India, and also was desperately trying to stem the advance of both the East African Division on the Kalewa road, and that of the 5th Indian Division which was pressing on to Tiddim. Both the Tiddim road and the Yedok–Yazagyo road converged on to Kalewa, and as the two divisions advanced, the Japanese worked furiously to maintain their rearguard. It was plain that the enemy was in a very difficult position regarding reinforcements and fresh units. He was pushing up troops from all over Burma in an effort to keep up his fighting units, but the numbers were quite insufficient. Probably he was saving his best troops for the battle of Mandalay, and it was considered that Mandalay might fall swiftly, once we crossed the Chindwin.

Rumours, known in the division as 'latrinograms,' or for short, 'latrinos,' flew thick and fast. But we had little doubt that when the enemy had found time to move up new troops on to the Chindwin front, and had really got over the chaotic retreat there would be hard fighting to reach Kalewa.

It was also established that the Japanese ahead of us were also engaged in the construction of log roads, and were having the same trouble with their remaining transport as we were having. Great numbers of enemy trucks had been abandoned and some of these had been put into working order by the sappers. One Japanese staff car, which had contained the body of a senior enemy staff officer, had also been repaired. Equipment that the enemy could hardly spare was being abandoned, or smashed and left beside the road. Seventy-five-millimetre guns and stacks of ammunition were left in the jungle. It was all he could do to to drag his men out of the debacle with what little personal equipment they could still find the strength to carry. Over them all flew the Allied planes, blasting them with high explosive, so that they moved in the jungle like terrified animals, and could only march freely at night, hungry and dispirited.

In the front line dinner was eaten at half past five in the evening and all ranks had retired to their foxholes by six o'clock. There was no talking and no smoking, and ears strained for the slightest sound. Around each unit encampment lines of *panjis* were planted, and behind these the machine-gunners waited and listened. The *panji* is a long bamboo stake sharpened to a needle point, and hundreds of these were planted to take the place of barbed wire. In Burma booby-traps made of *panjis* run into many types. One favoured by the enemy was made with a *panji* after the point had been buried in putrefying matter for some time. It was then lashed into position so that pressure on a root or wire released it with force enough to drive the point into the body of the unwary. The wound ensuing from this would be of a highly poisonous nature. Men who fought in the Arakan through the long stalemate know a great deal about these things, for the war round Buthidaung and Maungdaw became like the fighting between two savage tribes, and every device was used in order to kill or maim.

The Japanese used the small shell-like grenades from their grenade dischargers as booby-traps, by placing the grenade nose first in the ground after the pin had been removed. If you stood on this, you had 'had it.'

The enemy was fond of using 'jitter parties' at night, and these sneaked around the perimeter of the camps and made noises, threw grenades, and fired occasional bursts of machine-gun fire into the area, in an effort to draw fire. It takes keen discipline to hold fire when this happens on a pitch-black night, and after the first usual fusillades of rifle fire, the askaris learned the game quickly and lay still. Often the Japanese ran into each other and opened fire, and fought running actions in the jungle.

The jungle at night is immense. There is a darkness that is like the darkness of a big sealed room, for the trees shut out all light. In this mesh of vegetation and pitch blackness, figures moved silently at night, watching and listening. Like some crazy dream, the war went on in the darkness, and men tried to snatch sleep while they held their rifles and bayonets ready to leap into action. On all this the rain went on falling, and the stink of dead teak came up out of the soil and was almost indistinguishable from the smell of dead men.

A European creeping out of a wet foxhole in the dim morning light looked as tired as he felt. The face was grey and dirty, if it was not smeared with black paint, and there was a crust of beard that joined with the slightly sunken eyes in the picture of a jungle soldier at dawn. The green battledress was wet and crumpled, and the equipment smeared with mud. Tea, the eternal British army tea, brought life into the tired skin and eyes, and gradually the face cleared. The African does not show the same signs of exhaustion or tiredness as the European, nor his black skin did not mirror the effects as faithfully. But he showed a yellowness in the eyes, and there was a lack of lustre in the usually lively eyeball. He also revived under the stimulation of hot tea. When he strapped on the mass of kit and had slung his rifle, he was ready to move again.

The stiffness and pains in the joints do not show now. The troops are young. Those whom the monsoon had affected may feel it when they are forty and fifty. But now, the tough sinew and muscle can burn this pain away and push it back into the secret recesses where the body hides such things.

On each side the walls of the Khabaw Valley rose in jungle and mountain, and like ants in the vastness of vegetation, the troops of the 11th Division moved on, as the sun rose to fight again with the rain-clouds.

CHAPTER TWELVE

'If you go down to the lines near Tamu, sir,' said the British sergeant-major, 'you could get down to the front with the mule company. It'll be some trip, sir, but you'll get there, which no truck will for some time.'

Mule Companies had arrived to work with the division, and they were now assembling near Tamu for the march down the Kalewa road to the front line. It was said that these were among the most experienced in Burma, and a great number of the men had been in the first retreat out of Burma in early 1942. They were from the Indian Army, and the troops were nearly all Punjabi Mussulmen. Sometimes at night we could hear their wild singing, which was higher and thinner than that of the more melodious African voice. They sang the nasal and somewhat heart-broken songs of Northern India, and sometimes one thought they would weep. As a body of hardened and physically fit troops they were splendid, and a high proportion of them were regular soldiers.

As they were now attached to the East African Division, they would be carrying rations and ammunition in the forward areas, and would be doing what they had been doing for nearly three years—walking for hundreds of miles with their little mules.

We could smell the mule lines when still half a mile from them. They were camped down a side track off the main road, and the country around here was strewn with mines and booby-traps. The mules were highly trained and had learned a great deal about the war, and they did not wander far from their camps but, even so, the Indian muleteers kept an eye on them always.

The camp was deep in the jungle and surrounded by trampled mud. Hundreds of mules were lining up as we arrived, for it was feeding time, and the patient Indians talked to them, coaxed them and had no trouble at all. They wore their hair long and thickly plastered with grease, and their flashing eyes moved quietly and never urgently. They worked like men who knew their jobs, and in their faded green battledress they looked seasoned and very experienced. Some were piling manure into a great high bank, and though this was the jungle, the camp was scrupulously clean. Not far away from the barbed wire enclosure was the 'truck's graveyard,' and this was one tremendous dump of rusting cars and trucks which had been abandoned at this spot by refugees from the 1942 retreat from Burma. They had all turned red with rust, and we were able to reconstruct the scene of 1942 when harassed officers had directed all cars to this spot, for there was no more petrol and the road was impassable. As the trucks and cars had piled up, the refugees started to walk, or paid great sums to ride in a bullock cart towards Palel and Imphal across the mountains. Now, inside many of these rusted vehicles, lay Japanese who had crawled into the shade to die. Some of the mules feeding contentedly nearby had retreated past these vehicles when they were still piling up in 1942, and now they were heading back into Burma with the spearhead of a victorious army.

The officers' mess still smelt faintly of the Japanese who had also used it as an officers' mess, but the smell of good Indian curry was gradually hiding all that remained of the curious and cloying smell of enemy food and equipment. The graves of several Japanese officers were neatly laid out near the house. Much care had been shown to the graves, and the long carved poles that stood up from them were covered with Japanese ideographs and probably spelt the names of senior enemy officers. There were four of them together in the gloomy shade of the jungle, and they looked weird and somehow forbidding. The tall poles looked like totems, and the neatly stencilled Japanese characters almost certainly said something about loyalty, or magnificent death, or splendour.

Near the graves were two abandoned enemy trucks and a gun tractor. The trucks were painted green and on the turret was stencilled the white flag with the red sun of Japan. All around them was the usual scattered equipment and picture post-cards now sodden and rotting. Foxholes, shelters and trenches were everywhere, and as usual they were skilfully dug. The Japanese are the best diggers in the world.

The major commanding the mule company was as lithe as he was lean. His brown face with a small reddish moustache held many years of sun, and he told me that he had spent twenty-three years in India. In his fluent Urdu he ordered curry for both of us, and as it was nearly lunch time we drank a bottle of Indian beer. This man had hardly stopped walking since the Japanese attack on Burma. He had walked through Burma from Rangoon via Mandalay and then on to Kalewa on the Chindwin, and from there to Imphal. Then he had marched back to Tiddim and had then retreated again and now was walking back over the same route over which he had retreated in 1942. He liked walking, and I was to find out that he was one of the best walkers I have ever met, and with an energy that seemed to come from a dynamo inside the slim, tough body.

He said that I could march to the front with him when the mule company moved in a couple of days. We would march through mud, and sometimes the going would be very hard for the animals, but he promised me that I would enjoy it.

'Don't bother about rations,' he said. 'I have plenty.'

This was typical of him. He was an experienced officer on this front, and he saw to it that he always had plenty of everything, but the mules came first, and when they were well provided for, the major and his troops started looking after themselves.

Indian troops grow on you, and after a short time with them you come to like them, and when you leave them you miss them. These muleteers worshipped their major as only Indian soldiers can, for they show it in many ways, and the major saw to it that they got everything that could make life good for them. They relied on each other, and this reliance made them a good unit.

They were all experienced troops, and all had seen fire and had been in some kind of action against the Japanese. Many had been lost in the jungle for days and even weeks, after ambushes on mountain tracks, but they had returned to their sahibs eventually.

With us on the march would go about fifty askaris who were learning to be muleteers.

'In many ways,' smiled the major, 'it should be an amusing trip.' Anybody learning to handle mules is amusing, whether he be Indian, African or British, and not the least amused is the mule.

While we were eating the hot curry (there was a cooler, sweeter type beside it in order to bring relief to the tortured throat), the Africans arrived to start learning their new job. They made it quite plain from the start that they would watch the mules with eagle eyes until they knew all the tricks. The mules also made this plain, for they stared at the Africans from the sides of their eyes, and were intelligent enough to know that these black people did not understand them as did the brown ones. Therefore they shifted uneasily on their small feet, and the Africans shifted also. Men and beasts eyed each other covertly, and the Indians burst into high-pitched laughter. The Africans grinned sheepishly.

Among the learners were askaris from Nyasaland, Kenya and Tanganyika. The Nyasas, born mimics, started right away to imitate the mules, and did it to perfection, until the African corporal became annoyed, and said so.

'The mule will know you are imitating it and will be furious,' he said. Everybody became serious, and an Indian havildar came and showed them how to tie loads on to the back-saddles. Africans learn quickly after the first puzzled look, and soon they were all tying and untying loads with the competitive spirit that eventually the army produces in every soldier.

The mimicry of Nyasas is something to see and hear. At night, when you lie in your blanket, you will hear a familiar sound. It is the sound of a voice, and there may be laughter accompanying it. After a time you realise that it is a perfect imitation of your own voice, and you are able to listen to yourself, or the nearest approach to it possible. Then you will hear the officers of the company being imitated. The irascible type of officer is imitated with great glee, and you have to laugh, for mixed in the general impression of the officer's rage is the waggish humour of the Nyasa. There is no harm in this. Often during *ngomas* (dances) the troops will imitate their officers while the officers sit and laugh.

I could see that the imitation of the coy mule was going to become a 'turn' on the march down the road, for already the Indians were interested. They stared at the Africans with their black, melancholy eyes, and the contrast between the boisterousness of the askaris and the gravity of the Indians was striking.

The Africans would accept much more of life than would the Indian, and would do so more swiftly, for he was untied by the long tradition that made up the Indian way of life. The African would leap into the machine age without qualms, and would eat all the fruit that came with it. He would also accept medicine and education more quickly, for he was not tied to taboo or a complex philosophy. The Indians showed plainly that they came from an older race, but the Africans were like children who would mature early, and who could enjoy all that life offered, under the right guidance. It was curious to see this proved among the soldiers of two entirely different races, in a morass near Tamu in 1944.

'Mules,' said the major; 'mules are the answer every time in Burma. In and out of the monsoon, they can reach places where no other form of transport can go. They are tough. They can carry heavy loads, and they don't need petrol and oil—though the way some commanding officers order the mule companies to do the impossible, you'd bloody well think they *did* run on petrol. Some people think you can load a tank on a mule, or a couple of thousand pounds of ammo. Still, we deliver the goods, and on time too.'

At this time the Supply Corps of the division was also using elephants as transport, and they went off laden with supplies for long distances to outlying patrols in the jungle.

Near Tamu was a Field Maintenance Centre which was run by a Rhodesian officer. It was in this place that I first saw the Burmese elephants. They were lined up in the mud, near a lean-to store, and while they waited they nuzzled into the mud for the rice that had been spilled during previous loadings. The mahouts were tiny men, who looked like old women. They were lean and brown, with black, silken hair piled high on their heads. They smoked opium when they could get it, and it was said that Europeans who looked after these people usually saw to it that they received a supply. Without it they could not work efficiently.

They sat well up on the elephant's heads, and in their right hands they held Japanese bayonets. With these they struck the elephants on the bony part of the skull, making a dull, sickening noise. They were impassive and stared into your eyes, not seeing you at all.

Already a field bakery had been established at Tamu, and fresh loaves from this bakery were now being passed up into the big baskets that hung on each side of the elephants. Tins of meat, flour, salt and ammunition were hoisted up and packed.

The head mahout, who spoke English, told me that the elephants do not start work until they are five years old. When they are five they start doing light work, and they continue that kind of work until they are about twenty years old. At twenty they start on big tasks, dragging huge teak trees for bridges, and the mahout told me they can judge what size of tree they should bring for the task.

The working elephant eats six hundred pounds of food a day. He loathes heat, and is never worked in the full heat of the day. Though he falls a victim easily to anthrax, he is not prone to many sicknesses. When he is sick, he will not lie down voluntarily but will lean against a tree until he is better, or until he drops. He knows, said the mahout, that if he lies down when he is sick he will never get up again. Once a year, he goes *must*, or crazy, when he bleeds from two holes in his head called *must* holes. During this period he is left alone and does not work until he is better, when he returns to his humdrum job. When the mahout called one of the elephants, he came like a dog, and with good nature.

'They are very affectionate,' said the mahout. 'They learn to love their bosses, and they are very, very intelligent.'

When the six elephants lurched away into the jungle, they were carrying thousands of pounds weight in supplies.

These elephants had been taken back from the Japanese in our advance, and it was found that the enemy had cut the tusks out of many of them, perhaps to make the signet stamps which every Jap soldier carries.

The collecting of stray elephants was still in progress and the local Burmese were scouring the jungle for them.

While we were using elephants as transport, the mules were still moving into the area, and now the two companies were ready to start work.

Last details about kit and load-weights were being attended to as I finished the last of the searing curry, and it was agreed that I would join the mule company along with two British sergeants from the division who were in charge of the African muleteers. We were to leave in two days.

One party of officers who had left on foot with several mules were still marooned between two rivers somewhere on the Kalewa road.

It was that kind of weather, and that kind of country.

CHAPTER THIRTEEN

From my diary

September 15th.—As we occupy villages, we hear reports and stories from the Burmese, telling of Japanese morale, habits and tastes. There is little doubt that the enemy behaved well considering that he has maintained a big force of troops in Burma for over two years. On the whole, they have respected Burmese customs, and have not attempted to interfere with their women. This is most likely the policy of the Imperial army, and has been worked out with the political branch of their administration; but policy or not, it has been well and skilfully done.

The Burmese consider the Japanese to be good soldiers, and they admired their fighting qualities. But they could find no *sahibs* in the enemy ranks. 'The Japanese have no *sahibs*. They are all the same,' said an old headman.

I was sitting next to a British colonel who knew the Burmese well. With him were several Civil Affairs officers, full-blooded Burmese and Anglo-Burmese, who had been government servants before the war in Burma. The Civil Affairs camp was down in the jungle, and a few old headmen had arrived after travelling on foot for over thirty miles, and they were smiling and bowing as I arrived.

The officers sat down on camp chairs, and the old headmen walked up when they saw the officers were ready. They bowed very gravely, and with great solemnity. One knelt down and pressed his forehead to the ground and remained there for several seconds. Their faces were impassive. It was quite impossible to say whether they were feeling any emotion. Probably not, I thought at the time.

The kneeling man was small, with a mass of coiled black hair pressed into a bun on the top of his head. He had a small heart-shaped face, smooth and brown like a polished nut, and two black eyes that twinkled and beamed. He moved about like a bird, while the other three old men fingered their chins and thought over their lines. There was no hurry, no undignified haste, no wish to rush this ceremony and get it over lest the officers be bored. There was that feeling in the air that if the officers were bored they could say so and the headmen would walk back through the jungle to their villages.

On a hill, some two hundred yards away, about a dozen askaris were watching this scene. They had not made up their minds about the Burmese yet, for they had seen few. The Burmese had slant eyes like the 'Jampans,' and a man could not be sure who was who. They were always interested in any Burmese they came across, and they noted eventually that the Burmese skin is much darker than that of the Japanese.

The old men had finished their bowing. There was no scraping. Nothing could have pierced or shaken their dignity. They were like old priests performing a ceremony as they moved round the colonel and his seated officers. Then they stood still and were ready to talk.

One important point that the onlooker could not miss was that the old men paid the same grave homage to the full-blooded Burmese officers and to the Anglo-Burmese officers as they did to the British colonel. This is one of the good things about the Burmese. They do not crawl along the ground on their bellies if they judge by a white man's facial expression that he might be the type who likes that kind of thing.

They also gave me the impression that they bowed because they were glad to see the British Government back. But the Burmese had a bad reputation with the British troops who retreated out of Burma in 1942, and this record has caused them to be called traitors. That morning in the jungle camp they appeared glad to bow to the British officers.

I had met many Burmese and Anglo-Burmese officers up to this time, and I found them excellent men. They were generous and without any of the preoccupations with skin-colouring that makes life in India so unhappy. The Anglo-Burmese were proud of their English blood, and said so. Both Burmese and Anglo-Burmese officers loved Burma, more than they could convey in conversation. They delighted in talking about their people and their history and customs. They made it plain in their stories of the country that there was a great tradition of the Burmese kings still among the people. Never once, during many conversations, did one of these officers start talking about colour, or skin, or racial differences. If they felt bitter about anything, they did not say so. They conveyed the impression that they loved Burma, and were happy to be going back as servants of the government. Burmese and Anglo-Burmese mixed together and were friends, and there was no difference between them.

Now, as they sat listening to the first headman talking, they nodded to each other and smiled, and the old headman smiled too. The colonel asked questions, and the old man replied, sometimes turning back to the other three who stood in line behind him. They nodded or shook their heads, and then they had a little conference like four small birds under a tree. They were arguing as to the numbers of Japanese who had died near their village.

One Burmese officer who sat on the right of the others was a lieutenant-colonel. He was very tall and strikingly handsome. He had not long returned from Tamu, and at Tamu the Burmese cried when they saw him and ran to his truck with greetings. They had mourned him as dead, for they had been told that he was killed during the retreat earlier in the year. An officer who saw this reception said that it was one of the most touching sights he had ever witnessed, and there was a similar scene in another village nearby.

One of the old headmen had a curiously shaped nose, and now as he came forward to speak I saw that the tip was missing. He pointed this out to the officers and then said something that caused them all to laugh. The colonel turned to me, and said: 'The tip of his nose was shot off in an R.A.F. fighter strafe, but he has got used to it now. He also said that one of the great things of life now the Japanese have gone is the freedom from R.A.F. raids.'

The headman described how the enemy troops had returned from the Imphal front like old men who had seen hell, and he told how they died all over the village, while many flung themselves into the river to drown. I could visualise the scene as the colonel translated. The Burmese villagers, dark and silent, standing under their houses watching the small, twisted men come in, shedding their equipment and falling into the mud, weeping. Some were hysterical and cursed the Burmese and their country.

'They made us bring elephants with mahouts, so that they could cross the river which had swollen. Most of the Japanese were sick, very sick, and when the elephants came they were loaded on to the animal's backs and taken to the wide river. But the mahouts were cunning, and when they got the elephants into mid-stream, they told the beasts to kneel down and when they did so, the Japanese were swept from the backs into the flowing river and were not seen again. Three times they did this, and still the Japanese officers did not know, and even when they went and could not find their men, they did not realise what had happened.' As he finished speaking, the headman gave what could only be described as a ghastly smile; the smile of a man who had triumphed when all seemed lost.

'The fit ones,' he continued; 'those who had not been through the same troubles as the others, sat down in our village and conscripted all the women into cigar-making. They made the women work day and night, rolling cigars for them, and as fast as they were rolled, they smoked them. The women were very angry. Then the Japanese took cloth from us and other things like boxes and anything we had that they wanted.'

So the Japanese had begun to loot villages in Burma, and this almost certainly meant that they did not intend returning to these villages, and there was no more need for discipline and politeness. They were withdrawing into central Burma, and one by one their outposts across the Chindwin were falling to African and Indian troops.

When the headman had gone, the British colonel spoke of the difficulties that would be experienced as we moved into Burma. He said that many people held the opinion that the Burmese were traitorous and had welcomed the Japanese into their country. This opinion was held also by those British troops who had had unfortunate experiences in Burmese villages during their long fighting retreat to India. There were stories that Burmans had killed British troops, had signalled to enemy planes and had laid out pointers on the ground to guide Japanese troops on to their objectives. The story ran that the Bhuddist priests had been most active in the role of fifth columnists, and had welcomed the enemy into Burma as liberators and racial brothers.

Many officers were now worried as we advanced into Burma lest embittered British and Indian troops vent their anger on the Burmese as repayment for things done to them in the 1942 retreat. One regular British N.C.O. said to me weeks before I entered the Burma theatre: 'The Burmese! Bastards and traitors. They nearly fixed me and my chums when we had the Japs close on our tails.'

Yet Burmese have hidden British and Allied soldiers for days and even weeks while Japanese combed the area. They had also helped many of them to escape back to our lines. Just how far the Burmese were disloyal has never been established, but it would appear that more bad incidents have gained more publicity than good ones.

The major in charge of the mule company had told me how the Burmese ripped open the big rice stores of plaited grass so that the rice flooded on to the road where the hungry mules could eat to their heart's content. They did this again and again. In nearly every village, when the local inhabitants had sighted the British columns retreating before the enemy, the Burmese had brought every pitcher and pot available, filled with cold water for the troops to drink. The major did not eulogise the efforts of the Burmese in this respect, because he told me another story of quite a different nature. He described how he found one of his Indian muleteers with his throat cut from ear to ear in a Burmese village during their long retreat. He described this as an incident that might have happened anywhere. But he did not fail to impress me with the fact that he had received more help than hindrance from the Burmese during that scorching march to India.

Another interesting story told me by the colonel of Civil Affairs was that whenever he sent men out to the outlying villages to inquire about life in general and difficulties over rice or some other affair, he never needed to issue rations to the travellers. It was a custom in Burma that the wandering stranger, no matter who, would receive all help, food and a place to sleep, and this without charge. The Burmese were not avaricious, nor did they possess the keen nose for money which distinguishes the Indian. For this reason, a Burmese officer told me, the Burmese dreaded the return of the Indian merchants to Burma. The Indians had fled in their hundreds of thousands when the Japanese came, and would return. They had owned the country; they had managed to put the Burmese into their debt and they had held the people in their power. This from an educated Burmese, with a definite bias against the Indians of whom he spoke.

'I assure you,' he said, 'that the people dread the return of the Indians to this country. They will put the screw on again, and the people are really afraid of them.'

Those who know that there are Burmese who love the Japs do not say much. There is not much to say. There were many people in the East, Chinese, Burmese and others who felt that the Japanese held the future of the East in their hands. Various Indians, various Indo-Chinese, and others, were lit with a sort of holy fire at the thought of spiritual and political communion with the Japanese. They have had all that the Japs could offer, and none of it was secure. It is always best to admit that one is in a certain place for a certain reason, like oil, rubber, or the furtherance of economic domination.

The Japanese did not say that. They said that they had come

to make East Asia safe for Asiatics. Instead it was made very unsafe, for the enemy could not guarantee a freedom from air raids or sea-borne assaults. The first few months after the magnificent victories of 1941 and 1942 were good, were pleasant, and full of promise. But the wheel turned, and Japan is pressed down and surrounded by enemies.

The Burmese saw the strange black troops from Africa advancing down the Khabaw Valley, and they came to the Civil Affairs officers, and said: 'These black men. They are good-natured. They are kind. Are they too, soldiers of the English?' And when they were told that this was so, they said it was amazing that the English could produce soldiers of so many kinds.

Troops from all over India, Britain and Africa, have held the Burma front for over two and a half years, while overhead an umbrella of British and American planes gave them eyes and ears and fire-power. Troops from India, Britain and Africa have fought and died in the Burmese jungles in order to free Burma from Japan. When you see the graves of all these various soldiers, you remember that it would be a good thing if these few facts were made known to the Burmese when they obtain their freedom. They should be reminded that half-savage men from the loneliest villages of East and West Africa travelled over unheard of seas in order to fight and die in that country for Burma's freedom. If she values freedom and is really glad to see the back of the Japanese, then she should remember all the peoples who suffered and endured to make her free.

This should be remembered none the less by the people of Britain, who have taken the Empire for granted for so long. Without the Empire, it is doubtful if England, not less than Burma, would have ever been free.

Wingate's Chindits, Merrill's Maurauders, and other forces which for the present must be nameless, have ranged farther than the most frugal Japanese could dream of ranging. We are liable to overlook the magnificent achievements of British, Indian, Gurkha, African, American and Chinese soldiers who have soldiered in a far country which once held part of the flower of the Japanese Imperial Army.

In Burma you do not think of these things. These thoughts come later when you are out of it, and especially when you realise that as a war correspondent you did not have to take half the risks that the officers and men took who stormed the bunkers and deeply dug holes in the hills. You realise too, that since October, 1935, when Italy attacked Abyssinia, death and the numbers of deaths had ceased to matter greatly. If three hundred people are killed in some European city you remember that we have seen bigger lists, like three or four thousand in one night. And death has become a cipher, a sort of number of which there are varying degrees of greatness or headline value.

But when you see a man die, no matter what his colour, in mud, horribly hurt, you wonder what value history will attach to his death. For those who knew him, for those twelve or so who came within the circle of his living, it is tragedy, but for the world it is part of the day's list. This is not the fault of the world. We feel more than do the enemy, who adore death with a kind of masochistic bliss, yet when I saw the first askari die, I wondered: 'What will this mean to Mr. Jones of High Street, Britain?'

The Burmese have watched them come and go. Small yellow men, who taught them to bow more gracefully, and black, white and brown men with a thousand tastes and a gift for soldiering.

All this suffering and stoicism can be made to matter; can be made to mean something, to all the peoples who have been fought for and freed from Germans, Italians and Japanese, and this includes the Italians. As far as the East is concerned, it concerns the Burmese, and fewer Burmese have died for their freedom than have Indians, British and Africans.

Some people feel that it is a matter of rice and oil. The askaris in the Khabaw Valley did not think about this. There was a surfeit of mud and sweat, and in Burma, they say that sweat saves blood. It was to save a great deal more, and the advance went on, through villages where the Burmese had seen no foreigner save Japanese since 1942, and the newcomers, African, British and Indian seemed more concerned with the supply of rice and cloth than anything else, and the Burmese, like any other unfortunate people in war, understood.

The askaris were able to eat bamboo-shoots cooked in grease, but they preferred soya link.

CHAPTER FOURTEEN

The machine-gun opened up with a long, chattering roar that was sucked down into the valley and cast back in rolls of thunder. Again and again it happened. Silence! In the dark, jungle night of the mountains there was more than stillness. There were eyes staring with every atom of concentration they could muster, and there were many fingers resting on triggers. Something that moved on the hillside, and thousands of men lay quiet as the echo of the machine-gun flickered away down the gulleys until it was lost. Then again the long, hammering roar of the machine-gun. It was joined by another, and then another, and with their echoes they joined in a tremendous sound. The valley could not deal with the echoes which clapped and rumbled until they drowned out the original sounds. Grenades began exploding with sharp detonations and these too, were seized up in the echoes and thrown back and forth from mountain and jungle. The grenades burst in twos and threes, rifle fire merged into the noise, then once again silence. Brooding, yet electric. One rifle shot, savage and definite because of its loneliness, cracked and thundered in the gorge. It was so definite and final that you were sure it had killed somebody.

The darkness filled every crevice of the night and was unlit by a single star. It filled the eye and the mind.

Both sides were feeling for the initiative, for the chance to drive in one powerful blow. The machine-gunner in his hole held command of the dark world in front of him, but it extended for only a few yards until the darkness began which blotted out all gleaming of steel and all movement of flesh and metal.

You have been alone in the dark, after a strange sound in a strange place. You do not move, and your breathing is a feat of labour. What was it? Did it really move? It was just like . . .

For the soldier with the rifle, staring out from his hole in the darkness, in the middle of a wilderness of mountain and jungle, it is like that. The trees seem to move. There is somebody out there who wants something, who wants to achieve a certain object, such as the capture of a prisoner or the killing of a few Japs. It is the same for the Japanese, who are as scared in the front line darkness as any other human being.

When the tree seems to move, the watcher may be wrong, and he holds the pistol-grip of the machine-gun firmly. If it is not a tree and he does not open fire, then he has had it, but if he is wrong, and it is a tree upon which he opens fire with the series of flashing detonations, he may still have had it. The eye that has waited for those flashes may narrow itself over the rifle sight and pin him down for the kill.

Troops of the Fourteenth Army have spent many such nights in Burma. If the Fourteenth Army had been an American army, there would probably have been a dozen films from Hollywood about it, and the British public would know as much about the

Burma front as it now knows about Bataan, Pearl Harbor and the Pacific war in general as viewed through the eyes of Hollywood's cameras. There would have been blondes in the film as well, as yet undiscovered in Burma by the Fourteenth Army.

The Chin Hills are wild, and are cut off from the rest of the country by lack of roads. One track led off from the main Kalewa road, and passed through a place called Tenkaya, into the hills. It was over this track that a separate East African force made its way to attack and capture Mawlaik on the Chindwin.

The force started under the name of 'Watforce,' and assembled at Witok on the Kalewa road in early September. They were to make a reconnaissance in strength through the Chin Hills towards Mawlaik where the Japanese were reported to be concentrating troops. These were a threat to the left flank of the East Africans moving down the Kalewa road.

Mawlaik, on the Chindwin between Sittaung and Kalewa, had figured in many intelligence reports. Some of the reports had spoken of hundreds of sick enemy troops passing through Mawlaik in an effort to reach central Burma. There were indications that fresh troops had moved up to Mawlaik and were making offensive preparations. Watforce was to probe as deeply as possible in the Mawlaik area. Watforce consisted of one battalion from Uganda, and it was considered that this would be able to deal with the Japanese at Mawlaik.

The Uganda troops practised loading and unloading mules, and checking the bulk and weight of stores. Medical stores, ammunition, rations and all other equipment were worked out with the number of mules available for the force. In the kind of warfare they were to engage in, every ounce of loading capacity would have to be used, and the colonel with his officers took pains with all these arrangements. They would be without any form of motor vehicle, and their feet would have to carry them across torrents, over muddy hills, and through a jungle denser than anything they had yet encountered in Burma.

The rain went on through the day and night, and the troops though soaked through, were cheery and worked as one team.

Tenkaya is several miles from the main road, and it consisted of about three derelict bamboo huts. From Tenkaya, the jungle country rolls on and on to the Chindwin, and there is one narrow track through this jungle. From the main road to Tenkaya the track was 'Jeepable,' and all stores were ferried in Jeeps from the main road to the starting point at Tenkaya. This work went on day and night without a stop, and the African drivers stayed at the wheel until they nodded into sleep. While the stores piled up at Tenkaya, the Indian muleteers took their mules to the loading place. While they prepared to move with their loaded animals, a screen of askaris moved into the wild hills ahead of Tenkaya in search of the Japanese. They found the country to be quite deserted, but rotting ammunition boxes covered with Japanese characters told them of the enemy retreat. They found bunkers dug into the sides of hills and look-out posts sited so that they commanded a view of the vast stretch of jungle and plains that reached towards India.

On September 12th Watforce became Watcol, and the first operation order was issued. The troops began leaving Tenkaya in groups, pushing into the bamboo jungle where the track wound upwards into the Chin Hills. They had given up trying to keep dry. They had come to regard the rain as something permanent in the life of troops in Burma.

Attached to Watcol for its operation against Mawlaik was a veteran Indian mountain battery. This battery had fought in Arakan and at the battle of Manipur. Without a break it came straight on into Khabaw Valley when the pursuit of the Japanese began. The troops of this battery were mostly regular soldiers of the Indian Army, and a good proportion of the Uganda infantry were regulars of the King's African Rifles.

In East Africa there is an Indian community of great size and power. Most of these Indians are traders, and between the Indians and the Europeans in East Africa no love is lost. The Africans themselves were often cheated by the Indian traders, and had come to believe that all Indians were cheats and crooks. They did not like the Indians. While the war continues the Indians in East Africa increase their power.

The askaris who had come to think of the Indians as traders who did not fight in the war were interested in the first Indian troops they saw in Burma. These were the Indian gunners and muleteers. Indian soldiers with long service and considerable war experience showed the askaris that India produced other kinds of men as well as traders. The askaris realised at once that these were different Indians to those who sold shirts and bought maize in East Africa. They looked different. They looked you in the eye, in absence of oiliness in their voices. Indians and Africans mingled into one force as they moved into the hills. With them went a detachment of sappers, a field ambulance company and a stretcher-bearer company.

One company of infantry carrying enormous packs started off for Atet some miles along the track. Atet had been reported clear of Japs, and the infantry were marching as fast as possible in order to contact the first enemy outposts.

When you start off from Tenkaya there is a march of perhaps half an hour through flat jungle, and then suddenly the mountain range starts to grow out of the trees. The troops had to drag themselves up the first slopes by gripping the bamboos and then scrambling up while others pushed and pulled. At times like this the equipment seems to weigh more than the body. Equpment is the curse of the infantry and has always been so. The full equipment is known as 'the Christmas tree.' The dark jungle let in no light other than the greenish light common in the thick jungle, but as they climbed higher, the sun burst through the bamboos and teak. When the troops came out on to the mountain track, they were able to see out over the rolling sea of bamboo to the plains. They could see the high, mountain walls of Khabaw Valley running away into the rain mist. They turned their back on this scene and marched into the jungle along the muddy track.

The rain poured on and on, lashing down for hours on to the troops who marched like hunchbacks under their soaking kit. The mules steamed, and the rain splashed from the oily gun parts which each mule of the battery carried. Attempts to dry clothes in the rare sunlight failed. So they marched on, and the feet of thousands of men and mules churned the track into a river of deep mud. Into this they plunged their squelching boots, got stuck, gripped trees and pulled, and floundered on after the column. To march in deep mud while carrying a heavy pack is to find out just how strong you are. It cannot be called marching; it is more a form of wading, or of hopping from one firm part to another until you slip, or hop quicker than your eye, when you flounder. The askaris cut bamboo sticks and used them as a sort of crutch, and laboriously the column moved forward.

The life amidst drenching rain and swirling mud in a jungle that sprayed showers of water when disturbed, became a procession of days for the division. It was especially so for the troops of Watcol who were slowly marching away from the main road and their parent body, the division, into practically unknown country. There was no comfort as people think of comfort. Comfort could be obtained from the most unusual things, like a dry towel, or a cigarette that would smoke properly. The snatched rest against a tree became one of the boons of life. When you are really tired, and you must rise to continue the march, with a water-logged set of equipment that makes the body ache, you know the real meaning of such words as 'comfort,' 'rest' and 'soldiering.' Behind every few hundred yards of victory in Burma, lies this greatness of consumed energy and extra effort. When 'the show' is over, when any hard war experience is over, generally only the best parts are remembered by the troops, and the thousands of minutes of strain are forgotten, or are blotted out by a bottle of beer (if they can get it) or half an hour at the cinema.

The African is not as sensitive as the European, and he does not concentrate the same imaginative powers on to a situation. He is unable to do so by virtue of his background and state of development. He is nearer to the grass and trees and earth than is the European, and his muscle and unsophisticated soul supply the answer to many of life's hardships. Where the white man can visualise the hidden machine-gun before it opens fire, the African seldom does so. Generally it must open fire before it becomes a fact. This is not to say that he is unafraid. He knows as much fear as any other man, but his memory is shorter, and his capacity for suffering is not as pronounced as that of the white man. The greatest hardship for the African soldier is that of being so far away from his home, his village, his wife and people. Few of them enjoy strange countries with that philosophical acceptance of soldiers in war. For the African, the *world* is a mystery, and a map of the world is only a coloured picture without the dimensions of the imagination.

The mud and rain, the sleeping in wet clothes and the hasty meal from the mess-tin for day after day and week after week did not depress him. It was just life. It was the war. One day the rain would cease and there would be sunlight and dry clothes. The chopping down of trees and massed bamboo, which labour is great, especially when wearing equipment, did not pull him down. The powerful arms rose and fell, and the gleaming matchets cut through the jungle. It drew the sweat from the body until it dimmed the eyes.

At Atet, high in the hills, the askaris began chopping out an air-dropping zone from the jungle, and the enormous stumps of the felled trees stood up out of a carpet of slain bamboo and tangled timber. Ahead of Atet the advancing screen of infantry was still in search of the enemy. The planes came in over the new dropping zone, and the parachute bundles of stores began dropping all over the jungle clearing. The planes dropped ten days' supplies to Watcol, and on the same day a part of the force pushed on towards Yezon. Atet became a supply base for the advance as the stores piled up.

Cases of bad feet began to occur. The prolonged wearing of wet boots and the lack of opportunity to dry the feet caused several such casualties. Whenever possible the officers and men took off their boots and socks and went barefooted during a rest. They tried to dry their socks but were generally unsuccessful.

Sometimes the loaded mules went over the escarpment along which the narrow, muddy track wound its way. One day six mules went over but none was hurt, nor were their loads damaged. The mule takes it all in the day's work.

The rain poured on from a dark sky, and the columns of men and mules, puny against the immensity of jungle, slumped on through the trees. They arrived in the area of Chinmagale, and there the patrols saw the first signs of the Japanese troops defending Mawku and Mawlaik. The country rolled in high, razor-backed ridges, and the jungle that covered them was often quite primevally dense, and the valleys that ran between the razor-backs were choked with bamboos. The Japanese had chosen this kind of country for the defence of Mawlaik. It was wild and desolate, with chilly nights, and the jungle exuded continuous damp. Without the monsoon the country would have been quite pleasant to live in. In the ceaseless rain it was difficult and miserable.

One massive razor-back hill called Leik had been turned into a strong defensive feature by the Japanese, and on the 28th four Japs were seen digging slit trenches on the top. Jap and African patrols exchanged shots, and the East African patrol withdrew. The enemy then fired thirteen grenades from their discharger cups, and Watcol replied with a shower of three-inch mortar bombs.

This was the first clash with the Japs since Watcol had entered the hills, and patrols had established that the towering and almost precipitous Leik Ridge would have to be captured before the column could advance to the Chindwin.

It took some askaris three hours to cover one mile through the jungle-covered hills, and the troops slashed their way through the bamboos with matchets. The enemy began feeling his way about at night, and trying to draw fire. 'Jitter parties' came to the perimeters of African defensive positions and tapped bamboos, screamed and fired into the areas. They moved along the dark valleys like hyenas, and as the small boy whistles in the dark for courage, they shouted and hammered bamboos together. As a reply to this, silence for the 'jitter party' is more nerve-racking than a misdirected hail of bullets. The 'jitter party' is never sure whether it is walking into a trap or not while the silence continues.

'Charge!' they shouted in English. 'Charge!'; but no charge came. They expected bursts of nervous machine-gun fire, but none came. There was only the powerful silence and the darkness and the uncertainty.

On the 29th one of the forward Uganda platoons was attacked by a party of Japs. It was half past one in the morning, and in the pitch blackness the Japs were able to reach the lines of sharpened bamboo stakes which separated them from the African weapon pits. They broke through the *panjis*, and the darkness began flickering with the flash of automatic fire. In the flashes the black shapes of men moved like enormous shadows. The Jap party got into the forward weapon pits and came under well-aimed fire from the askaris a little way up the slope.

During the fight, which continued for nearly four hours, the enemy cut the telephone cable leading from the platoon position to the rear. In the flash of bursting grenades it was possible for the askaris to see fallen Japs. Before light the Japs were driven out and they scattered into the jungle.

At dawn the officers and men were able to look at a Jap second lieutenant crumpled in one of the weapon pits. He had been dead for a couple of hours. He wore a pair of spectacles with extraordinarily thick lenses. The tall major commanding the askaris put the spectacles on and his eyes seemed to cross, so powerful were the lenses. As the major said, 'Wearing glasses like that, the Jap probably didn't even know he was in Burma.' Beside the Jap officer was a Sumurai sword, and this was the first one to fall to Watcol.

Five Jap privates lay dead around their officer, and with them was a brand-new light machine-gun; so new that the working parts were stiff and the blue of the metal unscarred. The clothing and equipment of the dead were new and in first-class condition. They were fresh troops, well fed and healthy looking.

A medium machine-gun began spraying the platoon position, putting in bursts all along the ridge. The Jap medium machine-gun has a very slow rate of fire, and there is a deliberation about it that allows the listener to count the number of rounds fired with ease.

It was still raining, day and night, and no one could keep dry. After the attack on the forward platoon the askaris began digging deeper, and over the trenches they laced logs and packed the spaces with earth. Then they cut communication trenches and deepened the rows of bamboo stakes about the positions.

Watcol was preparing to assault Leik Ridge, which rose like a great wall before them. The four three-point-seven guns of the mountain battery had moved into position and they opened fire on the enemy. The explosions rumbled in the gorges and then went hissing and rolling away with long echoings until they became faint whispers in the distance.

The Jap 'jitter parties' were out every night, and the little squat men who cried out in the darkness and fired grenades haphazardly had to be more careful these days. The askaris had sown booby traps all over the contested area.

One night a voice cut in on the field telephone and began calling excitedly, 'Want Brigade major. Want Brigade major!'

The Jap who had cut in to shout this was told what to do. It was doubtful if in his excited state he was able to do it, for this job goes to the actively stupid. He cut in again later, shouting, 'Want mortars. Want mortars!' He was told to do it again and there was silence.

An order was issued by telephone to the forward troops saying that if they needed mortar fire they must fire a green Very light.

That night green Very lights went up from the Jap lines, but the mortar officer was not to be caught and did not reply. The order was immediately changed.

Behind the East Africans the dropping zone was littered with parachutes, and the planes dropping the supplies had to turn over the Jap lines each time they finished a run in. The enemy must have watched them with bitterness, for though they had rations and ammunition there was much they needed.

At 10.00 hours on October 10th, Hurrican fighter-bombers dived out of the cloud and struck at Leik Ridge. The bombs burst in clouds of flame and debris, and the explosions covered one another, like thunder rolls. Trees, clumps of jungle and showers of earth rained down, and the planes which had released their bombs went in at terrific speed with their cannons flickering like glowing cigarette ends. The batches of cannon-shells burst in strings of white-hot flashes like the scintillations of hundreds of lights.

The askaris made three attempts to scale the cliff-like hill. Where the bombs had torn the jungle there was no cover, and the Japs flung showers of grenades among the climbing askaris. Twenty-eight African casualties lay in the undergrowth and they were brought away as the attacking force withdrew.

At a quarter past three in the afternoon the Hurricanes came again and blasted the ridge with bombs and cannon shells. In the evening a message was received by Watcol from its Brigade headquarters to say that the whole brigade would move against Mawlaik. It was appreciated that the job was too big for one battalion.

This brigade is one of the crack brigades of the East Africa Command, and it felt it all the time. The officers in this brigade spoke of *The* Brigade, and when Watcol heard the news that the other battalions were joining them, they were much heartened.

Leik Ridge was a feature that normally would have been battered by artillery prior to the infantry assault, had such artillery been obtainable. But because of the nature of the country the only artillery available to shell it consisted of the four small three-point-sevens. The R.A.F. could plaster Leik with high explosive, but could never achieve the steady and accurate hammering of well-sited guns.

The preparations for the assault went on. Ammunition in mule slings was ready to be rushed forward, and stretcher-bearers were sited in the places where they would be most needed. The Hurricanes came again and again and smashed the sharp ridge into a pulp of red soil and torn undergrowth. Gradually the ridge was stripped of its covering, and the red earth showed like wounds against the jungle.

Officers watched the Japs in their weapon pits during the aerial attacks. With fixed bayonets the enemy troops stared out to their fronts. When the planes came screaming down to the attack, the Japs dropped into the bottoms of their foxholes while the bombs burst in thunderous noise, filling the air with whizzing fragments and earth. As each plane's bomb burst, the Japs would sit up again and stare out at their fronts, ready to mow down the African infantry who might attack at any time. Well disciplined and highly trained, they knew their job, which was to try and kill the enemy no matter what form of hell he threw at them. But continued bombing of a small area can chew the nerves away of those confined in that space, and as the air strikes went on the Japs became jumpy and nervous, though they did not pull out of their positions.

At dawn on October 22nd the whole attack force was ready to make the assault on the ridge. They had practically surrounded the enemy position. Every askari carried two days' rations, and either an entrenching tool or a shovel. If they were stopped by heavy fire while ascending the ridge, they would dig in there and wait to attack again.

At 08.00 hours the flat, slow hammering of a Japanese machine-gun began, and it went on steadily. Searching fire that smashed bamboos into fragments went creeping across the ground, and the steady drumming of automatic fire increased until the whole area separating the two forces was lashed with it.

At 08.45 the mortars began throwing smoke shells on to the enemy positions, and twelve of them burst in white, puffy clouds.

At 08.57 two companies of askaris rose out of the jungle and went forward with fixed bayonets, led by their black-faced officers and British N.C.O.s, and at 09.40 a track junction of the greatest importance was captured.

The machine-guns now reached a crescendo and the air was alive with buzzing, whining metal. Long bursts tore into the ranks of the Africans as they pushed through the trees. From a tree-top a Jap sniper killed and wounded those who came into his sights. Grenades tumbled down and burst in groups as the Japanese troops picked them from where they lay in hundreds beside the foxholes, ready for throwing.

From one attacking company, only one officer remained unwounded, and it was nearly ten o'clock in the morning. The sun was high, and the murderous fire continued.

Nyasaland askaris who had arrived with the forward parties of the other two battalions began carrying ammunition forward to the Uganda troops. On the sides of the ridge the troops moved slowly forward, their uniforms black with sweat. Only if you saw Leik Ridge could you form an idea of the agonising climb, the increasing weight of the kit as the muscles tire and the salty sweat running into the eyes. Climbing through the curtain of machine-gun fire and bursting grenades, the troops were experiencing their severest test as soldiers, and they were doing well. They would remember Leik Ridge for the rest of their days, if only for the sweat it drew from them.

At half past eleven the Japanese began screaming and howling as though preparing for a counter-attack. The askaris waited for them on the slope, but the attack did not come. One company dragged its twenty wounded away, and in the heavy fire from the enemy machine-guns the stretcher-bearers did their nerve-racking job. A sniper in the tree-tops picked off several as they rushed forward to where a young officer stood over his wounded Africans. Then the sniper put a bullet through the officer's left arm. Those who had been hit by grenade splinters, but not seriously hurt, were dressed swiftly and went back into action again. The wounded lay in thick undergrowth and the stretcher-bearers searched for them like hounds. The streams of fire whanged and crackled in the air, and the chattering of the machine-guns was continuous. One stretcher-bearer dragged a wounded African out of coils of barbed wire where he lay struggling. While he disentangled this man, the other two stretcher-bearers with him were picked off by snipers.

The Japs stood up in their pits and flung grenades by the dozen. An askari told me that as he advanced through the trees near the summit he came upon a Jap sitting in a foxhole. The Jap had a cigarette in his mouth, and he beckoned to the askari to come nearer. Then he flung a grenade. The askari told me that it made his blood turn cold.

'He missed me,' he said, 'but we didn't miss him.'

By half past one in the afternoon fifty-five wounded askaris were being dragged out of the undergrowth by the stretcher-bearers.

At four o'clock a company attacked under a dummy air strike. This means that the Hurricanes dived at the enemy positions but dropped no bombs, so that the Africans could rush in as the Japs crouched in their holes awaiting the bombs which they thought would fall. But the attack was driven off by massed machine-gun fire and hundreds of grenades, for the enemy covered all approaches and they watched their fronts. They were determined to hold Leik at all costs.

Sweat had washed much of the face paint from the faces of the British officers and N.C.O.s, and the muscles that had strained all day were tiring, but still they continued to attack, feeling out the enemy positions. the Japs were tiring, too, and were nervous and excited as the day dragged on under a burning sun. As the sun went down behind the mountains, the askaris dug themselves in on the slope, and they lay clutching their weapons while the darkness filled the jungle. Not far up the slope the Japs chattered and shouted to each other in a sort of anguished excitement. At four o'clock in the morning a lieutenant went forward with some sappers and flung a bundle of gelignite into a bunker. There was no answering fire from the enemy.

When the first watery light of dawn crept into the sky, a company of askaris attacked and captured the ridge, and at half past six on the morning of October 23rd the bloody and sweaty battle of Leik Ridge was over. The Japs had taken their wounded with them, but had left twenty-three dead sprawled in the mangled undergrowth and foxholes. Twenty rifles, one light machine-gun and an officer's sword were found. And many documents.

The way to Mawku and Mawlaik had been prised open by

the capture of Leik, and the whole brigade was assembling for the push against those places. Leik was a mass of bunkers and foxholes, all sited and dug with the usual Jap skill. The askaris had beaten crack Jap troops, and as they peeled off their sweaty jackets and equipment and began to dig themselves in, they were able to think about it. It had been the hardest day of their lives, lives innocent till now of mechanical violence, and they knew there would be similar days before they finished their job. Ahead of them lay an ocean of jungle which must be captured before the division's task was done.

It began raining again, drizzling first, until the clouds swirled and the rain came down in sheets. The spades cut into the muck, and all ranks greased their weapons. The climate during the monsoon worked untiringly against metal, leather and flesh. All these must function efficiently, and oil, grease and pills kept all three going, helped by a first-class spirit.

What could they write home about to the families back in the villages of East Africa?

That it was raining again, and they were very busy.

CHAPTER FIFTEEN

On the main road, that is to say, on the main stretch of mud, the mule columns stretched for about six hundred yards, and three mule-carts laden with kit brought up the rear. They were pulled by the toughest of the mules. All mules are tough, but some are very tough, and they got their chance to prove it in the mud. We were nearing Khampat, and the forward troops were about twenty miles south of that place, pressing beyond a big village called Yazagyo.

With the Indian mule column, we had crossed rivers over bridges of teak logs laid side by side. Often, the legs of the mules slipped down between the logs, and it took half a dozen askaris and sepoys to extricate the loaded beasts. We passed lines of trucks which were hopelessly bogged in the mud. They had been there for days. Some of them had moved like turtles, doing a few hundred yards in a day, until they eventually sank above the wheel hubs, and there they stayed. Miles behind us the bulldozers were at work, cutting their way through, and carving the mud away until a comparatively dry road remained. But the going for them was slow and laborious.

The road ran through very thick, towering jungle which shut

out all sunlight, and it was here that the mules had their hardest time. In the jungle the mud swirled like a thick paste, and men and animals had a strenuous time, making the slowest progress. The mules floundered and plunged. Each was led by an Indian or an African, and each man carried a full equipment and a rifle. It is a rule in the mule companies that a man never burdens a mule with any of his personal equipment. He must carry it himself no matter how tired he feels. The muleteers led the mules, adjusted their loads when they slipped, and at the end of a long day the needs of the mules were catered for first, before the men looked after themselves.

From the Indians who had been years with mules the Africans learned quickly. They learned first of all to resist the temptation of hanging a haversack or a water-bottle on the already laden animal. Many of them were far more intelligent than their masters. They exercised considerable cunning, and if they had decided on one sure way of crossing an obstacle, they went that way, even when their mistaken masters tried to force them in the reverse direction.

In the evenings when we camped beside a swollen river, or in the jungle, Indians and Africans amused themselves by their mimicry of the mules. Then there were enormous meals of hot curry and rice, which the Africans came to love. The Indians had secret, grave faces. Their hair was thick and plastered with oil. It hung below their ears. The Indians watched the Africans for a long time before they unbent and laughed with them. Secretly they thought the Africans were childish, and in a way they were right, but they came to like them. They never learned much of each other's languages, but when they met the Indian usually said, 'Jambo,' in Ki'Swahili, which is the greeting used by East Africans, to which the Africans replied, 'Tig Hai,' in Urdu (is it Urdu?), meaning that it was all right.

In charge of the askaris with the mule column were two small, lean and hard-working British sergeants. Both of them were regulars, and they came from British line regiments. These two argued through the day and night as to the merits of this regiment or that one. They dismissed many regiments as 'showers.' A 'shower' is the word used in the army to describe a unit which is not considered to be a very good one. These two considered their own regiments to be magnificent, and to have saved Britain and the Empire for the past three hundred years.

The two sergeants marched from one end of the column to the other through the day. They roared here, and cooed there, and always they wore their equipment and grenades, with the rifles slung just so, and with the bayonet in the scabbard, just where they had been taught to carry it years before as 'rookies.'

One of them had served under Field Marshal Montgomery when the Field Marshal had been a colonel in India. Always, said the sergeant, wherever they had been, and no matter how far they had marched, Colonel Montgomery had never failed to send the cooks ahead of the column. The cooks would have hot tea ready for the troops when they arrived tired after a day's march in the Indian sun, and that, said the sergeant, was a bloody good show, wasn't it? He was not surprised that the Colonel had become a great Commander, because he knew what men liked.

The major commanding the mule company was the one with whom I had eaten the fierce curry near Tamu. He was one of the most hard-walking men I have ever met. He walked without ever growing tired, effortlessly, and with an unchanging step. At the end of the day, when the mule column would be about four miles behind us, he would pick a camp site and then walk all the way back to the end of the column in order to see his men and animals in. We, the guests of the party, would sprawl under a tree with a water-bottle each, and wonder how the major did it. We never found out. He was just a great walker, with much lean muscle.

We swam in rivers where the fish swam with us and nibbled our legs. Officers hungry for fish threw grenades into quiet pools and watched the stunned fish rise to the surface. It made a change from bully-beef and Soya Link. Even those who decried the practice liked the taste of the fish after a hard day.

As we passed through liberated villages we saw the timid Burmese. They drew back when we approached, or stared out at us through slits in the lattice work of their houses. Once we came upon a very lonely house far down a river in which we had gone to swim. Two Burmese women and a boy watched us approach their house, and then they came out and gave us fresh limes and a cucumber. They did not want money, so we gave them bully-beef. Nor did they smile or thank us as we thanked them. They just bowed and went away, like monks.

Burmese children tried to sell the Japanese occupation currency to us, but we had plenty of it already. At Tamu hundreds of bundles of these notes had been found in the jungle where they had been left by a starving army which could not buy food. The children were friendly, but the older men and women did not come out to see the troops until they had been passing through for a couple of days.

The life of the Burmese in peace-time must have been pleasant indeed. Quiet, tranquil and fruitful, it must have been a life of considerable safety from want and anxiety. Some of their bamboo houses on stilts, beside a quiet river, with the blue mountains and jungles as a background, looked like the delicate paintings of China. The bamboos hung over the water and trailed their fragile shoots in the running stream, and the mountains were sometimes striped with bars of blue and gold which moved like fluid light.

The bridge across one river was built of teak which had been laid on top of several Japanese trucks, and in the cool shadowy water near this bridge hundreds of Indian and African soldiers splashed about. The Indians were shy and wore loin-cloths even when they were on the water. They were Mussulmen. The Africans swam naked and laughed like children. They were pagans and Christians. On the banks of the river, their dirty battledress lay in heaps where they had flung it at the end of the day's march. Now they swam and dived and whooped, while some just lay with their eyes closed, letting the fishes nibble them.

This was far from the war, and though bones and rusty helmets lay about on the bank, the war was gone from here, had moved south with the retreating enemy. Far out on the left across the jungle the brigade that had been 'Watcol' was fighting for Mawlaik, and in front of us to the south, Yazagyo, a maze of Japanese emplacements was falling to the troops of another brigade. The monsoon had not ended, but it was beginning to weaken, and when it rained it was with an effort from the clouds. The rain would continue for another month, and then the inches of mud would turn into dust.

While we lay in the river watching the sky, there was a continual coming and going of transport planes, little two-seaters that could carry one wounded man each, fighters and bombers. Near Tamu we had seen some of the new American Super-Fortresses flying very high. They looked like slivers of silver as the sun caught them. They started to clear their cannons, and the rippling sound of dozens of these heavy-calibre machine-guns had filled the air. One of the big bullets had fallen into a camp where it killed an askari.

Accidental deaths near the front line were not uncommon. Booby-traps were thickly planted everywhere. One unfortunate officer had camped near a big ammunition dump which had been captured by the Japs and then retaken by us during the enemy retreat. This dump was filled with shells, mortar bombs and all kinds of ammunition. From a box of grenades the officer took one in order to demonstrate to his troops the correct method of throwing at close quarters. He wished to explain the technique of withdrawing the pin and holding the grenade for two seconds before throwing. He took out the pin and allowed the spring to fly off, but instead of the usual burning of the fuse, there was an instantaneous explosion which took off half of the officer's arm and wounded a couple of the askaris. This grenade had been primed with an instantaneous fuse and had been intended for booby-traps and had been mixed with other grenades.

The askaris became very careful in their handling of captured explosives and in the way they walked about in the jungle. Some had taken Japanese shells and grenades back to their camps and had been killed or injured. Japanese ammunition and explosives were scattered all over the countryside, and were gradually collected by sappers for destruction.

On the way down from Tamu with the mule column we had had no accidents, even when we crossed dangerous bridges which had been loosely constructed of logs and felled trees. And the mules never strayed far, for they seemed to know about mines and booby-traps from former experiences. Many of them had seen three years' active service. They liked to crop the green shoots of the bamboos, or roll in the jungle clearings at the end of the day.

We tramped on through the mud, and a column of light tanks which should have passed us was still in our rear, bogged, as we found out later. They had a date with a battle, but the mud defied all their efforts at haste. We saw an occasional Jeep which almost miraculously had managed to get forward, but sooner or later we caught them up and found them bogged. The officers in these Jeeps would grin good-naturedly and say, 'Yes. I've had it,' as we passed them. In any camp along the road there was hospitality and hot tea. There was a good spirit abroad in the Khabaw, despite the rain and muck and the general discomfort. A mess-tin of hot stew and a mug of tea worked wonders.

One morning as we were preparing to march one of the officers reported that his wallet had been taken from his battle-dress blouse. He had hung the blouse on a tree near the place in which he had slept. A search was made in the vicinity of the camp, but the wallet was not found. It must have been stolen, said the officer.

The Indian muleteers had known for a long time that there

was a thief among them, but they had never been able to find him. He took little things, needles and thread, a couple of rupees, or a new mess-tin. Now, said the muleteers, he has taken an officer's wallet, and in the wallet there had been a lot of money and all the officer's identification papers, the loss of which would cause him a great deal of trouble. There was a great stir in the lines.

The Subedar had a magnificent face. His beard was short, pointed and silver grey, and two piercing, black eyes were set widely apart over his small, hooked nose. He was lithe and fit, and he moved about like a cat. When he heard about the wallet, his black eyes burned with a curious satisfaction. He seemed to know what to do about it, and he looked like a man who feels that this is what he has waited for. He spoke to the Indian veterinary officer, and they nodded together for a long time. The Subedar had been in the army nearly all his life, and as is usual with a regular soldier, he seemed to know everything about his men. He walked to the lines with a thin mouth, slapping his legs with a riding quirt.

It was obvious also that the muleteers knew who the thief was, and they behaved as though they were waiting for the Subedar to act upon the knowledge which both he and they possessed. As the Subedar reached the men, three of them came forward and stood to attention. They were ready to help, and further, they knew where to go.

One wretched man stood away from all the others, and he did this quite voluntarily, because he knew that they had recognised him for the thief. He scratched circles with his toe in the mud, and he hung his head.

The major looked at the scene, and then turned his eyes to the man with the hanging head. 'From the mountains,' he said. 'Wild. Sometimes they do the most stupid things.' The major had been in India a long time, and was therefore patient. He understood the people.

'This one,' he said, 'is probably quite an accomplished thief, and they have been waiting a long time to catch him. Petty thieving has been going on since we retreated out of Tiddim.' He turned to the officer who had lost his wallet. 'You will get your wallet back,' he said, grinning. 'Oh, almost certainly you will get it back.'

The African askaris had gathered to watch this scene. There was no excitement. It was rather like a parade. The mules, ready to move, were cropping the bamboos, and the muleteers were drawn up in front of their equipment. They looked contented, almost smug. They had found their man at last. Then the Subedar shouted something to the three volunteers. They turned on the man with hanging head and seized him. A length of rope was thrown to them, and in a few moments they had trussed their man up. They trussed him in such a manner that he was able to stare out over his green-clad buttocks while only the small of his back touched the ground. A pole had been tied behind his knees and over this pole they had tied his legs. Now, staring out over his buttocks, he rocked slowly to and fro on the small of his back. The Subedar knelt down and stared into his eyes and asked him a question. The man shook his head. Then, raising the riding quirt, the Subedar lashed him with it across the tightly-stretched green trouser seat. He hit him several times, hard, until the man nodded violently. He wanted to talk.

This was a front-line area, and there was a shortage of the correct army forms, without which the machinery of army justice cannot function. There was no time for the calling of witnesses, and for the falling in and out of escorts. The mules were ready to move. In a few seconds they had untied the man, and he said that he would show the Subedar where the wallet was hidden. They went into the jungle together, and in a couple of minutes the Subedar was saluting the major and handing over the wallet intact.

'Count it, Sahib,' said the Subedar, 'count the money. You never know. Thieves are clever.' And the officer counted the money and found it right.

When the column moved about ten minutes later, the thief marched with the rest, free, yet not free. Nobody spoke to him. The justice had been swift and rough. The Africans clicked their tongues and shook their heads. They secretly admired the Subedar, and his administration of justice. It was the kind of thing all tribesmen can appreciate, whether they come from India or Africa. It was the way things were done at home, without papers, and quickly.

CHAPTER SIXTEEN

At Khampat the airstrip was crowded with planes. They were all of the two-seater type, piloted by British and Americans.

The Americans stood around in groups. They wore baggykneed trousers of tough green material with pockets down on the shins. They wore skull-caps of green cloth with long visors that they had turned up, so that they looked like curious birds. These caps reminded you of America, and if you had been to the pictures a lot and were educated, then you knew that they wore caps like this in films about Sing-Sing. The British pilots wore khaki shorts and shirts, and both British and Americans drank tea together out of mess-tins while they waited for their turn to fly out with wounded. Hollywood would have called them birdmen, and they would have resented this. They handled their small planes in the air as though they were bicycles. They made flying look simple. They flew out wounded and sick day after day, often making four and five trips from Khampat to the rear airfield from whence the casualties were moved into hospitals.

The wounded lay about in the airstrip while the pilots drank tea and waited their turn. Some had come straight out of action, and these lay contented, with slightly glazed eyes, silent like most wounded men when they are waiting to move. The Africans who had never flown before did not seem nervous. Most Africans accept the wonders of machinery with a surprising speed. They have a faith in the machine which, unlike that of the European, seldom allows them to wander if the machine will fail in mid-air. They watched the planes taking off one after the other. The aeroplane was just one more of the curious things used by the Europeans. It was a queer world in which they lived these days.

A big Irishman who had been years in the Irish Guards was in charge of the airstrip. He had a great faith in hot tea, and saw to it that the pilots and the wounded had plenty of it while they waited. He had a busy time. While planes loaded wounded, Dakotas were flying in and dropping supplies about fifty yards from the airstrip, and the showers of parachute loads mounted in heaps all over the grass near the jungle. The Supply and Transport personnel were gathering it up as the wounded were flown out. Gradually you came to realise that war is a business. From the managing directors to the office lance-corporal there is an appreciation of new methods and talent for organisation, though talent is not always appreciated in the army.

I talked with a couple of infantry officers on the strip and they said that everybody was 'sweating' on the arrival of the guns and the tanks. The guns were still floundering about in the mud some miles back. One regiment of British medium artillery which had fought in the Arakan and Manipur battles was making a few hundred yards a day. The gunners were regulars and many of them had come out of Europe via Dunkirk. I had seen them on the road, stripped to the waist and burned to a deep brown, straining with their enormous guns in an effort to move to the front. The twenty-five-pounder guns of the division were also struggling along, as were the light tanks. As the infantry moved nearer to Kalewa they were coming up against new Jap troops in well-dug positions, and they needed the guns more than ever. What the gunners went through in their efforts to reach the forward troops was everybody's business, and their arrival was eagerly awaited.

While the artillery crept forward, the R.A.F. figher-bombers went on battering the enemy bunkers and sewing their strings of explosive cannon shells among the Japs. From the airstrip we could see the African infantry marching forward to the front line. They sang their marching songs, and they were glad that the rain was slackening. It meant a lot to everybody in the Khabaw, but it meant more to the infantry who lived an even rougher life than the other troops. They sang loudly as they marched. The troops from Nyasaland are the most musical of the East Africans. The marching songs of the King's African Rifles are many and varied, and like all other soldiers' songs, some are unprintable.

The Nyasas are the singers of East Africa, or at least of the East African forces. Their songs have power and music in them, and one tells of the joys of 'Sweet Banana,' while another is called 'Gorile,' and tells of rich men and of the goodness of gold.

When East African askaris sing on the march, there is always one in front who sings a verse alone, in a high-pitched voice, and when he is finished the body of the troops roar the chorus. They are simple songs, and one verse will be sung again and again.

One song sung throughout the K.A.R. by troops from every territory, and in Ki'Swahili, which is the Lingua Franca of East Africa, is called *Funga Safari.*

Funga Safari means roughly, 'Let's go,' or 'We move.'

A *Safari* is a journey.

Let's move off;
By whose order?
By whose order?
The orders of the Captain, the orders of the Captain,
The orders of the K.A.R.

It goes on and on, and new harmonies are brought in as the march continues, and when the man in front sings, 'Let's move off,' the troops sing back, 'By whose order?'

Another one, from Nyasaland, and this is one of the best of all marching songs, has many variations of the words. This song is called '*Sole*,' and '*Sole*' is the Nyasa adaption of the English word 'sorry.' But '*Sole*' means much more than that for the Nyasa askari. It also means trouble. The song is sung to the beat of tramping feet, and when the Nyasa askari sings it it is splendid to hear, for their sense of harmony is highly developed.

Sole, Sole, Sole,
We don't know where we are going,
But we are going away;
Sole, Sole, Sole.
Perhaps we are going to Kenya,
We are sorry we are leaving home,
But it is the war. Time of trouble.
Sole, Sole, Sole,
Young men are going away to war.
We go to defend Kenya and Africa,
Because the enemy is near.
Sole, Sole, Sole,
Time of trouble.

That song is sung by the askaris from Northern Rhodesia and Nyasaland, and it was sung by them when the Italians moved against the borders of Kenya in 1940. Now they march against Japan, and the words are the same.

Another fine song comes from Northern Rhodesia, and is addressed to the Paramount Chief of the Tumbuka in Northern Rhodesia. It sounds uncomplimentary to the chief when translated straight into English, but it really is a jest with the chief, and behind the jest is a warning to him and to the people of Northern Rhodesia. This song is called 'Mwasi, Have you Seen the War?'

Mwasi is the Paramount Chief.

We are suffering because of the war,
Things are hard to get,
But Kenya is still the country of the King.
And Mussolini could not enter.
Mwasi, have you seen the war?
Mwasi, wake up, or you will lose your people.

Things are scarce because of the war,
When the war is finished,
We will go home again.
It is a long way to the war,
Mwasi, have you seen the war?
Wake up, Mwasi, or you will lose your people.

When they sing to Mwasi that he will lose his people, they mean that every one must fight, or the men of chief Mwasi will be lost and the enemy will win.

Another Nyasa song is called 'Lembani Kalata,' which means 'Write Letters.' The first verse is sung by the man at the head of the column and goes:

Askari, write letters home!
Ask is Nyasaland all right?
(Chorus by the troops.)
Oh, Yera, Yera, Yera, Yera,
Oh, Yera!
(Now the leading askari sings again):
We are helping the King,
Germany wrote to America
And asked her not to fight,
But Germany failed.
(Chorus.)
Oh, Yera, Yera, Yera, Yera,
Oh, Yera!
(Leading askari sings again):
Askari, have you received letters?
Are you all right, askari?
(Chorus.)
Oh, Yera, Yera, Yera,
Oh, Yera!

I was standing beside the river at Khampat with one of the Mule Company officers, and the sky was filled with the sound of the plane engines taking off from the strip with casualties.

We saw a Dakota coming in from over the mountains, and it was towing a glider. Indian and African troops stood up from their bathing places in the river and stared at the glider. This was the first we had seen down here near the Chindwin. Together the parent plane and the glider circled the strip and the long tow-rope flashed in the sun. The Dakota released the glider and flew down the valley out of sight. After turning slightly, the glider made its silent approach towards the airstrip, and the only sound we could hear as it neared us was the faint whistling of the wind. There was something almost eerie about it. The askaris stared, and shouted to each other.

'It has no engines!' they shouted. 'It has no engines! How can it fly without an engine!'

They had never seen a glider before, but they had heard about it, and for most Africans only the seeing of a strange object has impact. Hearing about it, but not seeing it, only magnifies the vagueness of the unseen object. And now as they watched the glider coming in, they feasted their eyes on it and talked excitedly.

As usual, one of their officers explained its mystery to them in detail, so that they were able to see the thing in flight, and actually flying without an engine. But they still did not understand it, even though it thrilled them.

The farmer's boy of song and story would have stared no less fixedly than these Africans, had he seen a glider coming down near his ploughed field. Nor would he have been less excited.

There was no magic in it for the askaris. The Europeans have a reason and a method for everything, and it only required careful explanation. So though they were too excited to understand much of what their officer told them, they knew that this was a special type of plane that could move on its own. But they were very perplexed, for there was every sign that the glider could land without any assistance.

We went through the trees to the airstrip, and the glider had landed before we arrived. The ground staff had started work already, and were preparing the inside of the glider for the reception of casualties. The two American glider pilots were sitting down in the shade of the wings, smoking cigarettes. They were wearing a new type of American jungle suit with dozens of pockets sewn all over it, and each pocket was zip-fastened. They carried the huge American Colt automatics, long matchets, water-bottles, first field-dressings and ammunition pouches. If they crashed in the jungle they would be fairly well equipped.

Flying on this front for all pilots is hazardous, for the mountains and the jungle are treacherous, and most of the air over Burma is meteorologically an unknown quantity in these days. The big bombers that make 1,500- and 2,000-mile trips by day and night into Siam to bomb railways and river targets fly over some of the worst country on earth. Since the retreat out of Burma in 1942, the Allied Air Forces in South East Asia have pursued what might be described as a long-term bombing policy. The big planes have struck into Siam and at Rangoon. They have nibbled and then chewed at the long Japanese lines of communication, while the short-range planes have hammered at the Jap front lines. The enemy lines of communication are tortuous, and when the sea route to Rangoon became too costly and dangerous, he was forced to develop the overland route through Siam, and as fast as he built and repaired bridges, the Allied Air Forces destroyed them. It took a long time for this policy to have its effect, but it did so when the enemy tried to maintain full-scale offensives in Burma.

The askaris asked often why no Japanese planes came to attack us. We told them that the greater part of the Japanese Air Force had been shot down in the fighting for India earlier in the year, and that the Japs were hoarding what remained for special occasions.

British and American planes were in the sky throughout the day, and it was clear that we had absolute command of the air. Dakota supply planes were to be seen flying in formation all day long, and it was they who kept the advance going. Without the power of the Air Force, the army in Burma could not have done the magnificent things it did in 1944. Air supply alone ensured that the advance would continue, no matter what conditions prevailed on the ground.

The two American glider pilots who sat smoking American cigarettes had made landings before in Burma, and had seen plenty of action while doing so. This was 'kid-stuff' for them. You landed your glider on a fairly well-cut airstrip, in daylight, with lots of people to help you. In other landings they had done, they had come tearing down in the dark, crashing down near the jungle with cargoes of fully-equipped infantrymen, and right in the Jap lines. This, then, was 'kid-stuff.' They watched the wounded askaris being loaded into the glider, and they shouted a few words of advice occasionally. Then they rose and began laying out cable for the 'snatch.' 'Snatch' is when the parent plane, a Dakota, comes in low and fast to pick up the cable, and snatch the glider into the air.

The two pilots laid the rope in a line from the glider for a couple of hundred yards to two small poles which stood like goalposts in the grass. The end of the rope was formed into a large loop, and then placed in such a manner over the posts that the Dakota could snatch it up with a hook, and then pass on with such speed that the glider left the ground with a jerk.

The Dakota began circling as the final touches were made on the airstrip. Then when everything was ready, the two pilots climbed into their glider and waited.

'They are sitting in the same way as the pilots sit in the planes that have engines,' said some of the askaris. 'How is that?'

'Because they must control the glider.'

'Control? But there is no engine. Why must they sit there with their hands on those wheels and on the stick, when there is no engine?'

The Dakota came speeding up the valley, close to the ground, too close for the slightest error, but he was about to make the snatch. We stared at the glider, and then our eyes went from the glider to the Dakota which came like a big bullet. We saw the two Americans press forward as though exerting all their strength, and then the glider was lifted straight from the ground, airborne. While the Dakota rose into the air over the jungle, the glider followed smoothly. It was a magnificent exhibition of flying, and the Europeans were almost as excited as the askaris about it. To be able to drop a glider and then snatch it up again was something that would change the war. It was changing it here and now at Khampat, for twenty wounded and sick men had flown out together instead of singly in a small plane. British and American co-operation around Khampat was one hundred per cent, and there was little doubt that they could produce a splendid machine together whether for peace or war, if they wanted to. On the airstrips at places like Khampat is the real and true co-operation about which Britain and America say so much. When men are stripped to the waist, and working in the middle of the jungle, nationality tends to slip into the background of the day and you either like each other or don't. Whether you do or not, the work goes on all the time.

The 'Amerikani' were of great interest to the askaris, for they had heard much about them. The askaris considered that they looked the same as the British, but their uniforms, rations and cigarettes were different. Very different. The 'Amerikani' chewed all the time, and they waved their hands and said, 'Hiya, Joe!'

Who was Joe?

The first tanks passed through Khampat after many days of struggle. They were plastered with mud from top to bottom, and the tired Indian crews stared out from the various trapdoors and turrets. These were Stuart tanks, thirteen-tonners, mounting thirty-seven-millimetre guns, and on their sides hung all the 'Kag' belonging to the crews. Steel helmets, sacks of rations, canvas water-buckets, rain-capes and even one collapsible steel chair hung by a length of rope. The modern caravan.

They needed petrol urgently, and the Supply and Transport officers of the division waited anxiously as still no aircraft appeared to drop the loads of petrol. The tanks waited, and the crews, when not maintaining their machines, snoozed when and where they could. The senior supply officer, like all Army Service Corps men, was very anxious. He waited for a reply to his signal for petrol, and the reply would be airborne containers of petrol, enabling the tanks to press forward towards Indainggyi, where the Japs were digging in.

While the tanks waited, and the crews were performing the endless task of maintaining and repairing their expensive and deadly vehicles, the brigade up on the Mawlaik front was preparing to fight the next action which would take it to Mawku, and then to Mawlaik. They were still based on Chinmagale, and were preparing to attack. The Japs were digging as only the Japs can dig. They dug in order to hold up all movement, and with the ultimate task of killing as many Africans as possible. Their task was to delay, to save precious time, for the Japanese army in Burma was in a bad way, and as fast as they tried to move troops and supplies into Burma from Siam and Indo-China, they were bombed by the Air Force. Therefore the Jap troops holding out around Mawlaik had been ordered to fight for as long as possible, and to deny that part of the Chindwin river to the Africans attacking them. They dug in. They prepared bunkers and trenches, and the crack East African brigade that was ordered to capture Mawlaik was preparing for the next strike against the Chindwin positions.

I decided to go up to that part of the front. There was only one way of getting up there, and that was on foot, for no airstrip was in operation as yet. The way the troops had gone. With Dick Elley, who had served in Greece, Libya, Syria, East Africa, Madagascar and other places that come under the repatriation scheme, I arranged to get to Tenkaya, and from there to Chinmagale.

We had a Chev truck with an African driver, and before us we had the terrible muddy road to Tenkaya, over which the bulldozers had not yet worked. Dick Elley had been in all kinds of country, and he took life as it came, and in Burma it came in dribs and drabs, and if you took it that way it was easy. If you did not champ at the bit, and curse uselessly, you would get on. If you tried to rush the monsoon, you would be wasting your time and would fail. If you accepted the monsoon, and still tried to take it philosophically, you would reach your destination and would not have dyspepsia.

We each had an askari orderly, both of whom were trained soldiers, and one African driver. When we reached Tenkaya we would have to walk for a couple of days to reach the brigade headquarters at Chinmagale. At that time little had been heard of the troops around Mawlaik. Though Divisional Headquarters knew what the conditions were like for those troops, the ordinary rank and file of the fighting battalions on the Kalewa road had no real idea of what was going on up there; they were too busy with their own problems.

We drew rations and checked our kit. Early one morning we rolled up our small tents and packed them in the Chev truck, and about half past eight that same morning we were churning through the mud and heading for the Tenkaya turn-off. We had a long way to go as the mud flows.

All the day we slithered, churned and twisted through the deep mud. The same mud across which we had walked, and in which the trucks were still bogged. We stuck often, and infantry marching past us laughed when they saw us knee-keep in the mud, trying not to look too helpless. We put chains on the truck and then took them off again. We packed trees, Jap boots, branches and grass under the wheels, and still the Chev would not move. About four hundred yards ahead of us were several British Tommies of the artillery, straining at their enormous black and glistening medium guns.

They had travelled four hundred yards in two davs—and with the aid of winches on the fronts of their big trucks. They still pulled and pushed, and were making a few yards an hour when we saw them.

At five o'clock that evening, we in the Chev had done three miles since half past eight in the morning. We sat down to smoke a cigarette.

'Forget it,' we said to the African driver, who still worked at the wheels. 'Relax and lie down.' We decided to stay for the night. The three muddy Africans dropped down beside the truck and lit cigarettes. We stayed where we were for that night, and the mosquitoes came in hundreds. We had dinner of Soya Link Sausage, a tin of tomatoes and a tin of Australian potatoes. The potatoes were a bit blown but they went down very well.

As we were about to turn in for the night, a small but stocky British Tommy appeared. He saluted and said, 'What about some dinner, sir? We noticed that you were stuck here near us and we thought you might like some dinner. We've got bags of stuff over there, sir. What about it?'

We told him we had eaten. But we gave him a couple of tins of stuff that his party had not been able to include in their stew. That is one of the great things about the war in Burma. The comradeship that overrides all rank, race and religion. 'Come and join us in a feed. Have a cup of char, chum. What about a tot of rum?' You will always hear such invitations if you are lost, or stuck without food somewhere on the road.

We had tea with those Tommies in the morning, and being regular British Tommies, to whom all the rules of the army are second nature, they cleaned their rifles while they were waiting for the dixie to boil. They were not really conscious of the fact that they were greasing and cleaning these rifles. They had done it for so many years, and also Burma was such a dangerous place that it was an automatic action. Greasing their rifles was as much a part of their life as breathing or drinking tea. The sight of them sitting there cleaning the rifles before breakfast was not missed by the three Africans in our party. They cleaned their own when we got back to our truck. They always did, but that morning they cleaned them with a new interest. We told them that the Europeans they had just seen had been soldiering for about twelve years, and were very experienced in war. The three askaris, one of whom had fought at Moyale in Northern Kenya during the 1940 Italian attack, were impressed. All soldiers are impressed by other soldiers who show a little something extra in their turnout, and not the least impressed are the Africans who can be as good soldiers as any in the world when well disciplined and well led.

Gradually, as their service increases, soldiers lose the tag-ends of civil life; the worries and wishes, and the ambitions to go back to the old life—which has gone for ever. The old life can never return as it was, it can only come back changed to changed men. As their service in the army lengthens, it is noticeable that soldiers, whether they be white, black or brown, all tend to become soldiers mentally. Though there is still the hankering for the old life, they begin to talk to recruits like old-timers.

'You'll get over that,' they say. 'It's only a question of time. You'll get used to the idea.' (The sergeant-major whom you once cursed throughout the day is not so bad when you get to know him, as long as you do what you are told.)

It was now mid-October, and the monsoon was ending at last. Old-timers who had lived in Burma said that it had not rained like this for ten, twenty or thirty years. Old-timers always say that.

The brigade on the Mawlaik front was in front of a position called Longstop. The troops on the Kalewa road were pressing down on to Indainggyi. On the Tiddim road, out on the right, the Fifth Indian Division was breaking into Tiddim itself.

The Japs were desperately trying to keep all the escape routes open. They were trying to keep them open in the South-West Pacific, and for Japan the good old days were fast disappearing in a rain of high explosive, and in a realisation that the Imperial army was being beaten.

Near the Chindwin their resistance stiffened.

CHAPTER SEVENTEEN

Thirty-six Hurricane fighter-bombers passed overhead. They flew in threes with the speed of darts, and the R.A.F. liaison officer with us said, 'There goes Brigadier So-and-So's air-strike.'

'How do you know it is for Brig. So-and-So?' we asked.

'Because he's the only brig. who uses aircraft on that scale. He uses it in a big way. He asks for the limit and gets it.'

The fighter-bombers streaked away into the clouds.

We had now done seven miles in two days with our Chev and the mud was still thick. In another minute or so those Hurricanes would be diving on to their targets, and we were heading for those targets but would not reach the area for a few more days. We went on packing branches under our wheels, and we lurched forward for a few yards and stopped again. As we crept along we came upon gun after gun of the British Medium regiment, and around each of them the gunners slaved with ropes and winches. The jungle smelled of rotten vegetation and of stagnant mud. Dozens of churned-up tracks ran from the road through the trees where many vehicles had tried to escape from the mud. Many of the trucks were stuck deep in the jungle. Tanks and Bren-carriers roared and clattered in an effort to get through. One carrier ground its way back and forth over about twenty yards of mud until it, too, began to sink. The British driver stood up and wiped his face with the back of a muddy hand.

'We've had it, chum,' he said to his companion.

'Aye, we've 'ad it, all right.'

They drew out a packet of biscuits each and a tin of beans. They ripped the tin open with a bayonet and then began to eat.

They were stripped to the waist, and their tattoos were faded under the deep sunburn. They watched a column of East Africans slouching through the mud, burdened with full equipment. At the head of the Africans an officer with a huge brown moustache grinned at them and passed on. One of the Tommies in the carrier said to his mate:

'These black men are the boys for this dump, chum. They don't feel the bleeding 'eat, and the monsoon is just another shower of rain for them.'

'Aye! Proper mud-wallopers. They seem to like it down 'ere. Nice little week-end. Feller told me the other day that these black men will eat anything. *Anything.* See what I mean? See those bloody big knives they got there in their belts? Well, I mean to say——'

They drank from their water-bottles. One of them dozed off. They were waiting for a breakdown gang. Or a bulldozer might arrive soon. The carriers had been on the road for nearly a fortnight now, and there was still a lot of mud and high water before them.

A truck came towards us, stopped, and out of it jumped a very small British sergeant. He had hair like yellow string, and he grinned cheerfully. He offered us a tow, and in a few minutes had fixed a cable on to the front of the Chev. He told us he had been on the road for three weeks and had been stuck so many times that he had quite lost count of the number. He said that the bulldozers were advancing rapidly and were cutting a new, wide road out of the jungle as they came. There were over a dozen of these machines working as one team.

The sergeant got us out of the mud and then went to help the gunners. He drove expertly in the mud, never making a mistake, never picking the wrong kind of rut. He handled his truck as though it were a horse.

We stopped for a mess-tin of tea with the tail-end of the British gunners. They had cleaned and oiled one of the big guns, and they opened the breech and let us see the barrel. The barrel flashed like silver under its film of grease. They were very proud of the gun, and explained its capabilities at great length. They seemed to lavish the same affection on their guns as they once did on their dogs. Even after dragging these weapons through the Khabaw jungle they had not lost any of their affection. One of them picked up a medium shell and showed it to us. It weighed one hundred pounds and was painted a vivid orange colour. He handled it like a toy.

'This,' he said, 'this is a shell. The twenty-five-pounders fire bullets.'

Then the sergeant-major patted the gun and said, 'And this is a gun. Twenty-five-pounders are called Flit-guns, and three-point-sevens are called cap badges.'

The cap badge of the Royal Artillery is a small brass gun.

'When the Japs get a few of these in the back garden, sir,' said a bronzed corporal, 'they don't like it. They start looking for a bus. We gave them quite a doing around Kohima. One of these shells alters the shape of a bunker in no time.'

The Japs now retreating to the Chindwin would soon be on the receiving end of these guns, but already the mud had saved them from bombardment many times.

'The only trouble is that we hardly ever see the damage we do. We always like to know just what we've done to those little——, but it's difficult to find out.' The sergeant-major voiced what seemed to be the sentiments of the other gunners.

Later one of the officers described how he was present at what must have been one of the heaviest bombardments ever 'laid on' in the Burma war. He told how massed artillery fired about twelve thousand rounds on to a Japanese fort in the Arakan. The target became a swirling mass of flame and smoke, and the ground shook under the explosions. When the bombardment finished, the infantry attacked with the bayonet, and the Jap machine-gunners, dazed automatons, opened fire. Many of the Japs were running about out of control, but others fought on.

'That's the funny thing about the Japs,' said the gunner officer. 'They are just bloody slaves to their army, but they try and fight if it is at all possible.'

We talked about the Fourteenth Army and its achievements, and about the Japs. I had now met all kinds of soldiers who served with it. Indians, British, Africans, Gurkhas. No doubt at all this army was one of the finest that Britain had ever had. Its fighting spirit was of the kind that would eventually destroy the Japs in Burma. It was the spirit that would hang on for a few minutes longer than the fanatics opposing them, in the rain or in the most intense heat.

The 11th East African Division now found itself in company with famous British and Indian divisions of the Fourteenth Army. With the Fifth Indian Division, a veteran formation, they were approaching the Chindwin. The advance was more of an ordeal in mud and rain jungle than a battle against a Japanese defence line. The Africans were pursuing a beaten enemy, but were doing so in the greatest discomfort they had ever known.

On the Tiddim road the Fifth Indian Division put up a road block behind the retreating enemy. In the darkness half a dozen enemy vehicles stopped, and a Jap came forward with a torch to investigate. He was killed immediately, and then sixty of the Japs attacked. They were driven off under heavy fire, leaving many casualties screaming in the mud. It was the same on the Kalewa road. Small but ferociously-fought actions, and then a fading away into the jungle.

This kind of warfare continued into October with the enemy growing more desperate as the two divisions stayed on their heels. They left tanks and guns behind which they could no longer drag along, and their burning trucks were surrounded by their dead.

'It looks as if the Japs have really had it,' was the general opinion of the troops.

A couple of hours after leaving the British gunners we came on to the bulldozers. They were the biggest we had ever seen, and behind them they had left a new road. It was wide, dry and flat. It was amazing. The bulldozers were driven by Indians, and we stopped for a couple of minutes to watch them. Gangs of men armed with shovels, or working at the drains, or gouging the jungle away with bulldozers fascinate people from London to Lashio. The bulldozer can hold a crowd for hours, but there is not much time to spare in Burma and we were only able to watch the removal of a few hundred tons of mud, soil and trees. This only took a couple of minutes for the team of bulldozers. They pushed the enormous piles of black mud and smashed trees into the jungle and the road took shape. Ahead of them sappers blasted teak trees and the bulldozers pushed them off the road.

We bounced off the mud on to the new road, and straight away the Chev picked up speed. Already transport and guns were rolling along towards the front—in clouds of dust as the new road crumbled under their wheels.

At the rear headquarters of the brigade we found the Staff Officer sitting over his maps in a small bamboo hut. On the maps there were red markings for our troops and blue for the Japs. The blue patches were spread around Mawlaik quite thickly, and there were even one or two blue patches behind our lines. These had been by-passed in the last couple of days and were now being mopped up.

The Staff Officer described the difficulties of communication with the Mawlaik front. The difficulty of evacuating casualties by mule over the mountain track, and just now there were plenty in the jungle dressing stations up front. Fighting was becoming fiercer, and the Africans had come up against the main Jap defence line, which had been dug into all the commanding hill features barring the way to Mawlaik.

We arranged for a lift in a Jeep to Tenkaya, and from there we could walk. We packed groundsheet and mosquito-net, rations, mess-tin and shaving kit into our packs, and the staff officer promised to pick us up in the morning. We then strolled over to watch an African transport sergeant putting the finishing touches to a Jap truck he had salvaged and repaired. The Japs had stripped the truck of many essential parts, but the African sergeant had scrounged and hunted for over a week until he had collected the necessary parts. In his spare time he had worked on the truck and now it was nearly ready. This sergeant had been quite a primitive human being some five years before, but he had learned much; an example of perseverance and adaptability of the African engaged in the war. Like many thousands of his people he was caught up in it, and was showing that although he was slower than the European pupil, he was sure when well trained. The sense of responsibility was coming to him. All Africans have a sense of responsibility, but a peculiar one, and suited to their peculiar lives. When Europeans say that Africans have no sense of responsibility, they mean that the Africans do not think like Europeans. It takes time for them to adapt themselves, and there is a danger in 'Too much too quickly.' That is why the African appreciates a patient European.

Some of them clapped as the sergeant put the truck into gear and she moved forward. He had worked for ten days to achieve this, and one or two of the officers looked on with pleased expressions. Perseverance had never been one of the African virtues. They had tended to give in if a machine was stubborn, but in the army they had learned to persevere, generally because they were made to. It appeared that discipline could promote ambition and the will to try again. It cannot be understood by those who have not seen Africa, just how much has been achieved in the training and teaching of Africans by the army. The officers and British N.C.O.s who had wiped the sweat from their faces on many barrack squares throughout East Africa had often cursed the fate which had transferred them to this place to teach primitive recruits. The recruits did not know that difference between right and left, and when you taught them they forgot it quickly. So you went on and on until they mastered it. The unbuttoned collar or shoulder-strap were buttoned and the trailing bootlaces tied a thousand times before the recruit realised that he must watch out for these things. And they spent their money like water if allowed to. They bought coloured rags or tin boxes because they liked the look of them, and they could not understand for a long time that if they did not draw all their pay the army would save it for them. They were lined up in a new world and dressed off from the right, and it was strange.

There were many who got lost and tangled up in the jungle of steel and rubber, in the new world which they entered without the gift of restraint. The new life went to their heads like a strong draught, and they were hurt in the ensuing trouble. Out of all this the army produced troops. The shell of discipline hardened gradually, even though the primitive lingered underneath.

Those who had worked for settlers before the war had learned a good deal already about the white man's world. They knew how to count fairly quickly, and they had a fairly well developed sense of proportion before they reached the barrack square. There are many in England who view the white settler in East Africa with suspicion. But the East African settler with his wife and family has probably done as much for the Africans as has the expert who weighs the calories and who knows all about the leatherwork of certain tribes. The personalities of many good men and women who have settled in Africa have helped thousands of Africans who have come in contact with them. These people have friends among the Africans, but not many in parliament. Africa has seen many poor types of white man, but she has seen many more good types. But the poor type gets the headlines the good type does not.

African soldiers have learned something more than the most efficient method of killing. Those who knew settlers and those who did not are all lumped together, and they have learned to live together and to help each other. They have also learned to ignore the differences between tribes and to treat each other as men. The African sergeant who had made the Japanese truck work had achieved perhaps more than he realised. He had drawn upon his short experience as a mechanic, and had shown considerable resource. He had not been helped by any white men while he had worked on the truck, but the officers had shown great interest in his progress.

As one officer said, 'The Africans are not ready for *everything* we have to offer, but they are ready for plenty.'

The officer who teaches things, who advises the perplexed, is appreciated by all African soldiers. When they have grasped the meaning of discipline and order, and can differentiate between good and evil, they make good soldiers. They will make good lives when the soldiering is over, if there is a plan for them.

In Burma they were homesick, for the African has a great affection for his home and his family. They wrote more letters as their advance continued. Thousands learned to write and read in Burma. In one artillery battery the literacy among the Africans was fifteen per cent when they arrived in Burma. It jumped up to eighty-five per cent after six months. They wanted to learn, and their thirst for knowledge was no passing whim.

At seven o'clock the next morning I left for Tenkaya in a Jeep. We left the main road and bounced along a jungle track in the loaded vehicle, heading towards the Chin Hills.

CHAPTER EIGHTEEN

'It's like this,' said the colonel. 'The Japs think that by throwing jitter-parties they will demoralise us. They are greatly attached to the jitter-party and they use it whenever they can.' He piled up a small heap of brown soil as he talked. This colonel was young, and he was very enthusiastic. 'The Japs are afraid of jitter-parties,' he continued. 'That's why they use them so often on us. They have such a faith in it that it made me wonder just how they would take one from us.' He had now made a small hill out of the pile of red soil. A Jap with one side of his skull pitted with grenade fragments was led past us, and a machine-gun began stammering beyond the hill. This was battalion headquarters—holes in the ground, and the jungle was very thick. It was early morning, and the jitter-party which the colonel was describing to me had been a success. The Nyasa troops had just captured a hill from which the thoroughly scared Japs had run, and there was an atmosphere of excitement among the troops.

'It was like this,' said the colonel. 'The Japs were on this hill, and our task was to capture it. They were well dug in, and we had had jitter-parties every night. So I decided to give them a bigger one, and it worked.'

A Jap jitter-party is composed of a few men usually, some of whom may carry pieces of bamboo, while the others carry rifles, a light machine-gun and grenades. The object is to cause panic, to upset the dug-in enemy so that he will fire indiscriminately into the darkness in a nervous and undisciplined manner. They tap the bamboos together as they go creeping up the valley like hyenas, and this weird sound in the silent night may cause many trigger-fingers to tremble. Again the bamboos tap, and then a burst of fire. A few grenades. If the dug-in troops are inclined to fire because they think they have seen something move (and the jungle moves when you are scared), then it is possible that all hands will start blazing away into the darkness while the Jap jitter-party lies still and laughs. That would be a successful coup, and it is not unusual for new troops to fire nervously when they are having their first deal from the Japs. But silence in answer to the tapping the bamboos and the bullets and grenades must be more frightening for the Japs than the nervously aimed streams of fire going harmlessly over their heads. Complete silence upsets the enemy nerves.

'Charge!' they yell. 'Charge!' in English, but the enemy do not charge. They are at a loss for the next move. One officer I know managed to get two Jap jitter-parties firing into each other at close quarters for quite a long time.

One morning near Chinmagale they found a small Oriental foot in a Jap rubber jungle boot. The owner had trodden on a booby-trap while on his way to jitter the Africans.

The jitter-party is as nervous as the dug-in guests, for to creep around in thick, booby-trapped jungle, not knowing whether you are observed or not, must draw the sweat on to the brow in great beads.

When the Nyasas staged their big party, it was with the object of demoralising the Japs on a hill called Longstop and capturing it. Two companies surrounded the hill and in the darkness they began howling and screaming. They sharpened their matchets together, and threw dozens of grenades. The Japs did not like this. They did not keep silent. They became very excited, and their jabbering was audible among the crash of grenades and rifle fire. One party of Africans would yell and sing from their side of the hill, and the nervous Japs would concentrate their fire on that part. Then from the other side of the hill another party of Africans would howl, and this went on for a long time. The Japs became increasingly nervous, and began showing terror. Many cried out and whimpered. The darkness around them was filled with screaming black men who were waiting with sharp matchets and bayonets. Longstop was small, but well defended. Hurricanes had blasted it for days, gouging great slices out of the red hillside, and flinging trees into a tangle. Despite this concentrated battering, the Japs did not pull out, but now as their nerves jumped in the darkness they were beaten. The weapon they loved so much was as powerful as they had imagined it to be. The Africans took a real and savage pleasure in their jitter-party, and when the time for attack came, they were singing war-songs of their tribal territory. The Japs chattered and shouted to each other, waiting for the expected attack. It did not come when they expected it. The jittering went on and on.

When the signal for attack was given, it went in with a rush, and the Nyasas swarmed on to the hills with matchets and grenades. The flash and explosions of hundreds of grenades died down as the Africans got into the positions. The Japs who were alive had managed to scurry away through the thick jungle, leaving their foxholes to the Africans, who shouted, 'Sokolei! Sokolei!' which is the war-cry of the Nyasas.

Their colonel, who had heard them going in from his command-post, said that he breathed a sigh of relief when the firing died down. He told me that he could hardly bear the thought of any one of his men becoming a casualty. He was very fond of his troops, having spent eight or nine years with the East African forces.

I went on to Longstop with a major just as the Nyasas were digging in. They were enlarging the Jap foxholes and digging others so as to face the next objective—a hill some six hundred yards away called Sadwin. We looked at a well-dug Jap foxhole which was cut so as to give a very wide field of fire. It was triangular, and hundreds of grenades were heaped beside it, most of them with the pins pulled out, ready for throwing. The plum-coloured paint on their brass necks glistened in the morning sun. Cunningly dug at the back of this foxhole was the sleeping-place for the defender when relieved at his post. It was filled with dry grass, and it stank like a stable. Defending a bunker or a foxhole under fire for a length of time does not allow much freedom to the defender, and a bad smell in a war is better than a bullet. The steel helmet and equipment of the departed Jap was stacked at the bottom of the hole. His water-bottle lay where he had had it ready on the parapet. It was torn and riddled with grenade fragments. We stumbled on over the littered grenades. One of our three-point-seven shells lay on the ground, its nose bent. We made a wide detour round it. Smashed rifles, ripped mess-tins and water-bottles lay everywhere. This place had been covered with high explosive, and the dust from the explosions coated the gashed and ruined trees.

A Jap soldier lay on his back and the sun flashed on his golden grin. Every tooth in his head was of gold. He was covered with red dust, and his close-cropped hair was thick with it. The two red collar patches and the three white stars showed that he had been a first-class private. He wore only one boot, and his body was torn open by a grenade that he had obviously received as he lay crouched. Probably he had been taking cover in the last moments of the attack. Near him lay a broken paper fan.

The Jap dead lay where they were, and the troops dug deeply. The Japs might counter-attack. Already a Nyasa patrol was out probing around Sadwin, which we could see from where we stood. The Nyasas on Longstop rammed their spades into the soft red soil, and the sweat flew from them. Hill by hill the advance to Mawlaik was making progress, but it was hard going for all ranks. Drive the Japs off one hill and they fight on the next. Bloody, tiring and maddening, but it had been that way for the troops in Burma since the beginning. The Nyasas filled the air with the sharp scent of their bodies, and they talked hardly at all; just grunting as they drove the spades home. If they felt exultant they showed it only in the occasional grin. On the sides of the hill the Bren-gunners stared out at the bamboo and teak which clustered about Sadwin. A Jap medium machine-gun began firing long bursts into the jungle. They had spotted the Nyasa patrol approaching, and the Japs were already on Sadwin. There had been a hope that the patrol would get there before them, but the Japs had moved according to plan. There was no doubt that they intended fighting from hill to hill as they fell back on Mawlaik. The Jap medium machine-gun had been chased for a week, but it opened fire from every fresh hilltop as the enemy was driven back. It began putting bursts right and left into the jungle, and the patrol drew off.

'——,' said the officer near us. '——'

'Exactly!' said another.

The Japs, with that skill they possess for swift movement and the shifting of weapons and stores, were already dug into the Sadwin cliff. They would have to be gouged out of there as they had been gouged out of Longstop and Leik. We climbed up on to a rock and had a full view of Sadwin. Nothing moved on it, and there was no firing. No doubt every Jap, save for one or two look-outs, was digging feverishly.

The country around Sadwin was greener and fresher to the eye, and the clear waters of the Mawku Chaung were sparkling.

From these hills overlooking the Mawku Chaung you could see the Chindwin like a band of dull metal in the jungle.

We came down from the rock and sat in the command-post, where the company commander and some of his officers were eating a hurried meal. They were all black-faced, and they looked tired and drawn. The major was shouting orders into a phone. He was calling for fire from the three-point-sevens. While a lieutenant slashed a tin of cheese open, another opened packets of biscuits. The command-post was simply a hole in the ground left by the enemy. It looked out over the Mawku Chaung and on to the rolling jungle below. Firing began in the jungle beyond the Chaung, and grenades started thumping. A platoon of the Nyasa battalion had bumped the enemy.

We sat in the foxhole while the major shouted into the phone. 'I must speak to the F.O.O.,' he shouted twice. 'On his way here, is he? What about some stuff coming over? I want fire on to the target now. It's urgent!' He put the phone down and offered us some cheese. An African brought us tea in cigarette tins. The officers ate hungrily, yet unconsciously. Eating was a duty, a necessity. It stopped certain pangs and allowed them to concentrate on their jobs. They wore no badges of rank, and their sweat-stained battledress was torn and crumpled, looking frowsy and as though the wearers had worked unceasingly in it for days. Out on the left the firing continued.

'That's old Johnny. He's bumped something.'

'M'mm!' said one of the others with a mouthful of cheese. Then there was a fluttering note in the air behind us as shells from the three-point-sevens began coming over. They burst with a low roar. An intelligence officer came up to say that they had seen three Japs standing on the top of Sadwin. They were lounging about and did not look excited, and they were having a good look at the African positions. They were probably trying to draw fire, but nobody opened up on them. The distance was too great for accuracy.

One of the officers in the command-post said to me, 'Ever come across my brother? His name is John Nixon and he's a war correspondent.'

I told him that I had seen his brother in Kandy once, but that I thought he was now in the Middle East.

'That's right,' he said. 'He gets about. I move a few yards a day. If you see him, tell him to come and have a holiday with me!'

The shells were coming over in twos and threes as we made our way back towards battalion headquarters. For the Jap it had started again. The hammering of one position after another. Later in the day the air-strikes would begin, and Sadwin would be clouded in dust and smoke. There would be jitter-parties, just like yesterday and the day before, and snipers up trees.

The Japs had always pressed their warfare home, and had exploited success wherever they had found it. They had prided themselves on the ability to drive everything before them. Nowadays the Central Chindwin front was symptomatic of what was going to happen to Japan itself. They were on the defensive, and disaster had overcome and wrecked one of their finest armies. They watched nowadays for an enemy who might strike from anywhere. The enemy soldier, staring out from a bunker and waiting for an attack to come, was only one of hundreds of thousands of Japanese troops who watched like that from New Guinea to Malaya. A new time had come, after years of victory against the unprepared and the trusting.

I walked back with the major to the small hill into which the Nyasa askaris had now dug themselves. They had dug their pits all round the hill, and it bristled with weapons. The enemy kit still lay everywhere, and we opened one Jap mess-tin and found it full of the finest cooked rice I had yet seen. The grains were very big and snowy white. The Jap mess-tin has a tray that fits into the top of the tin, and this was filled with sliced, pickled cucumber. There was good food in many of the mess-tins, and the askaris finished it off quickly. They praised the rice. It was the best rice they had ever tasted.

'The first thing the askaris go for when they have dug themselves in and prepared for the next phase, is the Jap rice,' said the major. 'They love it. I don't blame them, for there is no doubt it's the best rice we have seen in Burma.'

Burma was the rice bowl of this part of the East, and the askaris said that the rice in Central Burma must be splendid indeed.

The Jap troops always carry their mess-tins full of cooked rice, with vegetables, if obtainable, in the mess-tin lid. They also carry in their packs, when possible, a long bag filled with uncooked rice. These troops around Mawlaik were well supplied. Their rations were brought up to their front line on elephants, and we found the tracks of these beasts around the newly captured position.

The hill positions in the country around Sadwin were named Longstop, Nelson, Tom, Dick, Harry, Nuts and behind them all was the towering Leik Ridge. All these positions were now in the hands of the East Africans, and they faced Sadwin cliff.

Some time to-day the Hurricanes would start battering Sadwin with bombs and cannon shells. Far out on the right of the Sadwin positions was a battalion from Northern Rhodesia which was making a long, circular movement. This battalion had carried all its equipment on mules, and was heading for a place called Kun village, which was on the Jap line of communication to their forward positions protecting Mawlaik. The Northern Rhodesians would disrupt this line of communication, and would attack any Jap troops they found down there. Their job was a hard one, and much depended on its surprise value and speed.

Back behind Leik Ridge in the jungle was the hospital where lay all the casualties from the battle for Leik. For them the trip back to Tenkaya would be long and painful. The track was a couple of feet deep in mud, and it ran over the ridges and hills. Most of them would stay in the jungle hospital under the care of the unit doctors, until an airstrip could be cut out of the jungle in the flat country around Sadwin. One of the main benefits from the capture of Sadwin would be that planes could start flying in on to the flat, paddy-field country there, and when they had dumped their supplies, they could fly the casualties out.

We left Longstop and walked back to the battalion headquarters. On the way down I was introduced to an African platoon sergeant-major named Selika Walani. This Nyasa N.C.O. had led three bayonet attacks on to a Jap bunker the day before. He had done this with wonderful courage, leading his men each time through very heavy fire. When his ammunition and grenades ran out, he withdrew his men into cover and reloaded the Bren and Sten magazines, and had issued fresh grenades. Then he had led them at the charge again. The third charge got them on to the Jap bunker, but many of the askaris were falling under the intense machine-gun fire. Selika Walani was wounded twice through the left arm, but he pressed on and eventually got on to the top of the bunker. There, with four dead Japs lying around him, he blasted the position with grenades. The Jap machine-gun was silenced, and Selika drew his men off under covering fire, taking all his wounded with him.

Selika Walani told me he was twenty-eight. He had served with the King's African Rifles for nine years. When I saw him his left arm was bandaged, but this went as stiffly against his side as did the other before he saluted the major. He did not want to talk about the bayonet attack. The colonel had congratulated him on his bravery, but as far as Selika was concerned, it was what he had joined the army for. A man joined to fight. If a man became an N.C.O. he must lead and show example. He had done both of these things, and that was his duty. It was very simple.

'I must go, effendi,' he said. 'I must issue ammunition for the next show.'

All around us troops were breaking open boxes of ·303 rifle ammunition, and grenades were being primed and issued. Selika Walani saluted and went back to the job. He was one of the most impressive soldiers I have ever met. His face was dark-brown, young, yet very experienced. It was calm too. It was the face of a man who knew where he stood in life, what to do, and the best way of doing it. He was a disciplinarian, but with it he combined the human quality of understanding. One felt that law-breakers would receive help as well as punishment.

A recommendation for the immediate award of the Distinguished Conduct Medal to Selika Walani was being written out in pencil by one of the African clerks at battalion headquarters. The colonel was dictating. Nearby an intelligence officer picked up a Jap haversack full of material which had been sent back for examination. He emptied it out on to a groundsheet. There were albums of photographs, charms from Japanese temples, diaries, letters, post-cards, badges, maps, bottles of pills (the Japs are very fond of pills) and drawings on cream-coloured rice paper of stalking tigers. The intelligence officer picked out the stuff which interested him, and the rest he stuffed back in the bag. The charms from the temples were tiny tin swords covered with Jap ideographs, and each tiny sword was wrapped in a packet of rice paper. These were probably to keep the owners from harm.

The Jap prisoner with the grenade fragments in his skull had just been patched up by a medical officer. The Jap prisoners are always surprised because they are well treated by the Allied troops who capture them. There is little doubt that they are taught we kill all prisoners. Their bewilderment changes to depression, and they appear then as though suffering from some sickness, but this is usually the effect of intense mental strain and worry. One prisoner I saw, and he was not one of the walking cadavers from the Manipur shambles, sat down on the ground and then pressed holes in his shin-bones with his thumbs.

'Kakki!' he said, and then looked up at us as though he had just performed an interesting trick.

This was his way of showing that he had Beri-Beri. He then lay down on the stretcher and began to whimper. Two British corporals, who had dealt with all kinds of wounds in their time, looked puzzled. What can you do for a man who lies down and whimpers? What bandage can you put on this mental wound?

The colonel of the Nyasa battalion was very proud of his troops, and his enthusiasm was infectious. He talked rapidly of what the troops had done, and he spoke of his anxiety for them during the attack on Longstop. The troops of this brigade were certainly well picked. Each battalion in it felt that it was *the* only battalion in *the* only brigade, and you got this impression wherever you went among the brigade troops.

Well picked, well disciplined, and highly trained African troops can be relied upon to fight with great spirit. When there is a feeling of pride in a unit, it is evident in the way a soldier tells you the number of his brigade, as though you must know that unit well.

I walked back through the jungle with the major, towards Leik Ridge. We met the brigadier coming forward with some of his officers. He was wearing the bonnet of the Cameron Highlanders, and his grey, good-humoured eyes missed nothing. He must have been feeling proud of his troops, for Leik Ridge towered near us, and ahead was Longstop and the other captured hills. Out in the jungle, his Northern Rhodesians were moving against Kun village. His brigade was really on the move. Despite the hardships of the last few weeks, and despite those that were still to come, there was a good feeling in the air. The brigadier passed on up the muddy track with his officers. Shells still whistled over to burst on Sadwin cliff. They burst with the sound of slamming doors. In their foxhole, the company commander and his companions would have finished their cheese and biscuits, and would be watching the shells registering.

The mountain battery had moved forward, and was well hidden by bamboos and cleverly-placed camouflage. The Indian gunners, nearly all bearded and grave-faced, only smiled when you smiled. Their turbans were neatly wound, and they stood by their guns waiting for orders. India has produced some first-class troops in this war, and these were a handful of them.

The little three-point-sevens are very powerful, and they had proved themselves to be excellent weapons in this type of campaign. Old artillerymen who had watched many new-fangled types of weapon—two-pounders, six-pounders, seventeen-pounders, five-point-fives and others—come into the limelight, had put their word in for some of the solid and well-tried weapons they had known. The three-point-seven was one of them, and I heard a gunner with twenty-five years' service say, 'Well, it's a treat to see the old three-point-seven get another chance and do so well.' Loyalty to tried weapons among time-serving soldiers is a real thing. Many feel that there will never be a rifle like the short magazine Lee Enfield, and they will use no other. Many are certain that they can do more damage with it than with a sub-machine-gun which has come in with the new battalion gang-warfare. The three-point-seven can be dismantled swiftly, packed on a mule and moved to a new site.

The battery mules were the biggest I had ever seen. One of them carried a load of four hundred pounds. On the way up to the newly won positions several mules fell over the cliff and three radios were broken. This did not deter the mules. They plodded on through the mud and then went back for more stores. The shifting of a brigade's stores through thick jungle and over mountain ranges is a trying task. It takes patience and skill from both men and animals to do it again and again for months. The brigade moved like a machine, for it was now experienced, and it knew just what was needed to perform certain tasks.

The sunny days had come, and had evaporated that dark, wet gloom of mud and rotting dead which had marked the first two months of the campaign. The anti-septic and cheering sun now burned the rain-pools out of the ground, save in the deep jungle where the mud would stay for months. Dry clothes gradually became commonplace, and the cheerier atmosphere of sunny hills and jungle made up for the ordeal of August and September.

On the hills the green bamboo leaves rustled and seemed to grow greener and brighter as the clouds disappeared from the sky. Over in the Jap lines the little men must have stretched and felt the warm sun after the manner of cats, as did the Africans. Warm earth to sit on, and soil that is dry and easy to dig, is appreciated by soldiers after months of mud. Such small things as this become of the greatest importance to soldiers who must live like clever animals in holes.

Flight after flight of Hurricanes passed over, like sharp and deadly birds against the sky's blue. They began diving. We heard the ground-shaking thunder of the explosions.

'Go on! Give it stick! Give it stick! Get stuck in!' said a lieutenant to the planes. He sat near me on the hill. 'Wait until they open with those cannons, you bastards,' he said to the Japs.

The bombs burst in twos with great detonations that shook the valleys. Then there was a whining note in the plane's engines, and their cannons began crackling. Some fired long bursts, and others fired five and ten rounds at a time. One plane fired what must have been every round of ammunition in it, and the burst went on until we all looked at each other. He had probably found something moving in his sights and had pinned it down. We could imagine the pilot with his narrowed eyes, sitting in a thunderbolt of powered engines and pressing the buttons as he lined up a row of human beings in the sights. When he pressed that button it set the plane shuddering and the air crackling with fire.

'We like to get them in the gullies,' said a pilot to me during conversation. 'We like to get them in the open and then go tearing in with the old tit pressed hard down! Sometimes, if you're lucky, they go flying into the air when you give it to them, or they go flying around like washing.' He had stirred his mess-tin of dark tea and then smiled fondly at his thoughts. 'Another good one is when you get a smack at a petrol dump.' He spread his hands. 'Whoof! Up she goes like a flash, and you can see the blokes scattering all over the place.' He described the strafing of river craft on the Chindwin. That had been fun, but the best of all was when you got the Japs in the open, and you went in with your finger on the old tit.

After the strike by the Hurricanes, a signal came from the R.A.F. to say that one of the pilots had returned with blood all over his windscreen. This meant, said one of the intelligence officers exultantly, that the pilot had dived practically into the bunker with his cannons going. Outside in the world it may sound savage and brutal that a man is pleased to find blood on the windscreen of his plane, but to pilots who are trained to kill Japanese it is a proof of something successful. You don't seem to think of the Japanese as people—they are the Japanese, with a curious savage code. They don't act like people. They act like Japanese, and no other people act like that. If their blood smears the windscreen, it is the blood of the Japanese who fought without mercy, and whose deification of blood and death has caused the deaths of countless hundreds of thousands.

The R.A.F. were keen. They wanted to come in again and again, and to strike the Japs wherever they could be found. The Fourteenth Army, which was spread across Burma, used the Allied Air Force whenever it could find a target or a dropping zone. The offensive spirit of the army and Air Force in Burma left nothing to be desired. It was keen, alive and tireless. The feeling of a great mass of men when they have shattered an enemy army, especially one like the Japanese Army, cannot be distilled into a phrase. It is a feeling, and even troops do not discuss it much. After two and a half years of patrolling, ambushes and hard living, it is a feeling of power. It achieved its full stature when it held the Japanese offensive against India and then smashed it.

Back at brigade headquarters, which was still at Chinmagale but packing up to move, there was a large red-pencilled notice. This notice was posted outside one of the staff dug-outs, and it said: EXPECT JAP AIRCRAFT IN TEN DAYS.

It was quite surprising for all who read it. It meant that the Allied Air Force had found something out. The Jap Air Force, broken during the Manipur offensive, had somehow recuperated, and was ready to strike. But in view of their weakness in numbers, they would probably only strike when there was cloud to hide in, or when there was a definite and easy target. The red-pencilled notice hung outside the dug-out in that deep jungle country looked very strange. The tentacles of the intelligence and of the Air Force reached right out into the most remote and seemingly forgotten areas. The yellow and red field telephone cables that snaked along beside the muddy tracks held a high place of importance in the lives of the army in Burma. When the signallers patrolled endlessly along the cables, looking for breaks and repairing them, it was in order that intelligence officers could write such notices in red pencil.

An R.A.F. officer told me that the Jap Air Force in Burma, though small, was very mobile, and had lots of airfields to which they could fly after a raid. On each airfield were all the spares and ground staff they needed. A small Air Force was mobile and elusive. Allied fighters and bombers would have to chase them and seek them when there were many dozens of airfields to which the enemy might have retreated after a raid.

It was the general opinion that the Japs would strike from the air only when we had reached Kalewa on the Chindwin, when we would be easy targets from the point of view of location. At that time we had not experienced one Jap air-raid.

Camouflage and air-raid precautions reached a new point of efficiency. Those who had given up all idea of ever seeing a Jap air-raid now took to digging slit trenches and deepening holes. There was a new atmosphere about the jungle. That red-pencilled notice caused a quite new outlook among the troops. It meant that you could not listen to an aircraft engine again and know for certain that it was 'one of ours.' It also meant that when aircraft engines were heard over the lines, all ranks would take a look before they went on with what they were doing.

I started back with Dick Elley for the main road, when Sadwin cliffs was turning red under Hurricane attacks and the jungle was being ripped from it. We walked back over the hills, and were furious to see a small plane flying over us when we had been one day on the march. It meant that Sadwin had fallen, and that an airstrip was already being used for the evacuation of casualties. If we had waited until all the casualties had gone, we might have been given a lift out, and would have been with the troops on the Kalewa road in half an hour's flying time. The infantry on the Kalewa road were in front of Indainggyi, and were waiting to assault that place. Reports said that all the artillery had got through, and were now ready to open fire on the Jap warrens which ran around Indainggyi. It sounded as though the Japs would get a pounding.

We passed through Yezon and Tenkaya, and the mud still sucked at the boots and gaiters. It was quieter around those places, and somewhat deserted. At Yezon we stopped the night with an officer of the Uganda battalion that had taken Leik Ridge. He had been wounded, and was now having a 'rest.' His camp was at the top of a very high hill, and from his bamboo 'basha' you could look out across the jungle to the Chindwin River.

He told me about Private Wafula. Wafula was a regular askari of the K.A.R., and had served for about twelve years. He had a very big moustache, the same kind of moustache as had been worn by Bairnsfather's 'Old Bill' in another war. Wafula was known as Old Bill by all ranks of the battalion. He was always on a charge, which, in the army, means in trouble. His conduct sheets ran into four or five editions. They were a history of trouble. He was a worry to the officers. If there was ever trouble in a village in Abyssinia, Somalia or Ceylon, Old Bill was always in it. Then, when the battalion attacked Leik Ridge, this officer decided to take a chance on Old Bill. He made him a lance-corporal, and found that in the front line Old Bill was worth his weight in grenades. He was courageous, steadfast and cunning. He knew all the infantry weapons, and he could handle them as other experts handle spanners, books or cooking-pots. They were part of his trade as a regular soldier.

In the final attack on Leik Ridge, when they had been in the rain for weeks, it was found that Old Bill had cut strips of tin from a petrol container and had turned them into removable covers for his Bren gun so that it could be used without a chance of rain leaking into the working part. The officer who had liked and trusted him, and who had seen how that trust was not misplaced, had heard Old Bill's Bren gun firing all through the battle. It fired without excitement. The trained ear can tell what a gunner is doing with an automatic weapon—with or without excitement. Old Bill's Bren gun stopped and the officer did not notice it during the closing stages of the battle.

When he went to Old Bill's weapon pit, he found his new lance-corporal dead across his gun, shot beween the eyes. Everything in the pit was as it should have been. Kit was placed where he could find it at once, and the magazines were greased and stacked.

An old, black soldier, from Uganda, had died in action; the way he had been trained was the right way. Four conduct sheets may tell an interesting story of trouble, as did Old Bill's. But the officer's story was better. When he had finished telling me the story, I had the impression that he missed his lance-corporal very much. He had been right about him. The war is like that, even between Africans and Europeans, who, though they are so dissimilar in so many respects, were fighting as a division from Mawlaik to Indainggyi in 1944.

CHAPTER NINETEEN

A long line of anti-aircraft guns rolled along in the dust clouds, and their canvas covers were now a bright yellow from the layers of dust that covered them. When a vehicle stopped, the dust trickled from it, and when it started again it once more became covered with the swirling powder. This road had not seen so much traffic since the 1942 retreat out of Burma. Medium tanks mounting seventy-five-millimetre guns clattered along in tall dust clouds, and the crews sat around the turrets with their faces masked in cloths or scarves. From the air the road must have looked like a long trail of drifting yellow smoke, and there was no way in which the dust could be kept down.

We were nearing Yazagyo, and the going was slow because of the hundreds of trucks, guns, tanks and even amphibious water-craft. The movement of anti-aircraft guns checked neatly with the red-pencilled notice we had seen in the depths of the Chin Hills a few days before. During a halt at a broken bridge I mentioned this to one of the British ack-ack sergeants.

'Jap planes?' he said. 'Yes. They made a raid yesterday on

—— airstrip up the road. They lost two shot down by Spits and another damaged. The R.A.F. were sitting up there waiting for them!'

Fast Jap fighter-bombers had dived on to —— airstrip, but while they did so, several Spitfires dived from a greater height on to their tails. The sergeant said that it was a piece of cake.

'We're going down with ack-ack as far as you blokes go!' said the sergeant. 'It seems that the Japs are getting busy upstairs.'

Some of the ack-ack gunners had fought in the battle of Britain, defending London, and many had been in France. All had seen service in Burma.

Eighteen Dakotas flew over us and started to drop supplies a few miles ahead. They were dropping on Yazagyo, and the parachutes burst like white blossoms against the cloudless sky. It was very hot, and very dusty, but everybody agreed that it was better than the monsoon. We beat clouds of dust out of our clothes and wiped it from our faces, but at least we could move along in our trucks. A major on the road told me that Indanggyi was due to fall any time now. Indanggyi was said to be the headquarters of the Jap 33rd Division which faced us.

We drove through the jungle along the new, wide road with its thick layer of dust, and on each side of us the deep tracks made by hundreds of straining trucks during the monsoon ran into the jungle. The piles of sliced mud and felled timber which the bulldozers had pushed off the road were now beginning to dry. There was the usual smell of rotting teak. It did not look the same place, and the noise of engines in the jungle was almost deafening.

At Yazagyo the divisional headquarters was scattered through the trees and camouflaged with grass and leaves. It was dusty, and the dry heat was intense—but it was better than rain.

The Information Platoon had set up its headquarters beside the road, and it was this platoon that printed one news-sheet for the askaris in Ki'Swahili called 'Maendeleo,' and one for the Europeans called 'Rhino Review.' The Rhinoceros head on a white background was the divisional insignia. The Information Platoon had also set up a tent in which all kinds of magazines and papers were placed for the use of Europeans and Africans. There were maps of the Burma front and the South-West Pacific, and of the East and West European front. They were kept up to date.

'Maendeleo' ensured that askaris of every unit would know what other units of the division were doing on all the sectors of the Central Chindwin front. The askaris thirsted for news, especially for news from home. This came to them from their various territories after collation and was distributed to every unit, in their own language. It told them of the rain, the cattle and the crops. It told them of all the things that had made up the African day in peace-time.

The editor of 'Maendeleo' struggled for paper, and for more paper. The askaris liked to read as much as possible, and through their divisional news they were able to grasp the significance of what they were doing on the Chindwin, and why.

On the left of the road at Yazagyo we came upon the huge air-dropping zone. Parachutes hung in hundreds from every tree, and they were piled in tall heaps all over the dusty grass. As fast as they were collected for return to the rear, the Dakotas came in and dropped more supplies. Red, blue and white, and then yellow and black parachutes came down. The heat on the dropping zone was terrific, for there was little shade in the white space between the trees. All day, Europeans and Africans, busy picking up the supplies, sweated and talked little. There was an urgency and business around here as the weather improved, and the roads were choked with transport. Dumps were growing everywhere, and as new types of transport and weapons arrived, so also did the spare parts, and the staff to maintain them. The road was carrying increasing forces of men and material that would be pushed into central Burma. We could see this mass of material, and this increasing force of men, growing daily, and it was obvious that the crossing of the Chindwin would mean an intensification of the offensive, as the monsoon finished. All the staggering along through mud, the fighting without enough artillery, the cloud that stopped fighter-bombers, was now over and finished. Under the new conditions, the guns could move fast, and could mass for a heavy concentration of fire on any given point within range. It meant that the infantry would be able to ask for gunfire, tanks and planes, and get them every time. It also cancelled out the worry of cloud when bombers were needed, and it was certain that the enemy would suffer greater casualties. The guns would not have to be dragged about and pushed through mud. They would roll along without trouble, and the ammunition would not be a burden. On bad roads the problem of supplying ammunition to the big medium guns was difficult. These shells weighed a hundred pounds, and twenty of them weighed two thousand pounds. In the good weather the supply problem would be solved by the more normal methods of road transport as opposed to air supply, and there would not be the worry about rain and dark skies.

All over the Burma front at that time supply officers must have been feeling more jovial, if only because the monsoon which had tired all their drivers out, worn trucks down, and caused the slopping over of supplies, was over. Supply in Burma is hard at any time, but after supplying a division through a monsoon advance, any conditions slightly better seemed almost perfect.

That week heavy bombers attacked Rangoon twice.

At night we heard what sounded like medium bombers going over our lines and heading for central Burma. They were carrying bombs and leaflets. We found some of those leaflets on the Japs who were killed or captured. One of them showed a red flame encircling three falling Jap soldiers. To pick up such a leaflet and read its significance translated into air and artillery bombardment prior to the infantry assault, must be an impressive experience for the Japanese. Japs kept these leaflets, and read them often. They told the enemy that they could not win and that they would die. The encircling flame was not propaganda; it was something real, and it stretched from south of Myitkyina, down along the Chindwin, and into Arakan. It was moving faster as the clouds dissolved before the sun, and though each battalion, each brigade and division had its set objectives with unpronounceable names, and which would be wrecked with explosives, the flame was creeping towards Mandalay on the Irrawaddy.

The Japs fought, for they too could appreciate the good weather, and they began to fight harder as the Fifth Indian and the Eleventh East African Divisions advanced closer to Kalemyo and Kalewa.

Trucks carrying hundreds of tons of bridging material edged up behind the advancing East Africans, and with them came the Engineers. This was the bridge for the Chindwin River, and over it would go armour and troops—objective Mandalay!

While the Japs held on in Indainggyi on the main road, the brigade that had captured Sittaung in September was ordered to take Kalemyo. Kalemyo had been battered by bombs, and the Japs were camped outside of it. Both Indians of the Fifth Division and Africans of the Eleventh Division now began driving on to it. The Africans were hacking their way through the jungle. Hacking? It is a word now closely associated with the jungle warfare, and is misused. But this brigade were really hacking their way to Kalemyo, yard by yard. Kalemyo was the escape route for the Jap troops then opposing the Indian Division, and the East Africans were ordered to capture it, sit astride the road, and thus seal the escape route.

On October 7th I attended the funeral of an American pilot who had crashed in the darkness while trying to land on an airstrip. A funeral party of askaris stood by near the cemetery, waiting for the arrival of American pilots and American Field Service drivers. The cemetery had grown slowly. There were Africans, British and even one Japanese private soldier buried there. The dust blew up over it, and the crosses made out of sticks were red and drooping. Here had been hurried burials, without ceremony, while fighting went on around. The Jap's grave had a piece of ration box stuck in it, and in rough lettering the words, 'One Jap soldier,' were painted in grey camouflage paint. The days when the Japs had died in hundreds all over the jungle were gone. Then they had been burned in piles. Now they died singly in battle, and they were decently buried. As though sentiment and certain proprieties depended on weather, time and place, men reacted. One Jap soldier! A killer. A part of an unfeeling machine, but to their enemies, when they had the time to think, human beings, even though brutal and misled. This cemetery was very rough and ready, and parachutes were dropping all round it, while trucks and Jeeps roared and coughed nearby. It was a busy place to lie dead, yet, like all cemeteries it had its certain quietness, even amidst the terrific noise of an advance. The funeral parties marched up with their rifles at the short trail. They followed the four Americans who carried the dead pilot.

It seemed strange that on the edge of the dropping zone at Yazagyo, near the Chindwin, British and Americans gathered to pay their last respect to a pilot, while tribesmen from Africa paid the last military respect to one who had flown African wounded out for weeks. Overhead the Dakotas went on showering the supplies. A British officer, in the low voice that is usual at military funerals, gave his orders. He was dressed like a bandit, like a gangster. The wiltered, battered, oily and dirty slouch hat, the khaki neckerchief, the green, faded and ill-fitting battledress and the big moustache favoured by most officers. The Americans watched him closely. Though few of them admit it, the Americans like watching good drill. The bandit with his shocking hat gave them quite a good show. He did not know about that, but as we all stood there, and the Africans obeyed the crisp, low-voiced commands, it was good to see. It is better that a thing is well done than done half-heartedly as though in shame, and as though saying, 'This is just a formality —forgive me!'

His face glistened in the sun, the padre intoned the words. The Dakotas roared. One by one the officers stepped up to the grave and saluted it. The Americans in their swift, almost informal way, and the British with their measured salutes and turns. Everybody moved away again into the war. Into the dust, where tanks were grinding to Indainggyi, and into trucks that whirled them away to their various units of the advancing army. The Dakotas still droned on, and as the sun climbed, the askaris took off their blouses and worked on the removal of stores from the dropping zone.

The breeze shifted, and we heard the dull and flat sound of guns firing on Indainggyi. They had arrived, and more were following. Already they were battering the enemy. In that glaring sunlight, the Japs were crouched in their holes as the gun-muzzles turned and sought them out. They knew now that the mud was gone, and that their days and nights would be full of shellfire. Hurricanes began passing over, and they headed for Indainggyi.

A Jap prisoner who was brought in to the Nyasa battalion headquarters on the Mawlaik front while I was there had been flown to Yazagyo in one of the American planes. He was paralysed and could not speak. One of the best surgeons had operated on him and his condition had improved. But he did not seem able to live. He lay on a stretcher staring at the trees.

Another prisoner brought in to Yazagyo died while the interpreter officer was asking his name. Beri-Beri, hunger, fever and exhaustion were still killing the Japs in front of us. And the prisoners did not want to live. It was bad to live. It was disloyal, and it was something that the Emperor would not forgive. Nor would the ancestors forgive. They ate the food and felt better, but they moaned. Their chronic mental sickness lingered, grew from the fact of being alive instead of dead. Like no other soldiers on earth, they moaned and were miserable. The soldier of any nation who has fought to the finish and then been captured, feels that he has done well and that his government will still thank him for the fight he put up. But not with the Japanese. The soldier's reward is death. They must die rather than be taken alive. Many will refuse to do so as the war goes on, especially among the fresh troops. The regulars will probably go on being slaves, but many of the new troops will almost surely think for themselves. Nobody is quite sure about the Japs, even the experts. Not even the Japs are sure. Many of the prisoners taken in the hot days around Indainggyi area were fresh troops, but many were still of the units who had fought in Manipur. It was doubtful if the remnants of that Manipur debacle would ever again possess the same spirit of sacrifice and stupidity. They were all beaten men, who had found out that they were not really supermen, and it made them cry when they were captured. Most beaten men are pathetic, but the Japs are like Pi-dogs among fox-terriers. Pi-dogs always had a miserable life, though they did not know it until they mixed with the fox-terriers.

Local reports stated that about three hundred sick Japs had been killed by our planes which had bombed Mawlaik. These stragglers had been passing through Mawlaik from the Chindwin front, and many of them had been forced to wait there for days. Chaos still presided over most of the Japanese moves, and this chaos had been in existence since their collapse in Manipur. The brigade advancing against Mawlaik had now captured the northern part of Mawku on the Chindwin, and was then preparing to move on to Mawlaik, and a Kenya battalion had captured a position called Letsegan. This battalion was now pushing to make contact with the brigade near Mawlaik, and would come under its command.

The patrols of the Fifth Indian Division and those of the Eleventh East Africans were near each other in the region of the Palata Chaung near Kaemyo. When they linked up the two divisions would concert their plans even more closely. The enemy sent patrols into our forward areas, but were driven off, and the patrol war that had been going on around Indainggyi was intensified.

One East African battalion made an attack on a position but was met with intense fire, losing several officers. Indainggyi was hard to take, and it had been blasted by bombers until the ground was a mass of craters. At that time the division had killed over five hundred counted Japs. In Burma only counted dead are listed. The Japs were showing their old spirit about their dead and wounded. They tried to carry them out of the battle area as often as possible. The division had taken forty-nine prisoners, and in those days that was a large number. The bulk of these prisoners had been taken when they were staggering around, half-conscious, from wounds or exhaustion. Now, in the good weather, they were fighting a harder action, and they were becoming difficult to take again. Well fed, and well led, they were back on the old fanatical footing, and they did not totter about any more.

The casualty list of the division was not short, nor was it too long, but it was the casualty list of a division which was fighting a jungle campaign against toughening opposition, against a resistance that grew more determined as the weather improved.

We had no doubt that the enemy were digging their usual warren-like positions near Kalewa, and that when we got there the fighting would be harder. The artillery and the bombers could turn those positions into rubble before the infantry went in, and as the gunfire of the division grew in strength, so was it evident that an artillery concentration was going to be a murderous thing when the artillery officers had everything their way.

At that time General Fowkes, commanding the Eleventh Division, had to tell the British signallers that there would be no repatriation for them for some time. In South-East Asia signallers were informed that while other troops would be repatriated in the usual way, it would be impossible to do the same for the signallers. Signallers were short, for France was a big front, and at that time they were almost impossible to get. These men listened to the general and they saw the position. It was hard for them, very hard. But it was the war, and they went on with their very important job, repairing lines and maintaining contacts with widely scattered units in order to keep up the great flow of messages that increased as the momentum of the advance increased.

Repatriation was talked at all mess-tables, in all holes, in all trenches and trucks, and in all hospital camps. The Yanks did two years, the R.A.F. did three years, and why did the army do five? What did you tell your girl when she wrote and asked if you were really interested in marrying her or not. She was thirty-two now. It was getting tricky. It was a risk, etc!

The askaris were now trained troops, and they had seen some jungle warfare. They had felt experience come to them gradually, and now they dug holes and shelters without being told to do so. They did many things without waiting for orders, because if they didn't they might be unlucky. This is the way of most soldiers in action. They find the reason for everything, where once the sergeant had had to drive them to it, because it was training. But in Burma, if you had no hole to get into, you might stop one. It was best to have a hole. It was sensible to keep your eyes open all the time. If you didn't——

It is not possible to describe the serenity of eight British N.C.O.s who had been ordered to prepare for repatriation after over four years abroad. They walked about in a sort of happy daze. Everybody talked about them. They talked to everybody about it, and it really seemed as if the repatriation scheme was coming into effect at long last, and after many promises.

On November 9th the Jap Air Force went into action in cloudy weather. They operated for a considerable distance from their bases, and they made full use of the low cloud.

Twelve enemy planes came in fast and attacked a road junction near Honnaing. They dropped bombs and strafed, cratering the road. They then attacked a mule camp, killing five mules, and then shot back into the clouds. They finished up by shooting down two Dakotas which were dropping supplies. They did this by nipping out of cloud, firing short bursts and then disappearing before the Dakotas had hit the ground.

It was the only day that the Japs were to have in the air without worry. Spitfires, Hurricanes, Thunderbolts and medium bombers went streaking across the lines in the afternoon. There were a lot of medium bombers, and they flew to dump their explosive cargoes on to Jap airfields. Towards afternoon the tempo of the air movement quickened and there was hardly a moment when planes were not flying over the Jap lines. Bombing, strafing, photographing, and during all this the Dakotas began flying in formation, dropping their supplies while a couple of Spitfires circled overhead.

At half past four over Yazagyo airstrip a Dakota was turning under a ceiling of low cloud. There was a short crackle of cannon-fire as a Jap fighter came out of the cloud like a spider out of a web. The Dakota flamed and went down.

We began to take an interest in slit trenches. All over Yazagyo and down to Honnaing heads were visible above the earth while shovels flashed upwards with a mechanical monotony and flung showers of earth right and left. The air-war was on, and everybody was air-minded. An engine in the sky caused great interest. Nods, shakings of heads, and the usual scorn from those who could tell any engine of any nationality merely by the sound.

Askaris who had never seen an air-raid caught on to the digging idea. The digging went on through the days, but the Japs did not return.

Bombers smashed at Jap airfields, dumps, roads and transport. The heat increased, and in the eye-searing blue of the sky the Dakotas flew in tight formation and the fighters soared and dived.

There was less bully-beef and soya link these days. Canadian cheese, Australian meat and vegetables, and even American fruit cocktails came from the Dakotas. Occasionally we were driven back on to soya link, but less often than in the monsoon period.

Bottles of forty over-proof rum came down too, and many vulturine eyes watched it on its journey from dropping zone to dump. It was carried as though it were the grail itself, and there was a solemnity in the air as it was measured out in the various units by the experts on such matters. Every unit, every platoon, squadron or troop has one, if not two, who know just how much rum there is in a noggin, jill or nip.

CHAPTER TWENTY

Yazagyo was the first big village to be liberated from the Japs by the Eleventh Division. It had not been bombed. The jungle had been allowed to grow over it, perhaps because the villagers, or the Japs, realised that natural jungle growth would help to hide it from the air. The enemy staff officers used some of the houses as billets, but there was never any big Jap concentration in Yazagyo itself. It was the first big Burmese village I had seen intact. No dead bodies, howling tied-up dogs or shattered buildings, and no ragged Burmese fluttering about. It was very peaceful. In the days of peace it must have been an attractive place, and there had been gardens and well-laid-out trees. Now these were rioting into a green mass of creeper and vegetation. The big houses built up on stilts were set well back from the road, and from behind the lattices many eyes watched us. One or two of the Burmese women came out on to the verandahs. They were flat-faced, flat-chested, slant-eyed and quiet. Pin-up culture had not penetrated here. They smoked cigars, and they did not seem to care who came or went through their village. They seemed tired and bored with it all, and they wished to be left in their quiet way of life. Small boys and girls came out with handfuls of the Jap occupation currency and offered it for sale.

There were over five hundred Burmese in Yazagyo, but because of the jungle it was not possible to see more than a dozen or so of the houses. They liked it that way, for while the war lasted it might ensure an immunity from wandering or foraging troops. The main road was a few hundred yards from the village, and a few trucks came through Yazagyo itself. It seemed lonely and forgotten, but settled in the middle of it was a British officer who had begun to deal with the local people's troubles and problems.

The Civil Affairs officers were still back at Tamu, but the officer in Yazagyo was from the army and it was his job to keep the local peace, and to act as liaison between the army and the local population.

Living in the village was an old headman who had been appointed by the British Government in 1914, but he had retired from public life some time before the Japanese occupation. He still had in his possession a silver cup given him by the British Government for long and faithful service. This old man came to see the British officer, and he was able to give a good account of what life had been like for the past two and a half years under the Japanese.

Like most Burmese who had spent years in the battle area, he said that the greatest boon of the British Army's return was the freedom from air-raids. The roads had been dangerous. British planes swooped after enemy transport and marching columns, and if any Burmese had been close at the time they, too, were bombed or strafed. He said that the Japanese officers and men had had no sense of shame. They performed their natural functions anywhere and at any time, and in front of the villagers. The Burmese are very modest, and they were shocked at this kind of behaviour by people who claimed to have a religious and spiritual affinity with them. But they admired the Japanese Army because it was forthright and it fought hard, and it had seemed to win all the time until the last great battle for India. The Burmese had seen the Jap troops passing through to the front line, and the officers had shouted that they were going into India. Then they had come back, starving and dying, struggling along with sticks and crutches. They knew then that the Japs were finished, and would have to go. They had been defeated by the British, who were coming back into Burma, and thinking this, but saying nothing, the Burmese waited for the British Army. When it came, they were satisfied and retired again behind their lattices. They began to plough, and to cut the undergrowth from around their houses. There was no excitement, no rapture of welcome. There was silence, and the smoking of big cigars on verandahs as the troops passed through. It gave the impression that the British Army had done no more than its duty by coming back to Burma. The Africans watched the Burmese with suspicion, but if any one smiled, then all the Africans smiled too. They did not understand a silent people who looked at you with flat, black eyes, and changed not a muscle in their face. It was queer. They, the

Africans, would have beaten drums, laughed and danced, had they been liberated from the Japanese by a British Army. They stared at the Burmese who watched them pass, laden with equipment, not uttering a sound.

On November 9th Major-General Pearce, chief of the Civil Affairs Branch for South-East Asia, made a speech over the radio to all servants of the Burma Government in Japanese occupied territory, and the following pamphlet was dropped from the air over Burma:

> The Allies are now about to drive the Japanese from Burma.
>
> The British Military Administration, who will take over the administration of areas liberated from the Japanese, will work through the Civil Affairs Service (Burma).
>
> You will find in this service many officers of the Burma Government who are well known to you as old friends of Burma.
>
> If you have honestly done your ordinary civil job under the Japanese you have committed no crime *unless* you have either actively helped the Japs in waging war, or have been responsible for ill-treatment of Allied prisoners of war and friends of the Allies, or have shown open hostility to the Allies.
>
> Many of you will be required to continue your Government duties under the B.M.A., and if you are re-employed will be paid at the proper rates.
>
> Therefore as soon as Allied troops take over your area, or areas near you, *report to the first Allied military officer you can find. Tell him you are a Government servant and ask to be passed to the nearest Civil Affairs Service officer. Or, if there is no C.A.S. officer nearby to the nearest Burma Intelligence Corps officer.*
>
> *The era of face-slapping is over.*
>
> (*Signed*) C. F. B. PEARCE, Major-General,
> Chief Civil Affairs Officer
> (Burma).

The other side of the pamphlet carried the same message in the Burmese language. Showers of them went fluttering down, and the word went round among the people that the British were coming back, and were now driving the Japanese across the Chindwin. The Burmese were silent and patient, and as their lives under the enemy occupation had changed only for the worse, they were glad to hear that they would soon be able to live normal lives again. They watched the British planes flying over Yazagyo, and they were glad that the days of raids and air attacks were over.

Bombers were still going after the Jap airfields, and all motor traffic coming from the rear had been ordered to travel by night. The roads in the daytime were deserted save for a few Jeeps. The Japs would take every opportunity to find out what was moving on the roads, so transport moved in darkness. The dust was like a fog through which headlamps glowed with a dirty yellow flicker. Convoy commanders chafed at the delay caused by night travel. It gave everybody an idea as to what the Japs had had to put up with, chased day and night by our planes. Jap transport could hardly move at all by day, and when they took the chance, they were attacked from the air. Fighter-bombers were over their lines most of the day, watching for movement and strafing any if they found it. Truck drivers, churning along in thick dust, and listening for the sound of plane engines above their own truck engines, have an anxious time. For the Japs, it had been like that for months on end. Air superiority means that the enemy can never relax, and can never be certain that a convoy of vehicles will reach its destination, and a battle may be planned on the cargo which the convoy carries.

The medium guns opened fire along with the twenty-five-pounders. After their long and tiring journey, the artillery lost no time in going into action. The mediums rumbled, and the flatter, sharp voices of the twenty-five-pounders threw their rumbling into relief.

The Japs brought up one or two 105-millimetre guns, which throw a heavy shell, and they began shelling the air dropping zone at Honnaing. As the Dakotas dropped supplies, the Europeans and Africans waiting on the edge of the dropping zone could hear the shells coming over. When the Dakotas flew away, and the Africans and Europeans went on to the littered zone to pick up the supplies, the shelling became more accurate. They carried on with the collection of the supplies, creeping about in Jeeps, throwing in the bundles, and dropping when they heard the shells approaching. They evolved a drill, and despite the accuracy of the shelling, they cleared the dropping zone. Fighter-bombers went after the Jap guns, but they could not be found.

The mediums and twenty-five-pounders began putting down sharp and heavy bombardments around Indainggyi between one and five o'clock in the morning. The East Africans were firmly established around Indainggyi, and they were waiting for news of the brigade which had gone to attack Kalemyo. Indainggyi was flattened slowly under a rain of shells and bombs, and the enemy could not have known that the troops now near Kalemyo could turn and attack Indainggyi in the rear after Kalemyo had fallen.

Though they fought stubbornly, and tried every trick in order to delay the advance of the African and Indian divisions, it was quite plain that they were going to lose the Chindwin. At Honnaing near Indainggyi, the Jap jitter-parties were out every night. Bullets whistled across slit trenches, and figures scuttled about in the dark.

An order addressed to a Japanese major was captured. This document ordered the major to form a suicide party of one hundred men, and to take these men on to the British line of communication. Once there, they would cause chaos, shoot up convoys, destroy tanks and blow up supply dumps. They would be given one hundred drums of oil with which they would make a firebelt if attacked by British tanks.

It was presumed that if there really was a major and his suicide party, they would be somewhere near the road between Honnaing and Indainggyi. The captured order sounded quite in the line of Jap desperation, and from then on all trucks were escorted by infantry. A Jap party ambushed some Africans in the jungle and shot them up. It was thought that this might be the Jap major's party, but no one could be sure. Patrols ransacked the jungle, but found no trace of the suicide party. By jitter-party, ambush and offensive patrols, the enemy tried to stave off the fall of Indainggyi. They tried to carry the war to the attackers, but failed. If anything moved in Indainggyi area, the artillery opened a savage concentration on it, and the air strikes went on. The Jap positions were very cunningly placed. They had put a great deal of work into them. They now appeared to be thinning out, to be trying to slip away in small groups, while still holding up the African advance as well as they could.

A Jap sergeant was found lying beside the road with a bullet wound in his stomach. He had been part of a patrol which tried to pierce through to our rear. He was defiant and cocky. He was also pathetic, for his first words to the Japanese-speaking officer who bent over him were:

'When you shoot me, I demand a soldier's death. I am a soldier of the Imperial army, and I demand to be shot properly, like a soldier.'

He showed a remarkable disdain for his wound, which must have hurt him a lot, and he went on shouting that he was a Japanese soldier and wished for a soldier's end.

On November 12th the forward troops marching on Kalemyo were only three miles from that place. The news of its capture was awaited anxiously. The troops of the Fifth Indian Division were also close to it, and soon the two divisions would join up.

The Supply and Transport officers were having a busier time than ever before. New units were moving in continually and were applying for rations and various supplies. Though the drawing of supplies in bulk from the rear was now easier with road transport moving over good roads, the splitting and issuing of them at the front was harder. The growing bodies of troops and new units threw a great strain on the supply service. But nobody ever went without supplies or rations.

The ammunition officer of the African Divisional Supply and Transport was a South African. He was in his forties, and had left a lawyer's practice in South Africa at the beginning of the war and sailed for England. There he had joined the army and had been in Abyssinia and now in Burma. He was in charge of all ammunition for artillery, Piat-projectors, mortars and automatic weapons. When the batteries opened heavy fire, everybody pulled his leg. For him it meant a lot of work, and he heard the result of it in a series of echoing detonations.

Commanding the supply and transport of the division was a colonel who had been in Norway in 1940. He said that no matter how tough Burma was, the view was lovely. And a lovely view was a fine thing. This irony was lost on others. They did not agree.

At Yazagyo the bulldozers, working in a line, had made a tremendous airstrip in a few days, and Dakotas were landing as well as gliders and small planes. The wounded from both the Tiddim and Khabaw fronts were being flown there. At Yazagyo airstrip they collected, and rested in bamboo huts until their turn came to fly out. Bearded Indians, British Tommies and Africans sat together and smoked, some bandaged, others weak from malaria or scrub typhus. Around them, British and American ack-ack gunners watched the sky for enemy planes. The Dakotas took off in long trailing clouds of dust, while others circled waiting for the signal to land.

One African sat with his shattered right arm in a sling. His face was impassive, and his eyes were slightly glazed. He had come straight out of action, so swiftly that he probably could not catch up with his own movements. For the African, modern speed can be bewildering. His heavily nailed boots were spattered with dried blood spots. He had been caught in a burst of machine-gun fire at close range not more than an hour before. He would soon be in a hospital, and he was only one of many who were speedily evacuated. The Air Force was doing a magnificent job. These men would receive medical treatment that the Japanese could never even hope to have. When the enemy sickened they died or survived by their own efforts. The Japs did not work on the principle that there are certain limits to which you can drive men. The limit in their army was death, and it was a reward for service. In the Fourteenth Army, if you sickened or were wounded in action, you received the best treatment possible, and the machine that handled you, though up against many obstacles, seldom faltered. All the casualties sitting under the grass shelters on the airstrip knew that they would be in a clean, cool hospital in a couple of hours.

The American and British pilots stood in groups talking and smoking. Some of the Americans wore brown leather jackets on the backs of which were painted American and Chinese flags. When pilots talk together, it is as though they have no nationality. They talk a language that is peculiarly their own. The pilots and the soldiers in Burma admired each other, and they appreciated each other's difficulties.

On November 14th Kalemyo was captured. Patrols went in and reported it clear of the enemy. One Jap had risen out of the scattered ruins and had come forward. He was sprayed with Sten-gun fire by an askari. To this askari fell the curious honour of wiping out the whole Jap garrison of Kalemyo—one Jap. Indians and Africans of the two divisions mingled. Kalemyo was shattered and ruined, and the Japs had gone. The escape route for the Japs on the Tiddim road was now closed. They would be forced into the thick jungle, and the Jap front was cracking up. It was like a worn-out machine that tried to perform its usual function, but it broke down everywhere. Despite this, the Japs fought on and they went through the routines that the different situations demanded. Each hill was defended, but those that were most important were defended the longest. They still dug positions into which they could retire when driven from the one in front. One Jap was found dead in a captured position with his rifle still pressed to his shoulder. His right leg was ruined and had been in that state for easily a week. He had received no medical attention, but had fought on to the finish. They were like that. Their officers had no pity, because they had none for themselves.

A battalion from Uganda was forcing its way down to a place called the Bon Chaung. They would make a road block there and thus cut off the escape of the Japs retreating from Indainggyi. Troops who had marched down to Kalemyo were already moving back to take Indainggyi in the rear. The Japs had little information. Their intelligence system could not cope with the situation, and they did not seem to realise that they were threatened by encirclement. They lived in a glare of heat, in holes, amidst the battering of shells.

Just outside of Indainggyi I watched some Nyasa gunners of an anti-tank regiment. The duty gun-crews were alert, watching the road, and the resting crews were playing cards on a groundsheet. No traffic came beyond this place. It was fiercely hot, and card players threw down their sticky cards and wiped their brows. They had waited for a long time to use their six-pounder anti-tank guns, but their chance did not come. They had man-handled their guns through the muck and rain with the rest of the artillery, but the Japs did not show any armour. While the artillery plastered Indainggyi, the anti-tank gunners waited and watched, but no armour appeared. It was hard luck.

On November 18th the Hurricanes came in droves, and all day they hammered the Jap positions. The artillery joined in a crushing fire plan, switching from point to point, smothering each one with high explosive.

This was quite a different war from that of the past three months, a war in which the technicians of the artillery and the Air Force together joined in a tearing of the nerves and defences of the enemy. When the commander of the artillery wished, he could put down eight tons of high explosive a minute on any given target within range.

I went into brigade headquarters with a Colonel Hilton who had hoped to get into Indainggyi that morning. It was past midday and the artillery had stopped firing. In the intelligence officer's dug-out were two lieutenants. They looked tired. A wooden ration case was covered with maps and papers. They told us that Indainggyi had just been captured without opposition. Once again the Japs had faded out into the jungle. They had dug positions that could hold companies of infantry, but they had been unable to hold on in the face of the artillery and planes. Their job was to delay, delay, and delay the enemy again, to do anything that could hamper our progress. But they were given no rest and the advance went on. Out on the other front, Mawlaik had fallen on November 10th to the brigade which intended driving on across the Chindwin.

Indainggyi smelt of death. It was ploughed and cratered, just another area of churned-up soil and fallen trees. The troops pressed through it in pursuit of the Japs, and down at the Bon Chaung the Uganda troops had established their road-block. Towards this the enemy was retreating.

On November 20th the retreating Japs struck the road-block. They charged it. But there was no future for them there. They were cut down by automatic fire and twenty-three of them fell in the assault. It was dusty and hot, and their situation was very desperate. They must have realised that forces were closing in all round them. They filtered back into the jungle, while some fought on, trying to break through. The road-block was at Natkyigon, not far ahead of the Bon Chaung. The Bon Chaung was wide, with a thin stream flowing through it. Four ruined wooden bridges lay in ruins. Each one the Japs had built, and each one had been wrecked by Hurricanes. While the Japs tried to get away through the jungle, another force of Africans was moving to join up with the Uganda troops on the road-block. The enemy was outwitted, out-gunned and beaten. But he would still fight savagely, and he headed for the Myitthe gorge which ran down to the Chindwin. In the gorge the walls of cliff rose steeply on each side of the narrow road. The Japs began laying a few mines, but they were in a hurry.

There was speculation as to what the Japs had done with their artillery. We wondered if they had got their big 105-millimetre guns out and across the Chindwin. While we were wondering about that, the Japs started to use seventy-five-millimetre guns. They shelled a road junction which they had pinpointed with great precision, killing several men of a unit which was moving fast to join the Uganda troops on the road-block. They had also mined this part of the road which led to Natkyigon between the tall cliffs. The mines were small, about as big as a saucer, and they blew off the tyres of heavy trucks. I came on to a party of askaris digging for mines with fixed bayonets. The solenoids in their detectors had fizzled out, so they went on with bayonets. We chanced it in a Jeep and got through. It was uncertainty about mines that was the trouble for the advancing transport. They were never sure until the road had been well probed, though in a Jeep it was said to be less dangerous. But for the heavy truck-driver it meant that if he took the wrong chance, such subjects as repatriation, soya link sausage and medals would cease to interest him in the way they had always done. Nobody was unlucky about mines in the move to Natkyigon, though a few trucks were disabled.

Firing broke out on the right across the gorge. A new unit had come forward to learn jungle warfare, and had walked straight into a fight. The firing moved. It looked as if the new unit was learning quickly. We drove on until we came to the troops who were pressing towards the road-block. These troops were from Kenya, and they had done a great deal of hard work. They had marched great distances, having chopped their way to Kalemyo and then doubling back to Indainggyi. They were the same troops who had fought the division's first action at Jambo Hill on the Sittaung road. They were young troops, and, though tired, they grinned cheerfully among themselves as they waited to move forward. A few tanks rumbled along, and on the left of the road, in a patch of jungle, mortar teams opened fire. One of the troops picked up a shell fragment which was about a foot long. It had razor-sharp edges. He waved this and laughed, saying in Ki'Swahili, 'Just think of this hitting a man!'

The rest of the askaris laughed loudly. They thought it was really funny. They had been shelled in the open the day before and now it was funny. They had buried several of their friends who had been killed by splinters like this one now being waved about. During the shelling Sergeant Mwanza, a Mkamba tribesman from Kenya, had noticed a young officer approaching, and just then he heard the whistle of a couple of approaching shells. He jumped up and threw himself on the officer, covering him completely with his body as the shells burst. Mwanza was fatally wounded, dying a little later, but he had saved the officer's life. He did not know the officer. He had never seen him before.

When the Japs found that they could not get out of the trap they began digging in on the hills, determined to bar the way to Kalewa, now not very far away. It is possible that they even then did not realise their position. They did not even know that Kalemyo had fallen days before, for they despatched one party of Japs to Kalemyo as though they still held that place. The intelligence of the Eleventh Division had established that some of the Japanese infantry companies in front of them were down to ten and fifteen men. A Jap nominal roll was captured, and this listed one company's strength. It consisted of one second lieutenant and six men. They were short of food but had plenty of ammunition. The Japs dug in around a place called Kyigon, and they waited for the attack. Behind the Japs, at Natkyigon, the Uganda troops still held the road-block.

The fighter-bombers started making heavy attacks, and the infantry moved up, preparing to assault the dug-in enemy. They waited as the steel snouts of the guns turned to point at the long ridge held by the Japs. On November 21st, the guns opened fire on the ridge. African and European gunners turned their artillery into one great battering machine. Eleven hundred shells burst on the Jap-held ridge. It was the shattering bombardment of the kind made possible by the good weather, the dry roads, and the supply machine that could push ammunition through with ease. Between the shellfire the planes went in and dumped their bombs on to the mangled ridge. The Japs crouched in their positions, dazed in the hellish fire, and the African infantry attacked. The fighting was done in holes and trenches that ran through the fallen trees and bamboos, and the Japs resisted with their hopeless fanaticism. As they were blasted out of one position, they went into the next, and fought on from there, stupidly but dangerously. They could have gone, but they stayed. They had been probably ordered to fight to the finish. The jungle was thick, and in it Africans and Japanese fought with grenades, matchets and automatics.

During the night the mediums went on firing. They threw enormous flashes among the trees. In their fouled warrens the Japs waited for the next day, another day of explosions and heat. In the darkness three-point-seven ack-ack guns opened fire with a series of terrific thunderclaps. They were firing in a ground role, and their target was Kalewa. With a range of over twenty thousand yards, they are formidable weapons when used as field-pieces, having a very high velocity and giving little or no warning to those on the receiving end. They fired all night, and in Kalewa the Japs must have had a very worrying time, for they were certainly trying to ferry stores and weapons across the Chindwin to safety.

Brigade headquarters was a collection of scattered slit-trenches. The brigadier sat in the darkness and gave his orders in a low voice over the phone. He made a last check with the artillery about to-morrow morning's fire. The last-minute arrangements for another day of hell for the Japs.

At a quarter past eleven the next morning I sat with the brigade intelligence officer. He was elated. He looked at his watch and grinned. Another minute and the guns would start. We sat on a couple of ammunition boxes. There was deep silence in the jungle.

'Now!' said the intelligence officer.

Dead on time, the guns behind us opened up. It was like the

slamming of iron doors, and the shells went over in long, hissing and fluttering groups. They fired one minute slow, and then at eleven-sixteen they fired rapidly, so that every gun hammered and thumped as fast as its crew could operate. In front of us the infantry advanced slowly towards the moving smoke and flame of the shellfire, and at eleven-twenty-three, as the guns ceased fire, the infantry mortars took over. The infantry went in with bayonets, struggling through the tangled wreckage towards the dazed enemy. The smell of fumes and tree-sap mingled. It was hot. The troops took their objectives, and though sporadic firing continued as stray Japs were found, the combination of high explosive and African infantry had triumphed.

Down the narrow road between the cliffs the Kenya battalion was approaching Natkyigon. There were Japs in front, though they dodged about in an effort to escape. On either side of the road, patrols were seeking them out. Some light tanks passed us, and they were covered with camouflage. A dead Jap, wearing full kit and steel helmet, lay on the left under a tree. In front of him was a mess-tin half-full of rice. He was very big and powerfully built, and, lying there with a surprised expression on his face, it was evident that he had been shot while eating a hurried meal. He had probably been told not to but had chanced it.

We found pink Japanese army forms fluttering about the road in thousands, chests of ammunition, heaps of mines, and bundles of coarse, cheap green shirts. All the equipment was bundled together as if it had been flung from trucks by the desperate Jap quartermasters. The Africans cut the goggles out of the Jap respirators and wore them as they marched through the dust-clouds. Some came out of the jungle with brand-new bicycles. Somebody had found a dump of them, and they were good. Infantry cannot carry loot. It generally leaves it to the units who follow up. Loot is heavy, and it gets heavier on the march. But it is possible to ride on a bicycle, wearing all your kit, and some of the askaris pedalled down the road. An African sergeant came up to his company commander and said, 'Can I bring you a bicycle, effendi?'

'Do you think I am an old man, or something?' said the company commander with mock severity.

Boxes of saddles and mule kit were scattered all over the road. The jungle here was full of dumps. When we came to a demolished bridge the advance halted for a few minutes. The planks of the bridge were splintered and tangled together, covered with mud, and sprayed with a stream of blood. We looked over the side and saw a dead Jap lying below. He had committed 'Chota Hazri' as the bridge went up. He had done a neat demolition job, but the bulldozer cut a new road below it in a few minutes, and the advance poured on.

Automatic fire started up again in the trees ahead. In an hour or so this battalion would be at the road-block, and the enemy who had eluded it could be hunted down.

Transport was moving up behind the infantry, and the drivers sat in their cabs watching the toiling troops march past them as they waited. They were glad to be drivers, though they too had been through it during the monsoon. The infantry, their black faces glistening with sweat, wearing their Jap respirator goggles, looked like dusty gargoyles. Some carried Jap map-cases of light-brown leather. One wore a 'Sennin-Bari,' the belt of a thousand stitches, wound round his waist to the amusement of his friends. They trudged along in lines on each side of the road. Infantry who have marched far move with a curious patience. This patience is reflected in their bent knees as their feet rise and fall, and in the side glance at a tank or a truck. Despite the machinery, the battering artillery, and the planes, the infantry still have to go in and fight it out.

CHAPTER TWENTY-ONE

Jap deserters are still something unusual. One walked in and gave himself up to some askaris. He was carrying his rifle, but it was useless. He had broken it, and he held it above his head. He was a first-class private.

One morning while the artillery was firing on a Jap ridge near the Myittha gorge, this deserter strolled into the African lines. He was fit and well fed, and though his uniform was dirty and stained, it was new and in good condition. He did not have any of the symptoms of beri-beri and he was cheerful. Very cheerful. His red collar-tabs with their three stars of a first-class private were fresh and clean. As he held his hands above his head, he smiled all round him, nodding and bowing. It was a great surprise for everybody, for it had not been imagined that a Jap private would surrender unless half-conscious or badly wounded. Yet here was a private, grinning and waiting to be taken prisoner.

We wondered all kinds of things. Did this mean that the rot had set in at last. Did it mean that the Jap was beginning to think for himself, and to ask himself if being driven to death like cattle was glorious. Or did it mean that this man's unit was ready to mutiny or break, and that he was the first to come over.

It did not mean any of these things. It meant that this man was an individual who believed little of what his officers had told him. He was not a new soldier, for he had done nearly six years in the army and had served in China. It was still surprising that a Jap private should decide to desert and become a prisoner after six years' service. He said that he liked the British, and he grinned again. He had seen plenty of English people in Yokohama before the war, and he liked the way they brushed their hair and the way they walked. They seemed to move about as though they had not a care in the world. The English seemed to have a zest for life. He also said that the Jap officers hid the truth from their men, and that no criticism of Imperial policy was permitted among the troops. Grumbling was not permitted, nor was it possible to question any decision. Once, said this deserter, he had been reported by two of his comrades because he had said he did not consider the British to be as black as they were painted by the Jap officers.

He did not fawn or show servility after the manner of the Italian prisoners who had been glad to take part in the knifing of France and England when it was exciting and safe. He laughed a lot when he spoke about Japan, as though he spoke of an amusing foreign country. All Jap prisoners are voluble. They like to talk at great length. They are taught that they will never see Japan again, and they talk as if that country was a place that they had visited for a holiday, but would never see again. It was like the closing of a door in the mind. Once captured, you were finished. They talked without excitement, save when they wept because they had not killed themselves. But this deserter did not weep. He laughed. He bowed low from the waist to the British officers. He said that he wished to join our army and fight the Japs.

'I can never go back to Japan,' he said. 'I left my wife and family there, and I would disgrace them if I went back. They would cut off my head. All that is over and finished. Perhaps I could get a job as a servant to an Englishman after the war. I never want to see Japan again, and even if I wanted to, I could not go.'

In the prisoners' cage he took off his boots and cap and then squatted down on his heels. He was given a tin of sardines and a packet of biscuits by a scowling and suspicious African. The tin was already open, and then the African grinned as he saw the small, yellow prisoner smell the fish with great delight. Despite his short stature, the Jap was very thick-set and powerful. His hands, like those of most of the Jap prisoners I had seen, were very big and coarse, and with long, wrinkled fingers. His cheeks were pink against the weather-beaten yellow skin, and his long slit eyes were very black and lustrous. When he smiled, which was often, they lit up with a good humour. One wondered what sights they had seen and what cruelties they had witnessed in their six years of soldiering in the East. Because he was cheerful and open-faced, this did not rule out the chance that he had helped in the killing and wounding of innocent people. He was a Japanese soldier, and the name of Japanese soldiers stank of murder and cruelty. It was also associated with a kind of inferiority complex that made the Jap troops strip Europeans naked and ram their passports into their mouths during the China 'incident,' and had caused headlines in the *Volkischer Beobachter*. It had turned cities into butcher's shops in order to show what Japan could do when she was at war. This hysteria, this merciless obedience to orders and impulses was not present in the face of the Jap deserter. But no doubt he had often done what he was told. He said that he had waited for a long time for the chance to desert. No one else in his unit wished to desert. He had not voiced his feelings for over a year, since the time he had been reported by his comrades.

From a bush growing inside the cage the prisoner tore two straight twigs. He peeled the bark off their tips and began using them as chopsticks. He ate quickly with precision, picking pieces of fish up neatly between the two ends of the chopsticks. The Africans watched, fascinated by this dexterity. Then he stopped eating and turned to the two intelligence officers who squatted near him.

'The Japanese soldiers say that Tojo is finished,' he said. 'They say that the American advance in the Pacific is not being stopped. Tojo has made mistakes, and soldiers are tired of him. We all feel that disaster will come to Japan if Tojo does not go. But the Japanese soldiers will fight to the finish, no matter what happens. No matter what victories are won by the Allies, the Japanese Army will fight to the end. That is what every soldier says.'

He unbuttoned the greasy collar of his khaki tunic, and then went on picking with the chopsticks. With these two pieces of stick he was able to clean every single scrap out of the tin until it seemed as though licked clean. Then he drank noisily from the mess-tin of tea, and wiped his mouth with the back of his great paw. He was contented.

He half-crouched, and his eyes narrowed. Planes were flying overhead. They were fast fighter-bombers. The Jap stared up past the bamboo roof of his cage.

'British bombers?' he asked. His eyes glittered curiously. He was told that they were. 'I was in a terrific air-raid at Ye-U, and we lived in the slit trenches all day. Even the officers were terrified.'

The planes flashed past and went out of sight while the Jap watched them, hunched like a cat. He was glad to be in the cage, out of it all. He said so twice, while the plane engines hummed.

Then he said something which interested us all very much. 'When the survivors of the battle in Manipur came back across the Chindwin,' he said, 'we were not allowed to talk to them. We wanted to rush up and ask them all sorts of questions, but the officers forbade us to do so, and a guard was placed so that we could not approach them. They were in a terrible state, and we were able to understand that they had failed, and that thousands had been killed. Some of them crawled into the shade and they could not get up again. We knew that our army had suffered a great deal, and everybody was depressed.'

He changed the subject many times, aimlessly, as if glad to talk at last about anything he wished.

'My family will rejoice in my death,' he said. 'They will be told that I am dead in battle. They will be proud of me, and I can never return there. I have read many of the propaganda leaflets dropped by the British, and they have told us the truth, but not many of the Japanese soldiers believe them. Many kept them as souvenirs. The Japanese believe in the Emperor and the army, and they will fight on.'

'Did you never feel impelled to commit suicide?' said one of the British officers. 'Don't the Japanese soldiers usually commit suicide when they are defeated?'

'Yes,' said the Jap casually, as though discussing a meal. 'They take the grenade like this.' He closed his eyes, and a pious expression came over his face. He pulled the pin from an imaginary grenade and then pressed his hands against his chest. To imitate the explosion, he flung out his arm and then opened his eyes. He grinned, looking around him at the guards, as though he had performed a trick. It was a most horrible piece of mimicry.

'That is the way they do it,' he said. 'That is the way they do it when the end comes.' He beamed on us.

He was able to grin about it while he still savoured the taste of the sardines. He was alive, and he liked it. Despite the fact that he was one of the millions of cannon-slaves of Japan, he had a mind of his own, and he was not frightened of the future or the past. I wondered if there could be many like him in the Jap ranks, and if there were, what they would do about it when Japan was sealed off by the Allies.

The sun came through the roof. He blinked and stared at the beam, smiling to himself. He was one of the most contented people in Burma. What would the officers like to hear next? Nobody said anything. His grin and his merry eye had not wiped out the fact that he was a Japanese soldier, and if he felt this atmosphere, he did not show it.

He stared at the African guard, who stared back.

'Have you ever seen one of these black men before?' he was asked. He shook his head. He said he did not even know where they came from. He did not seem very surprised that a man should have a black skin. He did not care either. The future was full of peace and food. There would be no more shelling and bombing. No creeping about at night in the jungle, and no lice, mud and mosquitos. He ate another biscuit.

As we left the cage the huge African guard loomed. The African seemed disappointed with us. We had talked to the Jap, and the Jap had laughed. Frowning, the African stared at the Jap and the Jap stirred uncomfortably. Each to the other was a strange object. They were both suspicious, though the African showed it and the Jap did not.

CHAPTER TWENTY-TWO

On December 2nd the division broke into Kalewa and saw the Chindwin. It was like the sight of clear sky after bad weather. The Khabaw Valley had been long and difficult, and the Chindwin meant the end of the Khabaw. Japanese shells were bursting on the bank. One gun was firing. It switched on to new targets. Assault-boats laden with askaris were already crossing the Chindwin, and though shells burst among them, they did not halt the advance. The word Kalewa had been on every askari's lips since Tamu back on the Indian border. One came to think of Kalewa as a big town nestling beside the Chindwin. It had been a big place, but now it was destroyed. It stank as usual of the dead, and the craters overlapped each other to the river's edge. There were craters made by very heavy bombs and filled with stagnant water. Enemy kit was strewn everywhere, and sheets of corrugated iron had been flung all over the ruins by blast. A few dogs howled in the jungle. Their Jap masters had left them tied, and they were now yelping with hunger. On the gashed brown earth, the sun beat down, and on the river it flashed with an oily light. The Chindwin was wide, very wide, and the engineers were already at work unloading ton after ton of bridging material. Everybody sighed when they saw Kalewa.

The last big victory for East Africans had been Addis Ababa, under a different sun, and against an enemy who lived in great style and ate well. Addis Ababa had been a victory which slaked the thirst, and it had been romantic as well. The only smell had been from bad drains, but this was smothered in the scent, the heady and pleasant thrill of a big city.

Kalewa was a greater victory, but was a sordid and broken answer to a much greater physical effort than the campaign for Addis Ababa. The sun glared on it as the askaris marched through and prepared for the final phase of the Chindwin campaign. The division had to press on and take Shwegyin, a few miles along the road on the other side of the Chindwin.

The brigade which had taken Mawlaik had crossed the Chindwin at Massein, farther north, and when they crossed, they did so with four assault-boats and three outboard motor-engines. Three thousand men crossed, and fifty tons of stores as well. Five hundred mules went over also, and only one was drowned. At Massein the Chindwin was six hundred yards wide, but the whole brigade, its stores and animals, crossed in thirty-six hours, and the forward elements were fighting the Japs before the crossing was finished. The brigade was now coming down through the wild country on the banks of the Chindwin. The Northern Rhodesians had already arrived at Kalewa and were resting after their long journey. I saw some of the officers of the Northern Rhodesian battalion sitting at a bamboo table. They were brown, and their slouch hats were faded and crumpled. The table was built in the open near a brown hill, and from it the officers could see their men writing letters, or lazing about in the shade. The other battalions of that brigade were still in the jungle. They would come out on the main road across the Chindwin. A perimeter would be established around the Kalewa bridgehead, and fresh troops would pour through it to take up the pursuit of the Japs into Central Burma.

The Union Jack fluttered above the ruins of a pagoda-like building near the river. It was the same flag that General Fowkes had hoisted over Addis Ababa. In those days he had been a brigadier commanding the 22nd East African Brigade, and now as a major-general commanding the 11th East African Division he had hoisted the same flag over Kalewa.

While the engineers off-loaded the bridging material, the artillery moved in. The dust was now choking, and it was hard going to drive along the road in convoy. Traffic had increased, and the road through the Myittha gorge was one solid mass of transport, guns, tanks, troops and dust. The dust swirled until it hid everything from sight. The trucks that carried the bridging material were enormous, and after weeks of camouflage and hiding in the jungle, they had now come to the road, and they had priority. What they carried would make the biggest floating bridge in the world, and this historic bridge would take the boots, tracks and wheels of the British Fourteenth Army back into Central Burma after two and a half years.

The artillery settled itself in a long line, and where they poked their barrels out of the trees was known as 'Gun Alley.' They opened fire without delay, and the aerial observation planes wheeled over the Jap-held cliffs just across the river.

The enemy seventy-five shelling went on for about four days after the fall of Kalewa. Spasmodic, there being only one gun, it stopped altogether as our artillery made life too hot for the Jap gunners. They had dragged their gun from position to position, but in the end they pulled out. They could not stop the advance. The next stop was Mandalay, but before that place was reached there would be plenty of the bloody fighting that distinguishes the Japanese war.

The askaris stared hard as they came into Kalewa. They kept thinking that perhaps they had not really arrived yet, but they were told that this was Kalewa. The African is not profane, that is to say, they have none of the curious words that the British Tommy would use when they saw Kalewa. Where a Tommy might throw his kit down and stare at the smashed ruins he has fought for months to capture, and say, 'Well, of all the —— —— places I ever saw, this one takes the —— cake!' the African will shake his head and say, 'Mbaya sana! Mbaya kabisa!' which might be translated as terrible, awful, but nothing more profane than that. But the feeling is no less intense than that of the more fluently vituperative Tommy.

Officers and British N.C.O.s had said that the first thing they would do when they got into Kalewa would be to book a table at the 'Ritz' there, and then go on to a cinema or one of the night clubs.

'Personally, I don't see why you want to go to the Plaza,' one officer had said to another in a muddy bivouac six weeks before. 'We've seen that picture. Why not make it the Troc?'

The other had shaken his head solemnly and said, 'Don't let's go into that again. There are only four cinemas in Kalewa, but give me the Plaza every time.'

It was often like that. Their womenfolk might not have understood had they heard these conversations. They might have feared for their men's sanity.

There was no Plaza and no Troc. The R.A.F. had left one small hill on which to plant the Union Jack. The rest was flat.

One officer came out of Kalewa and said to another, 'Have you been in yet?'

'No.'

'It's terrific. People are going out of their minds with joy. Flowers, wine, cake, eggs, everything you can imagine. They throw it at you. The women fall around your neck and kiss you. It's the greatest victory that the Empire has ever seen. The askaris are feted, and the population is wild with joy. I return you now to the studio. . . .'

On December 7th General Slim, Commander of the Fourteenth Army, came down to Kalewa to see the bridgehead. The last occasion on which he had seen this part of the Chindwin had been in early 1942 after the retreat. He had come out with his troops via Shwegyin, and now Shwegyin was crumbling under our artillery. It was not possible to guess what his feelings were as he crossed the Chindwin from Kalewa. He carried a heavy stick, and he might have been a farmer crossing a river to see his crops on the other side.

Since June, 1944, he had been thrashing the Jap army. He had waited a long time to do so, and from Kalewa back to Ukrhul, Bishenpur, Kohima and Imphal, the bones of about eighty thousand Japanese troops were whitening, or were being covered by the jungle.

Though the great victory on the borders of India had been swamped by the invasion of Europe, everybody knew that the first great defeat the Japs had ever suffered had been inflicted on them by this general and his army. The pursuit and cutting down of the remnants had gone on in the worst weather in the world, and had been supplied from India across chasms, jungles and mountains.

The Chindwin glittered brightly. It was ours again. On the receding bank the bridge was being assembled. Already many sections of it were floating, ready for bolting together. The guns were rumbling, and the high cliffs that rose before us were in our hands. Only a couple of days before, they had been the target for the guns in 'Gun Alley.' General Slim leaned on his stick and gazed at the Chindwin as we crossed on the raft. The raft grazed on to the beach, and the askaris drove in the pins that secured it. They watched Slim talking to their own divisional commander. Their general was the *Bwana Mkubwa,* but the other general with the jutting chin was the *Bwana Mkubwa Kabisa,* which is even bigger than the *Bwana Mkubwa.* The two generals climbed into a Jeep, and a convoy of three Jeeps headed for the front line. It was not many miles up the dusty road.

We drove past the scattered remains of a Spitfire which had fallen here, and the British pilot had been buried only three days before. Though his plane had crashed there over a week ago during the Jap occupation, the Japs had not even attempted to bury his body, which had lain near the road. The ground was scarred by shellfire, and the palm-trees were split and gashed by fragments. The craters formed a sort of calendar. They stretched from 1942 to 1944, from dry greyness to fresh newness, and there were craters of a few days ago with the green fins of the bombs lying in them. A notice written in pencil on an American K ration packet said, 'Mines!'

At brigade headquarters, just behind the line, General Slim talked with some of the officers about the campaign. Everybody was glad that Kalewa had fallen at last, and there was a definite feeling of achievement. There had been times when we had thought we would never reach Kalewa, but would be stuck in the mud for ever. Kalewa was now behind, and was becoming a bridgehead, and was no longer an objective or a target. Shwegyin was the next objective, and in the front line Nyasa troops were preparing to drive the Japs back and open the road into Shwegyin.

The two generals walked up the steep sandy hill leading to the forward troops.

'Don't forget,' said General Fowkes to the battalion commander who was leading, 'The army commander is our responsibility.'

'Getting worried, Fowkes?' laughed General Slim, turning round to General Fowkes.

'No, sir,' said General Fowkes. 'But the askaris don't like anything to happen to their *Bwana Mkubwa.*'

He was right about that. The askaris watched their *Bwanas* as they walked up the hill. The two generals laughed.

The heat was intense, and the sand threw back the waves of warm air. Askaris in full kit were marching up to the line, and they sweated profusely as they kicked up the dust.

On a fallen tree over which we climbed, lay Japanese greatcoats, tunics and shirts. They had been laid there by the Japs to dry. They had fled and left them, and steam still curled from them in the sunlight. General Slim picked up a greatcoat and examined the buttons. He was interested in the material. Later, in the forward positions, he picked up some Jap rifle cartridges and examined the coloured markings which denoted tracer, armour-piercing or incendiary bullets. He did not say so, but he must have been curious to see Shwegyin again, where the tanks, transport and guns of the British Army retreating out of Burma had been destroyed so that the Japs should not have them.

The two generals looked out at the Jap positions. Below them flowed the Chindwin. The artillery was registering on the Japs and soon Hurricanes would be diving on them.

At the bridgehead on the way back cameramen took pictures of General Slim. Historic pictures; for the general who had brought his troops out of Burma was now back again on the Chindwin, after killing and wounding the best part of the Jap expeditionary force which had been told that the good times went on for ever.

CHAPTER TWENTY-THREE

The Engineers started the foundations of their bridge on December 8th. On the morning of the 10th a phone call from the headquarters of the 11th Division asked them when it would be ready. The colonel in charge of the task answered the phone. He said that the bridge would be ready at three o'clock that day.

One thousand and ninety feet of steel floating bridge, the biggest of its kind in the world, was ready at ten minutes to three on December 10th.

A doorway had been made which led into Central Burma, and the Indian engineers stood back, satisfied. The bridge threw off a dull glitter. Troops, tanks and guns, which had been forced to cross the river laboriously on rafts, would now pass in swift lines across the bridge.

Hundreds of forty-gallon oil-drums stretched in an irregular line along the beach on the opposite side. They had been laid there by the Japanese with the intention of creating an explosive barrier, but they never had time to use the idea. The drums now threw off quivering heat-waves.

When the engineers pronounced the bridge ready, General Fowkes and the colonel of the engineers climbed into a Jeep. They drove across together in the first British vehicle to cross since 1942. The general who had captured the place, and the colonel who had built the bridge, looked pleased. The troops clapped as the Jeep rolled on to the bridge. Everybody was pleased about the bridgehead. When the Jeep reached the other side, somebody opened a bottle of beer, and the general and the colonel toasted each other.

Trucks hauling guns began creeping down the incline to the bridge, and ten minutes after it had been opened, an unbroken line of heavy vehicles was moving across. It really looked like the big advance into Burma at last. The advance that had been promised and threatened for two years was really on. The Eleventh Division had been in action on the Burma front for only five months, but they had been five exhausting months. There were men who had come out of Burma on their feet, thirsty, embittered and defeated, and they had spent the time since that retreat on the Burma front. The Fourteenth Army contained many of these men. They did not say much, but they felt a lot. The trucks and artillery now crossing the Chindwin would smash their way to Mandalay. All the efforts of two years, and all the scroungings and beggings for equipment, had helped the Allies to reach Bhamo, Sittaung, Kalewa, and probably Akyab before long. The forgotten army would not be forgotten, especially by the Japanese. It was no use for the Japs to think they could stop the advance now. A victorious army was slicing into Burma from many angles.

The next day I went up the Chindwin in one of the first Ducks or amphibious water-craft, with supplies for the Nyasa troops then attacking Shwegyin. The Ducks were driven by British soldiers and they solved the problem of speedy supply to the front line. The right flank of the forward troops was on the bank of the Chindwin, within sight of Shwegyin. In front of Shwegyin several Jap units were holding out, delaying the advance. If you did not seize a hill at once, the Japs swarmed on to it and you then had to attack it. One hill on the Shwegyin road was occupied by Japs with machine-guns, and although an East African patrol had reached Shwegyin, the Japs on the hill still menaced the road. As the Ducks reached the beach near Shwegyin, we were hidden from that place by a slight rise. A colonel of the supply and transport and I went forward to look at the objective.

A tall cliff rose from behind it, and we could see Shwegyin, with a few small buildings, in the glaring sunlight thrown off the Chindwin.

The water started spurting up in jets on our right, and then in long lines. We heard the hammering of machine-guns and we drew back from the bank. Jap machine-gunners on the hill commanding the road were firing, and the overs were hitting the Chindwin. Shwegyin itself seemed empty and quite lifeless. Nyasa troops were unloading the stores from the Ducks. They were in a cheerful mood, for they had waited a long time for this load of rations and ammunition, and it was good for them to see people from the outside world establishing a link with them.

As the stores were dragged into the jungle by troops with slung rifles and fixed bayonets, the mortars opened fire on the Jap machine-gunners. An attack was going in later in the day, while other troops stayed ready to swarm into Shwegyin. The artillery fired on Shwegyin throughout the day, and the smoke rose in wisps in the sun-glare.

As Shwegyin was about to fall to the Africans, the Japs made their first air attack against the Kalewa bridge. This had been expected for days, and when it came it was swift and abortive.

I was talking to two supply officers in a dump near the bridge. The dump, containing ammunition, was hidden in the jungle which ran along the beach. We heard the noise of very fast aircraft approaching the bridgehead, and the note suddenly changed as the planes peeled off for the dive. We saw them, like speeding blobs of mercury, and their wings threw off a brilliant light as they dived out of the sun. There was a crackling and popping, and a sudden hammering of ack-ack guns. The shells burst into white patterns round the planes, like blossoms, and after four or five seconds, as the ack-ack concentrated with superb skill on the Jap planes, the enemy were thrown into confusion.

One turned desperately, trapped in the bursting shells, and then roared straight into the air against the sun, so that we could see the pilot's shock and fright. The ack-ack was intense and accurate, and had come up out of a silent and sleepy-looking jungle. One plane was smoking and it crashed some miles away. Two others were hit. There were about half a dozen planes in the raiding force, and one or two did get through to open fire with cannons and machine-guns. They wounded two askaris on the beach. Another dropped a couple of bombs very haphazardly, and then fled. The raid was over in half a minute, and was a failure.

The bridge was untouched, and everybody who had witnessed the raid praised the speed and skill of the ack-ack gunners who had waited patiently to show what they could do.

Shwegyin was captured, and the troops pushed on to Mutaik. The perimeter round the bridgehead was nearly completed. While the advance was in progress an East African patrol reported a big Jap camp holding plenty of enemy troops, and this news was sent by the brigadier to the guns. An aerial observation went over and found the camp, and in a couple of minutes the ack-ack guns which had shelled Kalewa as field-pieces before its capture were in action.

The pilot of the observation plane had directed a lot of artillery shoots, but he said that he had never seen one so successful as the one he directed that day. The first four high-velocity shells burst right in the centre of the Jap camp, which immediately began swarming with men attempting to escape. Under the pilot's orders, the guns lifted as the Japs fled, and forty shells burst among them, flinging them right and left. 'Up one hundred,' said the pilot into his radio, and the guns followed the Japs as they sought cover. One salvo made a direct hit on a dump full of ammunition. It blew up in a flash of fire and the camp was left blazing. It was quick and perfect. From the brigadier came a message for the gunners, thanking them for their fine work. Gunners do not often hear full reports of their shooting, but most people in the area heard about that shoot.

Shwegyin was a graveyard of British trucks, armoured cars, tanks and guns. They had lain there since the British troops had destroyed them in 1942. Shwegyin was completely flat. Just another Burmese village in the war zone. River-craft were unloading stores, and the askaris passed them from hand to hand and up to the waiting trucks. There was haste and excitement. Beyond Shwegyin and by the side of the road, stood a line of British tanks. They were drawn up in perfect line, like barrack-room beds for an officer's inspection. Their tracks were gone, and the marks of the flames which had destroyed them still showed against the faded green paint after nearly three years. Some twenty-five-pounders, with their barrels blown back, stood in tall, rank grass near the tanks. A couple of spiked ackack guns leaned crazily on the edge of the jungle, and all over the country surrounding them were the twisted and battered skeletons of trucks, armoured cars, and a few private cars.

When they got to Shwegyin in 1942 the Japs must have laughed with joy. Now, they too had gone, for the last time, and we went into their ration and ammunition dumps which were hidden in the jungle. The floor of one of the dumps was covered with the tiny biscuits used by the enemy. Hundreds of worn-out rubber 'tabi' type shoes were stacked in one corner of a room, and thousands of Jap army forms blew about in the breeze. One or two askaris mooched about thoughtfully, looking for a decent bit of loot, but they found nothing but a twisted cigarette-case made of coloured tin.

'Rubbish,' they said, 'rubbish. The Japs have nothing but rubbish.' They hitched their packs and rifles and then slouched away.

From the point of view of revenge, Shwegyin seemed more of a triumph than Kalewa. It was something more satisfying for the soldier, who could see the story of that first retreat in the mangled and sun-bleached ruins of an army's transport and weapons which covered the country round Shwegyin. Although Kalewa was the bridgehead into Central Burma, Shwegyin was where a new and powerful army had come back in triumph after a wait of two years, and overhead was an Air Force that we had not possessed in 1942. In striking power it was flexible and very powerful, and in its ability to supply a fast-moving army in one of the worst battlefields it was second to none. When you stood at Shwegyin and watched the tanks and guns move past, and the troops armed with weapons which had perhaps not even been on the drawing-boards in the bad times of 1942, you were able to realise that the Jap victory in 1942 was a cyclone and not a decision.

The askaris marched through Shwegyin, and their green battledress was now torn and sun-stained, and the dust that rose from their tramping feet got into their eyes and mouths.

They were singing '*Sole, Sole, Sole,*' and their voices were urgent, for this song of their country never failed to move them.

British artillery rolled past them and the tommies shouted, 'Hello, mate! How's Africa?' Those Tommies who had learned the words shouted '*Mzuri*? Everything *Mzuri,* chum?'

M'Zuri means good or all right.

'M'zuri sana,' shouted the Africans, meaning that everything was really good.

The Tommies lurching along in their trucks, sitting on heaps of kit and ammunition, were the gunners who had fought with the division beside the divisional artillery. They seemed to like the 'old black men' or 'the black chums.' They waved to them and the askaris waved back. The askaris knew that after a few more miles of marching they would come upon these gunners again, and their guns would be already firing on the next enemy position. There might be a drop of tea in the dixie too. The trucks and guns disappeared into the dust, and the askaris started to sing *Sole* again.

The division was over the Chindwin at last. Near Mutaik a dead Jap lay sprawled under a tree. He appeared as if pretending to sleep. He had not long been killed, and the rest of his company were not far ahead. On the edge of the road was a tall officer with a black-painted face. He carried a Sten-gun, and his African troops were standing by.

'Are you the so-and-so brigade from the Mawlaik show?' I asked him.

He grinned and said that that was so. He also said that it was good to see the main road again.

'The rest of our crowd are all here, and it's really good to be here, I can tell you,' he said. 'Even to hear Jeeps and transport again is good.'

The askaris heard a big convoy approaching, and they became excited. It was plain what it meant to this brigade to be back on the road again after months in the jungle, and after the fighting from Chinmagale to Mutaik. The job was now done, and the troops who were marching past us were heading for the front line again after a rest.

I came across the Uganda battalion which had taken Leik Ridge, and I met the major with the huge moustache who had shown me round their piece of front near Chinmagale. His face was painted black, for he had just come off patrol. He took off his jacket and sat down to a mess-tin of food. On the ridge in front the askaris were in contact with the enemy, who were falling back behind a light screen of automatics. They were being given a dose of three-inch mortar fire.

The brigadier came out of his bamboo office and asked about the bridgehead. He was glad to be back on the road, back with the main body. They had done a magnificent job, and all ranks were feeling happy. For this brigade, places like Chinmagale, Leik, Sadwin, Mawlaik, Massein and Paluzawa would remain as memorials in their memories of the campaign. The green and brown lines on the map could never convey what the country was like on the ground, when you were wearing a full pack in the rain and fighting a tough enemy.

For another brigade there would be Jambo Hill, Pyinbon Sakan, Sittaung, Kalemyo, Kyigon and the Myittha gorge. For the other brigade there would be miles and miles of stinking mud through Htinzin, the Khampat to Yazagyo. Indainggyi, Myittha gorge, Natkyigon, the Bon Chaung and Kalewa. Names on the map from which the buildings had been torn by high explosives, and yielding nothing save corpses and chaos.

Near Shwegyin, in the centre of a ruined village, I saw a Japanese soldier's head lying on the ground. It still wore a steel helmet, though this had been shattered by the steel that had killed the owner. A group of askaris were looking at this head, and they talked about the shape of the face and the curious eyes. They did not see it as something horrible, which it certainly was. They had passed that stage, and in any case they had never interpreted horror in the same way as their white *bwanas*. That scene seemed to explain that the askaris would not be changed very much by the war, nor would it twist their essential belief in certain things.

They moved off, leaving the head in the bright sunlight. It did not seem to matter. It was what they had come to Burma for. To kill, and to see things like that.

CHAPTER TWENTY-FOUR

Well, that was the Khabaw Valley campaign. After Shwegyin the country opened out, and the deep jungles which had distinguished the pestilential valley now gave way to more open country. The valley that had been so notorious for its diseases had not claimed the vast number of sickness casualties that had been anticipated. The diseases were certainly there, and malaria and scrub-typhus caused casualties, but very many less than had been expected. A battle against these two diseases was started by the army doctors as soon as the troops entered the valley. Mepacrine, which was taken regularly by all the Europeans and Africans of the division, did wonders. Anti-malarial precautions were rigidly enforced. Every askari carried a mosquito-net, and the anti-mosquito squads, though hardly noticed among the thousands of troops in the division, worked unceasingly. As soon as a unit broke into new country, they started work. There were others who spent their nights in catching mosquitos, and these they passed to army doctors who were engaged solely in the prevention of malaria.

While the Japanese were still holding out on hills and in clumps of jungle, Hurricanes swept low over the jungle, spraying the powerful bug-killer known as D.D.T. There was a loud pop from the aircraft, and clouds of white dust, like smoke, spread across the jungle, killing mosquitos and their larvae. This D.D.T. was sprayed over the Japanese lines on many occasions before an attack, so that when our troops broke into the area, it was already sprayed and considered safe.

The scrub-typhus squads, as soon as the troops entered a new area, started looking for the scrub-typhus. Areas they pronounced as unfit for troop concentrations were closed and a notice put up forbidding troops from entering it. Orders forbidding all ranks to move about without wearing shirts were enforced, as also was the wearing of long sleeves and gaiters which protected the ankles from bites.

The Africans stood the climate, the frightful weather and hard living conditions, cheerfully, and with constitutions that were considered to be more immune against malaria than those of other troops. The medical authorities with the division, both British and Belgian, did a magnificent job under very difficult conditions. Wounded and sick received the best treatment that could obtain under the conditions of the monsoon campaign. There was one night, in a jungle hospital near the fighting, when doctors had been dealing with wounded for hours under shaded lamps, and when the last casualty, an officer wounded by mortar bomb fragments, had been dealt with on the operating table. The sweating doctors straightened their backs as the officer was carried away, still drugged. One of the doctors said, 'Well, chaps, will you do me now?'

He was suffering from an abdominal complaint necessitating an operation, but had waited until the casualties were finished before mentioning it. So his friends put him on the stretcher, raised up on four stilts, and operated on him successfully.

In Burma there are even psychiatrists, what the doctors call 'trick cyclists,' who deal with cases of battle exhaustion. They work right in the front line, and they can deal with men on the spot before they become 'cases.' The Japanese wounded and sick receive treatment also as soon as they are brought in. It must be quite an experience for them after the treatment they receive from their own doctors.

In the Khabaw all the services contributed equally to the effort of the advance. Sappers worked until they were exhausted. They built bridges that were washed away by the flooding rivers, and then built them again. Pontoons were kept moving across fast torrents in order to pass troops and guns through with their transport. They worked all day in a burning sun, beside rivers that flashed in the aching eyes. And the roads, the nightmarish, heartbreaking roads, were their 'pigeon.'

The Supply and Transport, the Ordnance and the Military Police, and all the other services had their hands full all the time. The Military Police, usually imagined to be people who arrest soldiers for having dirty buttons, is one of the finest units in the British Army. In the Khabaw the Military Police of the division were responsible for the controlling of traffic, as well as the maintenance of good order and military discipline. When the advancing troops reached the Myittha gorge, near the Chindwin, they worked through the days and nights, on roads of choking dust-clouds, controlling a stream of military traffic that contained everything from Jeeps, mules and heavy tanks, to the weird and enormous amphibious Ducks. They had to be patient, and they were. I know one who ate his meals out of cans in the Jeep for days on end, and if there was a traffic jam, the M.P.s 'carried the can back,' or in other words, took the blame. One M.P., who had slaved for days in thick dust as the stream of transport grew bigger, cracked up and was taken to hospital. 'More trucks,' he kept saying. 'Get some more trucks across.'

'Dirt Causes Flies,' said a large notice beside the road leading into Kalewa, and 'Flies Cause Dysentery,' said the next. Beyond that was another which said, 'Burn all Dirt.' They were written in K'Swahili for the African troops, and put up by the hygiene squads, who were responsible for the removal of anything that might create flies, and the diseases they carry. Their horrible job in the first two months of the campaign, when the Jap dead were everywhere, was done swiftly and expertly.

All the troops working with the services were Africans. They had been trained with great skill and patience. What they knew, they had learned since joining the army. And they will take their knowledge into a backward country when they return to civil life. Africans have more than justified the toil that has been spent on them. To have produced large forces of trained men out of the primitive peoples of several East African territories, not simply trained infantry, but all the services that go with infantry, speaks well for the Europeans who did it. If you saw an African with a shaven head, wearing a red-ochred skin cloak, and strolling along with a herd of goats, and somebody told you that they would make a signaller out of him, you would be surprised. But it has been done. After immense labour and effort, it has been done on a big scale, and those men have fought alongside British, Indian and Gurkha troops.

The British officers and non-commissioned officers who led them, after training them, deserve special praise. Their responsibility was great, for they had to understand Africans as well as soldiers, and the African is not easily understood. He can be so simple that you would think him guileful, and so guileful sometimes that you would think him very simple.

African troops grow very attached to an officer who has been with them for a long period. They miss him when he goes. Leadership with Africans is very much a personal business. They do not consider that a man is a born leader because he had two pips on his shoulder. Very few trained soldiers think that, but with the African it is how a man deals with them that counts. If a European shows understanding and even if his decisions are hard, they will do more than their duty for him. And it does not matter if he is a sergeant or a general. They do not forget him quickly. In the queer and explosive world they now live in, they appreciate the leader, and when they went into the Khabaw they had the best that could be found. An officer who had been a long time with African troops knows all their moods and aspirations. And they know his. When you meet an African unit that has had its officers for a long time, you meet a family. That applies to most army units, but in an African unit it is a little different. An officer or sergeant is like a father, and he has about the same responsibilities. The troops rely on his decision about cattle sales and rain, just as much as about the setting up of a three-inch mortar. And when times have been bad, and their leaders have been wounded or killed, many of them have done great things, carrying on when the 'father' has gone, when the man who taught them a lot is no longer there. They can try the patience, but so can children. When they are trained and have been tried out, and are well led, they repay the understanding that has been shown them.

'My Africans,' says an officer, and he means just that. They are his Africans, and when he knows them well and they know him, he speaks of them possessively, for it is likely that besides knowing their regimental numbers, he knows how many children they have as well, or what songs they sing when the rain comes. I met one officer who knew and liked the Nandi tribesmen of Kenya. He knew their language; and nearly every Nandi askari in the division, and there are plenty, knew him too. They liked him. He is now dead, but he lives on in a lot of African memories. He wanted to live in the Nandi country after the war, but it was not to be.

When all the hectic days are over, when all the queer machines and weapons have passed out of their lives, the Africans who soldiered in the Khabaw will retain some of the things the army taught them. It is Blimpish and bad form to praise the army for anything other than winning battles, but whether the fact is considered sad or not by those who abhor regimentation, it is still a fact that the army has done plenty of good for a lot of people. It has served soup as well as steel, in many countries, and has brought order where many politicians caused disorder. In places like Greece and the Ogaden desert of the Abyssinian frontier, far apart, but misunderstood by critics on two sides of an ocean. And on the prairie of the African mind, where little grew save bewilderment. In that mind the army has placed a lot of things, like the appreciation of cleanliness and order, and anti-malarial precautions. The army in wartime is composed mostly of civilians, and what they have taught many people, without steel or fire, has done much good, and will do more. The young man in the very wide trousers, tight-waisted black overcoat and small pork-pie hat, who romped through the celluloid world of the thirties, has learned as much as the savage who thought that a river was a god. And there is no harm in this. The British, like the Chinese, have never really valued their soldiers until a time of catastrophe. But just as the wife who could do nothing about her husband's untidy habits thanked the army for teaching him to fold his clothes, so will the African whom the army taught to live with his fellows, even those of inferior tribes.

When an askari who was marching with me through a stretch of mud asked if I had taken my mepacrine, and I told him no, and he shook his head, I thought it said a lot for the army. The askari took a small box from his haversack and gave me a mepacrine pill from it, which I took. I asked him what he had done before the war. He said that he had herded his father's cattle near the River Juba. He did not think the mepacrine was magic. He knew what it did, about all the little bugs that swirled in the blood. His officer had told him about it. Not so much Captain Jones as Mr. Jones of High Street, wearing three pips. But they would not have met if Mr. Jones had not been a captain and Wanga had not been Private Wanga. So there is solace to be obtained even out of a devastating world war, fortunately.

The isms of this world have not hit the Africans . . . yet. They have fought a couple of the isms, comprehending only vaguely what they meant, but they were able to see certain aspects of them. The Italian ism, which they helped to kill in Africa, showed its face to them in the discriminations it made about tribes and about peoples. The Japanese ism was different. It just wanted to kill you, or be killed. It was easier to understand, being about life and death. A Japanese officer, made prisoner, *did* look very different when compared with Captain Jones. There was no doubt about it. What about the Japanese Captain Mitsuo ——, whom they captured one day. He was a regular officer of the Imperial army, and he was crazy, but his ravings were an expression of his attitude to his troops, and to life in general. He raved all night, screaming and shouting.

'Lieutenant Hazaki,' he shouted, 'Lieutenant Hazaki, where are you, you bastard? Shoot me with your pistol. Come and shoot me. You useless fool! For the sake of the Emperor we came to these filthy hills to be disgraced. Dragged on my behind by blackamoors. We came from Indo-China to be disgraced and clowned by blackamoors. Lieutenant Hazaki, you bastard, bring a machine-gun and mow them down. Our useless bloody soldiers. Hazaki, turn the machine-gun on these useless Japanese soldiers! Ah, the disgrace. A Japanese officer dragged in the mud. Hey, are you there, Hazaki. Shoot me. Shoot me. God save the Emperor. Tenno Heika Banzai! Koroshito Kure! Shoot me!'

That was a Japanese officer. His useless soldiers, who had eaten grass and roots in order to obtain strength enough for another attack, should be mown down. The Africans saw many Japs like that one, and they did not like them. They found out that they were fighting alongside people in a struggle that would ensure a return to the kind of life they had left in Africa. They love home as much as any soldier, though for them is greater because of the spiritual dimensions distance involved, and the inability to focus properly on some of them. But they are in Burma in their thousands, and have done well there. The Fourteenth Army has many races, many religions, and men from many countries in its ranks.

The Eleventh East African Division was one of many others who helped to drive the Japanese back through the jungles, of which they believed themselves masters. The jungle is a cemetery of the Imperial army, and of several legends. In its green darkness, from Myitkyina to the Chindwin, and down to Maungdaw, the slaves of Japan had fallen, before a better army, the Fourteenth, to which the East African Division was proud to belong.